The Lady and Her Tiger

With Chauncey the cougar

The Lady and Her Tiger

Pat Derby

with
Peter Beagle

Thomas Congdon Books

E. P. DUTTON & CO., INC. | NEW YORK

Library of Congress Cataloging in Publication Data

Derby, Pat.
  The Lady and Her Tiger
  1. Derby, Pat. 2. Animals, Training of.
I. Beagle, Peter S., joint author. II. Title.
GV1829.D37   1976   791.3'2'0924 [B]   75-43856

Published simultaneously in Canada by
Clarke, Irwin & Company Limited, Toronto and Vancouver

ISBN: 0-525-14275-4

This book is for Chauncey.

The Lady and Her Tiger

1

It has to begin with elephants. I was born in love with all elephants: not for a reason that I know, not because of any of their individual qualities—wisdom, kindness, power, grace, patience, loyalty—but for what they are altogether, for their entire elephantness. When I was a little girl in Sussex, I must have driven my father crazy, begging him eternally to take me to see the elephants at a circus or a carnival or a zoo sometimes halfway across England. We almost always got there, somehow. My father always knew how it was between elephants and me.

The trouble was that I hated circuses, and carnivals, and zoos. I hated the way their keepers and trainers treated the elephants—the other animals too, but the elephants most of all. Elephants bring out a fury in many men as no other creature does: a rage to dominate and to hurt.

My father eventually learned to take me to visit the elephants a day or so early, while the show was still setting up, with the elephants hauling on great cables and guy ropes, dragging tent poles into position, and carrying crates of equipment on their backs from this place to that. It was usually easy enough to find someone who would take a five-pound note to let the two

Neena likes to pick me up, as if I were her toy. I think she thinks she owns me. And in a sense she does. (Photo by Gary Brainard)

of us trail him around the lot all day, keeping more or less out of his way and out of trouble. We'd talk with the grips and roustabouts and share their lunches, and even help shift or shovel where we were allowed. My father was a red-haired, green-eyed man who stood almost six feet six inches tall, and if he hadn't been teaching Shakespeare at Cambridge, he would have had a very good time working in a carnival.

But what I came for was to be with the elephants. How much of their vast, gentle presence I was able to enjoy each time depended on my own quickness, on my father's diversionary actions, and on the occasional tolerance of an elephant man. One way or another, there would always come at least one moment when I would be standing alone in that shadow that was home, between those scratchy, gunnysack-feeling legs, while a trunk touched my face with a cold, sticky daintiness to see who I was, and as far over me as the ceiling of my parents' bedroom, a heart like an oven roared and flamed. I was never afraid. I breathed the elephants in, as they breathed me in, and I disappeared into their rumbling tenderness—so much so that I could never understand how my father knew where to find me, nor how he could see me at all when he came looking.

To this day, when I crawl away from a stupid, humiliating,

useless afternoon spent juggling bills, lying to creditors, and scrounging money from strange Hollywood people to pay for chicken necks and horsemeat, I can still cleanse myself by standing close to an elephant, leaning between her forelegs with the heat of her heart over me. Her name is Neena. She's fifteen years old, which is like being a fifteen-year-old girl. There are moments when it seems to me that it was an elephant who got me into this strange and arduous thing I do, and that it's only Neena who keeps me from getting into my car and driving away from all of it forever. *There's no other reason but that crazy elephant, who wouldn't understand.*

It isn't true, and I usually know it, even during the worst times. It's true about the first elephant, though. Her name was Taj. I'll talk about her later on.

I am a wild-animal trainer. I balk at the phrase, but it's the quickest and simplest way to identify myself, especially since what I think I do doesn't really have a name. What title is there that says, "I play with animals, and try to be like them"? The Lincoln-Mercury cougars and bobcats, the Enco Tiger in Your Tank; the lion, leopards, wolves, jaguars, and bears who have appeared over the last ten or twelve years in movies and television shows from *Dracula* to *Lassie, Gunsmoke* to Johnny Carson—how can I possibly say that I trained them, that I taught them anything? A wild animal is what it is, and knows what it knows. They trained me to understand that.

I try to be like them. Little by little, being no quicker about these things than anyone else, I am learning. It's taken a long time.

As I write this, I am sitting outside my house with Chauncey the cougar. He's been ill, and he's spending his recuperation lying on this patch of new sod that I had put in for him. The two lion cubs, Clancy and Mildred, are wandering cautiously around us, their normal yelping explosiveness a bit muted. Chauncey likes them, and would probably play with them as he does with the three dogs, but the lions are rather afraid of him. He is growling quietly, which is the way Chauncey always talks to himself, the sound shading in and out of a purr that jars sweetly through all my bones. He turns on his side to watch the sparrows that have nested in my four hanging flower-pots this spring—he will watch them coming and going all day without ever trying to catch them—and the sunlight turns the light fur on his belly to dandelion fluff. This is as happy as I get, this right now.

I am not at all sure that I have any right to this happiness. I am not sure that I have not done Chauncey a terrible wrong every moment of his life. He was born in captivity, of a line of similarly cage-bred cougars; and as a direct consequence of continued inbreeding, Chauncey's bones are comparatively frail, his whole frame far more vulnerable than that magnificently complete air could ever reveal. He spent his first year semiparalyzed, unable to use his hindquarters. The Lincoln-Mercury commercials in which he lies on top of a billboard, lashes his tail when I tickle it, and snarls on cue have provided most of my income for several years. I have been told that Chauncey is the third most-recognized advertising symbol in the country, after Coca-Cola and Ford.

Now he rolls his broad forehead commandingly against my cheek, and I put my arms around him, and we sit like that, talking in our throats. *I am like him. I am him. What have I done to him?*

2

Sussex is fairyland. Sussex is Middle-earth. J.R.R. Tolkien lived here most of his life, not far from Seaford, where I grew up, and Sussex is utterly present in the soft, rainy hills and downs, the haunted barrows, old roads and wild old forests of his Shire and the lands beyond. It's there, too, in the somewhat smug placidity of his hobbits, and in the sense of the sea's nearness. I left Sussex at fifteen, but it's all there in me still: not so much as a particular county of England or a time of my life, but as a synonym for a certain sort of quietness.

Buttercups. I remember being small and happily by myself in a surf of buttercups. Perhaps I'd been spinning around and made myself dizzy—at all events, the sky was buttercups too, and the buttercups around me were marching in the air, as alive as the lambs who had appeared at the same time, in the same noisy, shoving profusion, except that the lambs cried and the buttercups laughed. I told my father that the buttercups were alive, and he warned me that I must walk very carefully among them, because there were little people living in all flowers. He never called them *fairies* or *elves,* but always *little people.*

He wasn't playing with me, nor was he being properly droll with a young child. My father never treated me like a child. It was his way of teaching me to move quietly with everything, and not to charge through the grass trampling worlds I never saw. I walk carefully still, because of him; and if I don't believe specifically in little people living in the flowers, nevertheless I believe in what does live there, and I know that the child in the meadow was right about the spring lambs and the buttercups.

My father's name was Charles Boswell Shelley. He disliked both of his given names intensely, and he was never exactly overwhelmed by being a descendant of Percy Bysshe Shelley. My mother was Welsh, as golden as my father was fire-colored, with long, long pale fingers and blue eyes the color of lupine flowers, almost indigo. She was six feet tall herself, and all my life I've thought that she was the most beautiful woman in the world. We were never as close as I was with my father, and I think now that it may have been because I was so much in awe of her beauty, and of the serenity that was as visible a part of her as her blue eyes. What could have bothered my mother? what could I possibly tell her of my own bothers? I didn't envy, or fear, or want to replace my mother, in any respectable Freudian manner—but if the choice had ever come up, oh, I would have *been* her like a shot. Two seconds flat, and no questions asked.

My parents were both in their forties when I was born. Their only other child, my brother Derek, was twenty-two. He was killed in the war shortly after my birth. I don't know whether I was a planned child or not—and it hardly matters—but one way or the other, I must have been something of a shock. Instead of Derek, suddenly here came this red-haired little frog, bouncing and yelling and having to be pulled from the pond by my father's Great Danes—a changeling, a kobold, something undeniably out of another world. If the buttercups are perhaps my earliest memory, not too far behind comes the kindly whisper that I was supposed to be too young to understand:

"If only she weren't so small, and *quite* so plain—*such* a pity for Charles and Mary." Many children do grow up feeling as though they had been switched in the cradle, stolen at birth from their real families. I felt a bit like that, I suppose, except that I never wanted to be rescued and returned home. Frog or no frog, I loved these giant princes.

They loved me—I never doubted that—and in their different ways they tried hard to make the world comprehensible to their changeling. My mother would tell me very seriously, "Patricia, you have three terrible crosses to cope with—your red hair, your temper, and the fact that you're a Gemini." It looks silly in print, but it was my mother's idea of being some practical help to me; and, as it happens, she was perfectly right.

My father, for his part, took me for long walks, and turned me loose in his library. "Everybody has a different gift," he once said to me. "Some people have beauty, some have bodies that will do anything they ask them to do. Your gift is your mind, Patricia, and if you use it the way it was made to be used, it will be as good as all the other gifts put together." It was easy enough for him to say, who had all the gifts I ever knew about; but he meant it, and I believed it for dear life.

I read everything. Kipling, Poe, Hawthorne—*The House of the Seven Gables* is still my favorite book—the Brontës, Shakespeare, Thackeray, Hardy, Saki, Lord Lytton, Carroll, Chesterton, Donne, Byron, Jane Austen. I read thrillers, too, and lots of wonderful romantic trash that I always knew was trash, even as I cried so marvelously over it. I also read anything at all that had animals in it; and that, as any child growing up with the same fascination knows, is a peculiarly risky business. What prompts writers such as Mark Twain to write such carefully detailed stories about the willful torturing of animals? And why do they continue to be reprinted as "beloved children's classics" and forever pressed on children suspected of loving animals by doting relatives? To teach them about the uniquely human sin of cruelty, as though they hadn't learned it all long before, in the jungle of schoolyards? There is a special kind of lip-smacking sentimentality about these stories, which manages to make them even more horrible. I remember one absolutely maudlin story by Albert Payson Terhune, about a little border collie, almost by heart, and I wish I didn't; and *Black Beauty* put me in bed for a week. That wasn't the warm, pleasurable crying over silly romances, either—this crying was sickness and terror. My mother forgave the people who had given me the book, in time, but she never forgave Anna Sewell. I don't think I have.

Standing in the bedroom doorway, my Uncle Nigel, my father's brother, remarked loudly to no one: "If she gets that upset about suffering animals, how would she take on over *people* suffering?" It wasn't the first time I'd heard that particular challenge, and I've been hearing it ever since, in almost exactly the same words: as though one pain were entirely exclusive of the other, or even distinguishable from it. Suffering is suffering. I have never been confused about that.

Neither was my mother, heaven knows. Tramps and gypsy tinkers are said to leave secret designs on townsfolk's houses for one another—meaningless unless you know where to look, and understand the symbols: *"Friends here." "Old man, mean dog—stay clear." "Good food, but you have to do chores."* Animals must surely have a similar system—how else can one possibly explain why every hurt, lost, hungry, homeless, or simply footloose creature between Beachy Head and Chichester managed to find its way to my mother's long, slender hands? I can still see her sitting on the kitchen floor, spooning warm milk down the throat of the oldest, ugliest mongrel in all England, while a lamb that probably won't live the night whimpers in a quilt, and a one-legged pheasant, a badly torn fox, and two asthmatic stray cats wait their turn for attention.

She was the only person I've ever known who was consistently able to keep wild baby birds alive. We found them regularly—robins, thrushes, sparrows, wrens, vireos—pushed or fallen from their nests, or blown down in a storm. My mother had a special formula of her own that she fed to them all, and an astonishing percentage survived and grew to their first flight plumage in my bedroom. I have that formula today, exactly as she used to make it, but it won't work for me.

Once the birds were grown, she would have to teach them to fly. I love to remember her sitting in a window, one leg tucked under her, with four or five young birds perched on her shoulders and knees and the top of her head. "Come on," she would tell them gently, over and over. "Come on, it's time, you have to go." And the next spring, when the birds came back to our garden, she and I would sit together and try to determine whether any of them looked like one of ours, or seemed more at ease or approachable—or just wondering—than the rest. We were always sure about at least a few, every year.

My mother's deepest delight was an ancient African gray parrot who, in the best tradition, really had belonged to a sailor, and really did swear in four languages with a towering, gorgeous vileness from the moment that his cage was uncovered in the morning. We lived the most classic of English jokes with that parrot, hastily covering him two and three times a day on occasion, should the vicar drop in unexpectedly or the Garden Club march up for tea. My father had to be watched closely at such moments. Lecturing in America, he used to hook large numbers of Southern Baptist football players on Shakespeare by beginning with the bawdy parts; and I'm sure he must have felt that he was educating the Garden Club by liberating the parrot whenever he got a chance. He educated me, anyway.

The parrot had the run of the house, most of the time, and often he would sit outside under a tree with my father and me, watching us intently as we talked about everything that we liked to talk about, and now and then saying something nasty. It was part of the ritual that we always ate nuts together: my father shelling them very neatly with his penknife, one for me, one for him, one for the parrot.

The parrot died very suddenly one afternoon, keeling over with a final snarling obscenity. I remember my father's shock and sorrow much more than my own. The bird had been old enough to have heard some of Shakespeare's dirty jokes the first time, but my father was never certain that he hadn't died of a surfeit of nuts. He swore me to lifelong secrecy on the spot. It was the only secret we ever kept from my mother, and it was my first experience of feeling guilty about an animal's death. I remember all the others, too.

I've drawn myself so far as what I undoubtedly was then: a solitary sort of child, somewhat withdrawn with most people except my parents—once I got over my need to be demonstrably special all the time. By my Uncle Nigel's lights, though, I was spoiled, wild, and totally undisciplined. Uncle Nigel was regular British Army, and if anything was real to him besides the giving and taking of orders, I never knew it.

He was right, of course—I was quite spoiled, and it was the making of me. My father knew my temper, which was so much his own: he was forever in hot water at Cambridge because of his constitutional inability to obey orders. He was like a leopard. Leopards are the brightest and most easily spooked of the great cats, at once the most self-contained and the most high-strung. They have too much imagination—they can enrage and terrify themselves as a lion or a cougar would never do—and they throw blind, insane tantrums as resistless as hurricanes, out of which they emerge gentle and affectionate, licking their paws. You don't tell leopards what to do.

Disciplined in the normal way—let alone Uncle Nigel's— I might very well have become some kind of international criminal. I like to think so, anyway. I had the leopard curiosity and contrariness for it. My father was wise enough to let my love for reading, my fascination with animals and flowers, and my desire to please him and my mother be my discipline. The way I am with wild animals today is very much the way that my parents were with me. I've been accused, in my turn, of spoiling them.

Ballet and theatre were other regimens that kept me more or less domesticated. I began studying ballet at the age of four—largely, I think, because my mother wanted me to have the confidence and liking for my body that she must have already seen I was going to need. I stayed with it as I grew older, realizing that, if I wasn't beautiful, I wasn't as horrible as I'd thought, either; and dancing, I could be as beautiful and assured as anybody else. Like a lot of shy, self-doubting people, I always felt safe onstage.

When I was twelve years old, the Birmingham Repertory produced an experimental season of Shakespeare at Cambridge, with my father serving as a technical and historical advisor. One of the departures, for 1954, involved casting Romeo and Juliet to type. The Birmingham Rep might not have been quite ready to have Juliet played by a boy, as she was in the Globe Theatre; but neither would they compromise on a college-freshman Romeo and a pneumatic, earnestly nubile Juliet. Shakespeare's Romeo is barely fourteen, and Juliet is two years younger. They are children, not sexy teenagers, and it makes them terribly vulnerable and appealing to an audience. It also makes them almost impossible to cast.

"Let Patricia try it," my father suggested finally. "She knows the part, and she won't trip over anything." I had already spent two summers with the company, and I did at least know my way around both a stage and a line of iambic pentameter.

Actually, Juliet ought only to be played by very young girls. It's a beautiful part, but it's a soppy one too, soppy in a way that only a twelve-year-old girl can deeply understand and feel. The passion is real enough; but I sometimes think that if it hadn't happened to light on Romeo, it could just as easily have gone to a horse. I think Shakespeare may have felt that about Juliet, too—again, it's exactly what makes her gallantry and

her death so absurdly affecting. Anyway, she's not at all hard
to be, if you're twelve.

My father never saw me playing Juliet. He died months before the rehearsals began, of a heart attack, in his fifty-seventh
year. There had been no warning, no foreshadowing pain or
illness: it was now and over, like the old parrot's death. I am
not sure that I have ever truly loved another human being
since that day.

I was sick for a long time. It was like *Black Beauty* all over
again, but it went on and on: the tears and the awful dry wailing
that seemed to come from far away; the aching stomach that
couldn't keep food down, the feverish skin and the cold outrage
underneath, so cold that I shivered all the time, and someone
put more blankets over me. After a while, it became less
dramatic, I suppose. I didn't throw up so much, and I could
talk, and when I cried now I often didn't know that I was doing
it.

I sleepwalked through *Romeo and Juliet*, and through my
ballet studies and then two years at Cambridge reading English
literature. (In the English educational system, age is unimport-
ant if you can do the work, and at that time work was all I
could do.) During those years, the only thing that occasionally
brought me back from wherever I had gone was the prospect of
a good fight with Uncle Nigel over my manners, my dress, my
pets, or my attitude toward authority. Uncle Nigel was insisting on his responsibilities as advisor, surrogate father, and
general family pillar, and taking them with the remorseless
seriousness of a wrecking ball. It was a situation out of Dickens,
ridiculously melodramatic, and in a way we both knew it, but
it didn't help.

Yet I came to know my mother then, as I might never have
if my father had lived. She took me traveling with her in Scot-
land; in France, where she had old friends; and in Spain, because we both loved El Greco and wanted to see Toledo. We
went on picnics and walking tours, and we began to laugh to-

gether again, as silly as schoolgirls. But it was in the silliness that I understood for the first time how deeply she had loved my father, and how piddling and vain my long, noisy sorrow looked beside her in silence. I think I was jealous of her for a little while—how can you not be jealous of someone who knows how to love better than you do?—but we came home best friends, and the worst of the bad times were over for me.

I got on no better with my Uncle Nigel, however; and I began now to cling to my mother, rebuilding my old security around her. But she was too wise to allow that to happen: as she urged her foundling birds from the window when their feathers were grown, so she gently pushed me out of the nest by getting me interested in spending a summer in New York City, staying with friends of hers upstate, and perhaps studying ballet at the City Center school. I always used to wonder why she never kept just one of the wild birds as a pet. They seemed so contented to sit there quietly on her long hands.

So I went to New York, against my Uncle Nigel's express wishes—which, naturally, settled the question for good. I was not quite fifteen years old—too old, in my own estimation, to travel with toys, or I would have taken the one thing I most wanted to have with me. It was a dollhouse that my father had made for me one Christmas, working secretly in his office, carving every fixture and every piece of furniture, putting in the carpeting himself, and even decorating the room walls with miniature drawings and photographs. I did want to take it, but it would have been bulky and frail, and fourteen embarrasses easily. And I thought I was coming home soon, after the summer.

3

I loved New York. I wonder about that sometimes, as comparatively unsociable as I am by nature and by necessity. Raised in a country setting—content most of the time to be living with animals in these silent small-town cattle hills where ballet companies never tour and the hawks ride the same wind current all day—how did it happen that I was so immediately happy in that howling city? Today, in town to do an auto show at the Coliseum with Chauncey the cougar, I cling to my hotel, only scuttling outside for a sandwich and then scuttling promptly back again, as cold and fearful as anyone else, seeing muggers and maniacs all around me. But I lived here once. I used to know a few muggers, when I was fifteen.

That first summer, I enrolled at Columbia University, applied as a student to the New York City Ballet, and, now fifteen, even began cautiously scouting for an apartment of my own. Looking back, it seems an almost frantically impetuous commitment to a strange new world, one that I probably wouldn't have the courage to make again today. But I don't remember it as being a question of courage then: it was a waking after three years of desperate sleep, and the world dazzled me.

Perhaps it wasn't New York itself I loved, but the being awake.

I went home to Sussex for a little while before the Columbia year started. All I remember clearly of that time is going for long walks with my mother and talking endlessly about New York—telling her what Greenwich Village was like, and the Cloisters, and about all the plays, and how I was going to decorate my apartment, when I found one. Calm and golden as ever, she listened, smiled, offered suggestions, looked at me, helped me pack for good this time; and what she thought, I can't truly imagine, even now. I wasn't paying attention. I think she was happy for me.

I did find an apartment—a one-room walkup in the Village —and I furnished it exactly as I had told my mother I would. You have to imagine it with all the conventions of Bohemian poverty: cockroaches, peeling plaster, a defunct toilet, a sink from which the wall seemed to be gradually receding, like an old man's gums; a population of mysterious stains and smells, always spreading and advancing, and every possible bit of floor space taken up by genuine Victorian wardrobes, sideboards, Windsor chairs, breakfront bookcases, and horsehair settees. Some of the antiques had belonged to my parents, and had been sent to me by my mother; others I tracked down myself after school, bargaining for them out of my hoarded earnings as a waitress, nightclub cashier, or whatever I was being that week. The place looked like a cross between *The Lower Depths* and 221B Baker Street, except for the Irish wolfhound.

I didn't last very long with George Balanchine and the New York City Ballet, as I wouldn't have lasted with any company worth the name. Balanchine rooted out individuality among his corps de ballet like witchcraft: he demanded utter control of their bodies and their lives, on or off the stage. The ideal ballet dancer, in my experience, is a cross between a robot and a nun. I was spoiled. I'd been allowed to be a leopard for too long.

Like a lot of young would-be ballet dancers, I began looking for chorus work in Broadway musicals. I tried out for every

Here's the group we formed when I was sixteen, the Patricia Shelley Revue. We did a flapper routine to "Hard Hearted Hannah," and I was Hannah.

show that was holding auditions, and my list of rejections includes most of the famous musicals of the late 1950s. My wig fell off in the middle of my tryout for *West Side Story,* and I was advised either to learn to speak American or be resigned eternally to road companies of *My Fair Lady.* I remember being rather hurt at the time—I thought I made a striking Puerto Rican—but I dutifully enrolled in an acting class expressly to lose my British accent. I sound more Midwestern than anything now.

I did land a job in the chorus of *Goldilocks,* a Leroy Anderson show that came and went in a hurry; but what I eventually wandered into was nightclub work—anything from softshoeing in tiny piano bars to performing in fairly elaborate cabaret-style revues. I did whatever was going: sang, danced, did comedy bits, or just showed my legs and played straight women. My early cello training came in handy when I began to make a bass fiddle a regular part of the act. A small girl struggling with a bass fiddle is a long way from playing Juliet, but the laugh it gets is at least as old as the play.

The summer that I turned sixteen, six friends and I began putting together a comedy-and-music nightclub act—very light, highly acrobatic, slick, and unpretentious. We did astonishingly well from the beginning. Our agent had lined up several book-ings for us even before we were ready to perform in public, and we were given top billing when we opened in Las Vegas. My publicity photographs from that time show a sleek, long-legged creature with Debbie Reynolds hair (sometimes dark, sometimes blonde, but never red) and a thin, pink Ann-Margret grin: never beautiful, but so assured and moving so fast that you can't really tell. I don't look sixteen.

Our group stayed together for some three years, trouping across the United States and Canada, and eventually com-manding unreal sums like $12,000 and $14,000 a week. I spent most of my salary on antiques, and on fixing up the Village apartment, which gradually and inevitably began to accumu-late animals in the few chinks between the deal tables and the basket chairs. The Irish wolfhound had only been a boarder, but at one point I was traveling with a German shepherd named Phyllis, two cats, a racoon, and a parakeet called Cookie.

Eventually the act broke up. In Las Vegas a badly-moored trapeze came loose under one of the men, Mike Gentry, and crippled him. None of us wanted to go on without him, and we simply drifted back to New York, where the group dis-banded.

I went on living in the Village, eventually dropping out of Columbia, but still taking acting classes and going to auditions. Then I got a job in a road-company musical which brought me to California for the first time in my life, at the age of nineteen.

I liked California immediately. I knew I'd be back. New York was closing absolutely behind me, as the doors of my different lives always do. At the first opportunity I formed a jazz trio with Frank Tamarro and a drummer named Chuck Stevens—Connie Stevens's brother—mostly because they wanted to live in California too, and it was easy for us to get bookings in San Francisco and Los Angeles. I'd never sung seriously with a group before; but in those days I was always certain that I'd do well at new things precisely because of my utter inexperience.

Another reason for my eagerness to move west was that I wanted to study acting with Curt Conway and ballet with Carmelita Maracci, both of whom lived in Los Angeles. I settled into a small house in the San Fernando Valley and quickly established my normal sprinting, zigzagging Gemini routine: playing nightclubs, going to classes, gradually filling the house with stray cats, dogs, birds, and books; and, almost absent-mindedly, going into the antique business on the side. Having reached saturation point with the Queen Anne and William and Mary furniture that my mother loved to send me, I'd begun to sell some of it to my friends, and the eventual result was a shop on Melrose Avenue in Hollywood, with my mother happily buying for me in England. I had great hopes for my new trade, despite the fact that I didn't even know how to work a cash register.

Just before the antique shop opened, our trio went up to San Francisco to appear at the Thunderbird Hotel for a couple of weeks. The drummer-vocalist with the group working opposite us was a tall, powerfully built, curly-haired man in his late twenties, with a lion's light, faraway eyes and a lion's presence. He was an indifferent drummer, and he crooned throatily into his microphone like the last of the 1930s throbbers; but you couldn't not notice him, which annoyed me. I found him too pretty—like a slightly craggier and more saturnine Tony Curtis—and far too aware of his effect on the local women, whom he ran through as briskly as a pool shark clearing the table. I wanted nothing to do with him, and he was aware of that, too. His name was Ted Derby.

Ted set out after me from the day we met, with a sportsman's businesslike energy, but with no success. I wasn't interested. One afternoon, however, he found me exercising my dogs (Phyllis and another German shepherd named Hedy Lamarr) on the lawn of the Thunderbird, and he came easily over to hunker down and pet them, scratching them with an obvious understanding of where and how dogs like to be scratched. "I love German shepherds," he offered. "They're my favorite breed of dogs."

Uh-huh.

"I used to train dogs, you know."

Terrific. I'd known from childhood how I felt about animal trainers. Ted went on to explain that he had worked with animals for movie studios, and that he had turned to night-club singing only because the wild-animal ranch near Los Angeles that he had helped an old friend operate for several years wasn't making expenses. I didn't mind talking about animals, but I was too occupied with not committing myself to more than pleasantries to understand fully what he was saying. Patricia Shelley keeps her distance from beautiful crooner types, boy.

But he came back the next day with his scrapbook, and I was gone. The scrapbook was full of pictures of him wrestling with bears, sprawled out companionably with tigers, wolves, and jaguars, and being nudged in ponderous affection by the lions he so much resembled. I went to babbling pieces. "Can you really just walk in and pet them like that? Could I touch a lion? Where are they? Do you ever have any in your house? When can I see them?" He couldn't possibly have bargained on this sort of a conquest.

It wasn't him. It was the tigers—if you like, it was him with the tigers, him in the confidence of black leopards, whispering in their ears. That's a normal enough syndrome, to judge by the people I've met who would cultivate anyone, endure anyone, marry anyone, just to enjoy the slightest occasional sniff of power or notoriety. Ted could have been much less attractive and engaging than he was and I would have courted him just as ruthlessly, because of the tigers. He must have known that, somewhere, even when I asked for his phone number.

My group returned to Los Angeles three weeks after Ted's did, and I telephoned him as soon as I arrived. I might as well have asked to speak to his scrapbook, or if the tiger was in—my motives were that naked, and my method that shameless. More to be rid of me than for any other reason, he finally promised to take me to the ranch where his friend had the animals.

The compound, which I will call Peaceable Kingdom, Inc., was located in a remote area near Los Angeles. My first impression was of sun and dust, rolls of chain-link fencing, and dark, tense forms—too many to be anything but unreal and anonymous, not like the scrapbook at all—made clumsy by the constriction of the small cages in which they turned and waited. I had expected the magic jungle of a Rousseau painting, and my eyes hurt with disappointment. Where were the animals?

As we walked between two rows of cages, a large chimpanzee saw Ted and began to scream. Ted screamed back at him in the same challenging tone and ran over to the cage, where the chimpanzee clung to him through the bars, kissing him with his tusked mouth. In that moment they were two animals together, growling softly, moaning with affection, grooming each other delightedly, as all the great primates do. Ted turned to me, smiling for the first time in a way that had nothing to do with an audience. "I haven't seen this guy for two years," he said quietly, still holding the chimpanzee's hand. "He still remembers me."

He took me from cage to cage, introducing me to the other animals. Like the chimpanzee, every one of them seemed to remember him and was happy to see him, showing it by purring or yelping or whimpering hysterically, pushing enormous sleek or maned heads against his hands, or taking his arm gently between jaws that could have snapped it like a breadstick. And Ted talked to them, scratching their ears and stroking their throats, all but licking them as they licked his hands and face. I saw the best of him that first afternoon: a lion among his friends.

At this point, I think it's important to talk about the way I was with animals in those days. In the first place, I didn't know what they were. I loved them passionately and indiscriminately; but beyond caring for my cats and dogs, sighing at jaguars, and flying to the attack whenever I saw any animal being maltreated, I had no slightest understanding of what it was that I loved, nor of what such a love, to be real, must demand of me. "Animals are very basic," Ted would say; and again, "They're wild. You can't ever forget that they're wild." I didn't know what he was talking about.

Ted with one of his beloved lions, Joe. Ted is really a lion person, and he and Joe were alter egos.

My beliefs and attitudes were often utterly contradictory: for instance, I hated all zoos as implacably as ever, and yet it never occurred to me to question the whole matter of people owning wild animals at all, of people buying and selling animals like used cars. In New York I had once come very near to buying a baby elephant, deciding against it almost at the last minute. I'm certain that I would have unhesitatingly tried to raise an ocelot or a cougar or a bear in my Village flat without the least idea that I was being barbarously cruel and insensitive. In the last ten years I've received a tragically large number of sick, starving, tortured, and dying animals from people just like me.

Ted bought me a bear. By then we had begun a relationship based almost entirely on our mutual feeling for animals. Both of us were still performing in Los Angeles nightclubs, but I had gradually persuaded Ted to go back to working full-time for Peaceable Kingdom. Its owner, whom I will call Jack Krebs, had acquired two baby Malayan sun bears for use in a Walt Disney film, and Ted in turn purchased the female cub for me. I named her Babe, and I adored her beyond thought.

Malayan sun bears (they are actually found all through Indonesia, Southeast Asia, and southern China) are the smallest of all bears, seldom exceeding a hundred pounds at maturity. They're the ones with the wrinkly foreheads and the beige V-shaped collars around their throats. You see them every-where, in most zoos and many pet shops, because they're plentiful, easily captured—all the enterprising trapper has to do is shoot the mother—and several can be packed into one small crate to be shipped off to animal traders all over the world. Three-quarters of the cubs die, of course; but the sur-vivors look so cute and wistful, and the housewife just knows she can raise it in her five-room apartment, like a potted plant. I was no different with Babe.

Bears have only one real drive, and that is dinner. There

is no such thing in nature as a full bear. They spend most of their time in the wild foraging for food, and there is nothing in nature that a bear won't eat. I thought I was doing Babe handsomely on a formula blended from two cups of Gerber's Hi-Pro cereal, one cup of milk, two bananas, five slices of wheat bread, two tablespoons of Karo syrup, liquid vitamins, and one tablespoon of di-calcium phosphate. It was a good formula, and probably met Babe's nutritional needs quite adequately. Bears have no use for adequate nutrition.

Ted had warned me that Malayans have perhaps the quickest tempers of all bears; and I had even been perceptive enough to notice that Babe's brief fits of meanness usually occurred while she was watching me preparing dinner. For all that, I made no further deductions about Babe and food until what I still remember as the Night of the Strawberry Shortcake.

Briefly, there was a pastoral moment when I was whipping up cake batter at the stove, as a drowsy little bear cub watched me from the floor by my feet, her pointy-nosed head cocked enchantingly to one side. Then, with no transition at all, Babe was frantically climbing up my leg, digging her claws into me as she went, all the while muttering terrible little low cries to herself. She reached the dish of strawberries on the counter and stuck her head in, raging at the sweetness. I reached out to pull the dish away from her, and she lunged at me, sinking her teeth deep into my hand. I could hear her teeth hit bone.

I screamed and knocked her away, but she kept coming at me, biting my hands and arms, crying and crying. I had been bitten by animals before, but Babe was like a berserk child, and I was crazy with terror myself to see so much fury spilling out of such a tiny body. Then Ted came racing into the kitchen. He hit Babe with all his strength and knocked her off me. She fell against the stove and came up dazed, and Ted hit her again, and kept hitting her with sweeping, full-arm, open-handed blows until she backed into a corner, hiding her head and moaning.

I couldn't believe it was happening. My terror turned instantly to a rage as great as Babe's, and I ran between her and Ted, grabbing her up into my arms. "Leave her alone, leave her alone!" I screamed at him. "Don't you ever touch her again, or I'll wait until you're asleep and break your neck!"

Babe huddled into me, hugging me, crying now like any hurt and bewildered infant. Her face was streaked all over with strawberries. Ted was silent, catching his breath. Then he said, "Let me tell you something, Pat. Babe is a wild animal. If you let her get away even one time with biting you like that, she'll tear you to pieces some day. I mean that. That little bear will grow up to kill you."

"But it was my fault, I didn't know she was so terribly hungry. I haven't been feeding her enough, I guess."

"You probably haven't, but that's not the point. She'll pull that stuff on you again and again, because that's just what bears do, that's the way they are. If you can't learn to deal with what she is, I'll take her away from you, to save your life. Come on into the bathroom, I'll clean you up. You're bleeding all over your poor little bear."

I lay awake for a long time that night, my arms stiff with bandages, listening to Babe snuffling and grumbling in her sleeping cage on the back porch. I had never struck an animal in my life, and the idea of having to do to Babe what I had seen Ted do made me sick. More than I had ever wanted anything, I wanted to be with animals the way Ted was with them, to have them know me and call to me as that chimpanzee had cried out to Ted—*Did Ted ever hit him like that? how could any creature love you, or even look at you, if you hit it like that?*—yet, paradoxically, I wanted the trouble with Babe to have been my fault, not her nature. I loved her so much. I wouldn't let anything Ted said about her be true.

4

I did keep Babe as stuffed as a Victorian pantry from that time on, and the Night of the Strawberry Shortcake was never repeated. She grew increasingly gentler and more loving, especially after I began taking her with me to the antique shop every day. She spooked a few browsing customers, but she never damaged anything, or anyone. At home she played constantly with Phyllis, the German shepherd, who mothered her and kept her out of most mischief in a way that dogs seem naturally to do with baby animals. The instinct to guard sheep and round up cattle apparently transfers itself readily to young bears and tigers and jaguars. When in doubt, I most often tried to behave with Babe as I thought Phyllis would have done.

It was part of Babe's routine to wrestle and romp with Ted for an hour or so every evening after his job at Peaceable Kingdom. Then she would pad to her sleeping cage on my back porch. Still less than thirty pounds in weight, she was already too powerful for me to tumble around on the floor with, as Ted did, though she seemed consciously to hold back from exerting her full strength, except when she got excited and forgot. Coming in from the porch one evening, Ted exhibited his shirt with one sleeve entirely in tatters, and said, "You know, it's time we thought about having Babe declawed."

My stomach turned to cold stone. I said, "Why? She's never going to work at the ranch."

"There's more to it than just being in movies. As far as that goes, all the studios usually ever want from bear cubs is to have them sit and eat honey. It could be fun for her, but that's up to you. What's important is that she's beginning to play really rough. The way you take her around with you, one day she's going to grab some stranger, just the way she grabs us, and then everybody's in trouble. It'll happen, believe me."

"The shirt was an accident," I said desperately. "She never bites us anymore, you know that, she's as gentle as she can be. And I'll never let strangers come that close—"

"Right, she's as gentle as a bear can possibly be. It isn't her fault she's so much stronger than we are. Do you know how strong she really is, Pat? If we had to give her a shot right now, to save her life, we couldn't do it together. If she started getting mean with you again, she could open you up with those claws before I could get near her. She's hurt you a couple of times already—"

"No, she hasn't, those were just accidents, they were my fault both times, like bumping my head or something. And I'm teaching her not to use her claws, the same way I taught her not to bite. She learns so fast, I can't believe it, honestly." I was starting to talk very quickly, and to smile a lot.

"Pat, you can't do it. The biting's one thing, great, but there's no way you can train an animal with claws not to use them— it's cruel even to try. I've seen it over and over. She'll never understand what she's done wrong, or why you won't play with her anymore, or why she's got to be locked up in a zoo for the rest of her life." He paused, watching that go home. "If we declaw her now, while she's still young, she'll never know the difference, and you'll be able to keep her the way she is now.

Otherwise I can just about promise you there's going to be trouble. It's just what happens with bears."

"I'll think about it," I mumbled, and went off to play with Babe. The subject was dropped until some weeks later, when I pushed my face against hers, pretending that I was a bear too, and Babe ripped open my upper lip with one loving swipe that I never saw. Ted said, "It's only going to get worse. You think you'll stay friends once you become afraid of her? No chance."

"I'm *not* afraid of her. She didn't mean to hurt me." But I wanted to be talked around now, and Ted knew it. "Look, it's a simple little operation. Jack Krebs does it every day out at Peaceable Kingdom, and most times the animal's running around playing in a couple of days. Let me take her, Pat. We owe it to her. It's our responsibility."

I didn't go to the antique shop on the day of the operation. I stayed in the house all day, making empty chores for myself to keep from feeling the reality of what was happening to Babe: the anesthetic, the shaving of her fur, the cold smell of disinfectant, the thin knife slicing irrevocably through flesh, muscle, and tendon; the claws coming bloodily away, one by one, meaningless bits of horn and gristle now. But I had convinced myself that we were doing the best—the only—thing for her. I felt heavy with unhappiness all day, but I never doubted.

Ted came over very late that evening, and I ran out to meet him. I stopped in my tracks before I reached him, staring at the still little figure he was carrying in his arms.

"She's just sleeping," he said quickly. "She's all right, but she's had a rough time of it. A little too much anesthetic, maybe. They didn't want me to bring her home until she woke up, but I knew you'd want her back tonight. Let's get her inside."

Her feet looked pitifully small, swathed in bandages the

size of boxing gloves. There was a dankness about her fur, and she breathed with a sound like dead leaves. I wrapped her in a blanket and put her in a box by the side of my bed. I stroked her and whispered to her for hours before I finally fell asleep.

At about four in the morning she moaned suddenly and rose up in the box. I was awake instantly. Babe's breathing had a terrifying snore in it now, and she swayed dumbly over her swollen forepaws, looking for me and not seeing me. Even I could tell that she was in shock. I called Ted immediately, but by the time I hung up I knew she was dying.

I think sometimes that animals see death: that it has a shape and a presence for them, and isn't the blank, silent stopping that we dread so desperately. While their bodies know there is hope, they cling to life as stubbornly as we do; but when it is time to let go, they go nobly—always—and without fear. And, as always, I cry and mourn and become ill, as though it were Babe again. The animals taught me long ago that I am only crying for myself and my own loss, but I have never truly accepted what they know about pain and death. Edna St. Vincent Millay says it for me in a poem: *I understand. But I do not approve. And I am not reconciled.*

Ted and I went out to Peaceable Kingdom on the day Babe died. We just wanted to be going somewhere. When we walked into Jack Krebs's house I cried out in horror to see Babe's ghost: a cub who looked exactly like her tottering around the living room floor, his feet bandaged as heavily as hers had been, his eyes dazed with sedation. Jack explained that he was Babe's brother, who had been declawed with her the day before. I ran out of the house.

In the weeks that followed, I found it impossible to get through a day without crumbling into wretchedness over some merciless little token of Babe—a toy, a dish, a favorite hiding-place, a chewed-on chairleg, even a particular evening hour that had belonged to her. It's remarkable what a clutter of keepsakes and associations can accumulate around a small bear who lived only a few months. The house became my enemy, and I stayed long hours at the antique shop, dully preparing myself all day to go home.

I took a job with a nightclub act that was booked to play a month in Anchorage, Alaska. Two weeks before I was to leave, I was waiting at Peaceable Kingdom to pick up Ted when I recognized Babe's brother in one of the cages for small animals. I went over to see him, and he immediately started sucking on his front paw, rolling his eyes up at me and making a noise like a swarm of bees. Bears—even full-grown ones— do that a lot, the paw-sucking, especially Malayans. It seems to be common to many cubs raised in captivity without their mothers. I've seen lions, tigers, and cougars doing it; and once I knew an orphaned harbor seal who used to suck her flipper in the same sadly pacifying way.

I didn't want anything more to do with bears—or, really, with any wild animals. I walked away to find Ted, but the cub whimpered after me, pacing frantically back and forth in the cage. When I came slowly back to him, he sat up and began sucking on his paw again. I was still standing there when Ted got off duty.

"That's Booper," he said. "He'll probably be sold pretty soon, now that Jack doesn't need a Malayan bear anymore. They just got him and Babe for that one Disney movie, and there isn't much call for Malayans."

"Is that what happens to them? Take them out of the wild, use them for some stupid movie, and then just ship them off anywhere at all? All your friends in the scrapbook—is that what happens to them?"

"I didn't say I liked it," Ted said. "I wouldn't do it myself, but it's not my store. Jack's doing the best he can, I guess."

I took Booper home with me. Ted balked at buying him from Peaceable Kingdom, pointing out that he was already too old to be raised as a pet, and that he would never be anything like the affectionate spirit that Babe had been. He was right: Babe had loved everyone, but Booper cared only for a few people and—logically enough—detested most of the species on sight. Babe liked to please and could be conned into accepting almost anything but an interruption in the flow of groceries. Booper did nothing he didn't want to do, not for anyone. But he was a dear, solemn bear, and he loved to play with Phyllis and Hedy Lamarr in the back yard.

Ted had built him a large cage on my patio, and I would leave him there most days when I went off to the shop. Booper didn't like the cage, and simply refused to stay in it. No matter how elaborately Ted locked and reinforced the door, Booper would find a weak spot somewhere and, beginning with that, patiently unravel the heavy steel wire as though it were no more than a snarl of yarn. Whereupon he would step out and go looking for something interesting to do.

By a blessing, the place he found most immediately interesting—the house and flower garden next door—belonged to a wonderful old woman, herself forever in trouble with the law over her twenty or thirty loud little dogs. Most days when I came home, she'd call to me from her front porch, cackling with amusement. "Well, he got out *again* today. Found him in my tulip bed, same as yesterday, digging up the new bulbs. I just grabbed him by the scruff and marched him right back over home, put him on the chain. He sure does like them bulbs, that bear."

He sure must have liked her, that bear who could pick his cage apart, and whose fangs were nearly as long as my little finger. She always said he had a good heart.

I didn't want to go to Alaska, but I needed the money. The country itself was beautiful in a way I had never seen before, but my month there seemed endless. When I wasn't performing, I stayed in my cold motel room, writing letters to Ted about taking good care of Booper.

Two weeks after my arrival in Anchorage, Ted wrote me

that he had had to take Booper back to Peaceable Kingdom. Someone from down the block had spotted him pottering happily around in the old woman's garden, and had promptly called Animal Control. Ted had warned me that this was bound to happen if Booper kept getting out of his cage, but I was utterly stunned and miserable. I kept thinking about how much worse the ranch would be for Booper now. *If they just don't sell him before I get back. Please, if they just don't sell him.*

I couldn't sleep, and my performance fell off so obviously that the nightclub owner asked me what was wrong. Too down to offer a conventional excuse, I mumbled, "I'm worried about my bear."

He never batted an eye. "You like bears, huh?" I nodded forlornly. "Okay, tell you what. You be ready at ten o'clock tomorrow morning, I'll take you for a ride."

He picked me up outside my motel in an open overland jeep. We clattered through empty, frozen country for almost two hours, finally stopping in front of a snowbound farmhouse. The club owner led me around to the side, where an old yellow schoolbus was up on blocks. Living in the bus—in Alaska, in mid-March, with the temperature fifteen degrees below zero—were two bouncy, friendly African lions.

They certainly seemed to be in excellent shape, everything considered. Their coats were as thick as that of a polar bear or a Siberian tiger, and they played with the farmer with smothering affection when he came out to greet us. We stayed only a little while, though; for the club owner said, "That's not bears. I just wanted to show you, you never know who likes animals."

Another hour brought us to a dilapidated log cabin inhabited by an ancient fur trapper who looked exactly as Hollywood has taught us that ancient fur trappers look. He was gnarled and bristly and brown, with small, quick eyes, and he had the wild smell of Babe and Booper and the lions in the schoolbus. His name, inevitably, was Grizzly Pete.

"Old Pete likes bears," the club owner said proudly. "Girl'd really like to see the bears, Pete."

We followed the old man out back of the cabin, turned a corner, and found ourselves in the dark midst of four half-grown Kodiak bears. They walled us in and roofed us over, crowding us together, and they sniffed immensely at us, whoofing, shaking snow off their heads. I remember how silently and gracefully they moved, and that Pete called them all by name.

I was younger then. You'd never catch me today sauntering blithely among anybody's strange Kodiaks, and so I'll never have another experience like that one time of being considered by the wilderness. It was different from elephants: it shivered continually between menace and fear and a kind of babyish good humor. The bears lost interest in us very quickly and sailed slowly away like thunderheads, like sand dunes.

"Raised 'em all from cubs," Pete said. "Yearlings. Hunters kill the mothers. Easiest thing in the world, kill a bear with cubs."

"How many do you have? Do they come in the house?" I knew the questions were stupid even then, but I was thinking of Babe in the kitchen, playing with a frying pan.

"They ain't pets," Pete said severely. "Don't want 'em to be pets. Soon's they're big enough, out they go, let 'em be bears. I just take care of 'em. I don't have 'em."

He explained that these four most recent cubs were already inclined to wander off on their own for days at a time. Soon they would simply not come back, though they might visit him as adults if the food supply ran low, or if they had cubs of their own to feed. The club owner said, "You never do have any trouble with them, do you, Pete? Never turn ornery on you?"

"We understand each other," the old man answered.

I said slowly, "I wish I could do what you do—take care of them, but still let them be wild. I'm starting to think it was wrong for me to have my bears. Maybe people just shouldn't have animals, even if they love them. Especially if they love them."

Grizzly Pete looked at me for a long time, his expression at once kind and bitterly derisive. "People ain't gonna have to worry about it, a few more years," he muttered finally. "Them cubs been eatin' my food, they look all right now. Big ones out there starvin' to death. I seen 'em. Ranchers come in, loggers cut down the trees, miners come in—where the hell's a bear gonna live? No room. Bears got to have room, like anybody else. Got to eat, nothin' to eat. No room."

He stood glaring at us in the snow, a disheveled and angry bear himself, an old, uncertain bear, swaying on his hind legs. "Come after 'em in goddamn helicopters, shoot right down on 'em, still can't kill 'em half the time. Just cripple 'em so they walk around cryin', can't get food, can't even sleep, can't do nothin' but hurt and cry. I hear 'em."

One of the young Kodiaks came up to him again to push its great spade-shaped head against his shoulder. Pete pushed back without turning, and both he and the bear grunted softly. "Just take care of 'em the best way you can," he said. "It don't make no difference anyway."

The other members of the act agreed to stay on at the Anchorage club for an additional month; but I was so anxious to see Booper that I flew home on the day that my contract expired, which happened to be the day before Good Friday, 1964. The earthquake completely destroyed the motel where I had been staying.

"They sold him last week," Ted said. "I didn't want to tell you."

I didn't weep for Booper as I had for Babe. I couldn't. A kind of guilty numbness had begun to set in: the inevitable "ostrich" stage of not caring about anything, people or animals, trees or water or old buildings. The loss and suffering overwhelms you, deadening your nerves. Nothing can be saved, nothing can be protected; try to help and you only make things worse. So you blind and deafen yourself on purpose, and you march along. I wouldn't go near the ranch anymore, or any other place where I knew that I might see animals I couldn't help. I got very cunning about that.

But Ted kept bringing me animals from Peaceable Kingdom because they needed nursing. No bears, but a lot of lion and cougar cubs, and now and then a wolf or a fawn. Numb or not, I began to learn about taking care of them, because I had to learn. Ted's experience with very young animals was limited, so I read books and wrote letters and was forever telephoning anyone who might be able to advise me about diet and medication, especially the kind, harassed curator of mammals at the San Diego Zoo. And yet, whatever I know for sure, the animals taught me, without exception. There is nothing I know that hasn't cost some animal something.

Basic training. Lion cubs are loud and sweet and dumb. If they bump into a wall, or a piece of furniture, they promptly start pacing back and forth, exactly as you see the adults doing in zoos. They get bored easily and demand to be entertained all the time, while cougar kittens can amuse themselves perfectly well by curling up in a box and watching you move around.

Wolf cubs sing. I had eight of them in the house once, and the only way that I could keep them straight—staggering blindly into the kitchen at three in the morning, heating up their formula—was to put them all together in a box marked NOT FED, and then transfer them one by one to the other box that said FED. As each cub arrived, eyes heavy and tummy properly distended, in the FED box, he would begin to sing, leaning against his brothers and sisters and taking up his particular part of the harmony. It wasn't a howl or a whine, but an unmistakable lullaby of drowsy contentment and security, kept up until they all fell asleep. Human babies do it.

Two of the baby animals Ted brought me to nurse—Chui the leopard and Jambo the lion. It was my first experience at animal raising.

A practical tip—when you have animals, bathrooms are fine things. If I ever design a house for myself, it will have about fifteen bathrooms. They serve marvelously as nurseries, playpens, gymnasiums, hospital wards, guest bedrooms, and emergency hideouts. I know a good deal about that last. They clean up quickly, too, which is nice.

Eventually, of course, there was another bear. This was Candy, a Himalayan. I got her at Jungleland, which was a place like Peaceable Kingdom: no better and probably not much worse. There are a lot of such dealerships. The baby animals huddle in small, dank cages, clawing each other out of fear and hunger and sickness, and anybody who has the money can buy one, for any purpose. I was suddenly nauseated by even my own peripheral, well-meaning part in the whole horrible business, and I made a raging, screaming scene at Jungleland, holding Candy while she scratched wildly at my arms and wrists until the blood came. The dealers were so glad to see me go that I don't think they ever sent me a bill for one terrified, lonely, six-week-old bear.

Himalayans look quite a bit like sun bears, only they are much larger; there's the same pointed face and V-shaped collar; but a full-grown Himalayan may exceed six feet in length and weigh between three and four hundred pounds. Candy grew up to be as affectionate and trusting as Babe had been—benefiting, heaven knows, from all the mistakes that I had already made with both Babe and Booper. There was always a theatrical teasingness about her play, but there was no meanness in her, not ever.

When Ted and I came in together one evening to find her cage on the back patio open, I sat down where I was and let Ted go on alone into the house. I thought I might sit there forever, rather than start gathering up fragments of English Delft and Tang Dynasty equestrian statues. I was speculating idly on whether it would be at all possible to restore the needlepoint chairs, when Ted called to me from an upstairs window, rocking with laughter and insisting that I come inside. I have never entered a tiger's cage with such trepidation; but nothing was broken, chipped, or even displaced. At the top of the stairs stood the Abominable Snowman, nodding blandly, entirely covered with white feathers. Candy loved pillows.

Her good-natured sociability made me agree to let her appear, while she was still quite young, on *Disney's Wonderful World of Color,* provided that I went along with her. The sequence was simple enough: Walt Disney himself looking benignly on as a bear cub and a Malemute puppy romp together, and saying something benign about innocent friendship, or possibly about children the world over. I'm glad I've forgotten it—at the time I feared that the words were hacked forever into my cerebrum. With a rusty pickaxe.

It's a rule of working with animals—especially babies—that you don't ask them to do retakes. You get the shooting done quickly, or you don't get it at all. Whatever he's doing, a bear cub is going to want to be doing something else in five or ten minutes. Amazingly, Candy and the puppy hit it off so well that they played on a tabletop for a solid hour without stopping. Their energy and inventiveness would have supplied enough footage for an entire television show, not that they cared. They were just busy enjoying each other.

Unfortunately, Walt Disney couldn't remember his benign lines, even after almost two hours of mumbling and sputtering, cursing and starting over. The director kept saying loudly, "Just rehearsal, folks, just getting set up here." By the time Disney finally got the words out in the required order, the puppy had collapsed under the hot studio lights, panting, unable to get up. Candy had simply scrambled down from the table, and was beginning to bite me every time I tried to replace her on it. Disney looked up in annoyance—really seeing Candy and the puppy for the first time, I think—and demanded, "What's the matter with those animals? Get them back playing, we ought to be through with this stuff by now."

I moved the puppy out of the lights. "They can't stand the heat anymore," I said. "They're only babies, and they don't understand that they have to keep suffering until you get your lines right. Well, they're not going to, that was it. They're finished working."

Disney was famous for his own rages—I never met any Disney employee who wasn't afraid of him—but he was so taken aback this time that all that came out was a sort of strangled huff. "Well, I'm hot too. I'm hot too, but I'm not complaining."

"You've got nothing to complain about." Until I heard myself speak, I hadn't realized how angry I was: not merely at Walt Disney, but at Peaceable Kingdom, at Jungleland, at a trainer I had once seen set up a fine shot of rabbits in flight by shaving their haunches and spraying them with turpentine (they screamed as they ran); and at myself most of all for saying *If you think so,* and for saying nothing. "The animals don't get paid any more, they don't get any more food for exhausting themselves. You can just stand there getting richer every minute; it doesn't matter at all that you can't read, and the animals could die before you ever noticed them. And they'd just edit that last bit out, and there you'd be on television, loving nature and grinning at the children." I took Candy up under one arm and the puppy under the other, and I walked out of the studio. It was a long time before I was asked to go anywhere in any capacity for Peaceable Kingdom. I am not a natural at public relations.

I do try, though. When the neighbor who had betrayed Booper to Animal Control showed up one morning, asking brightly if her children could see my bear cub, I neither punched her in the eye nor poisoned her tea. Instead, I invited them all in, chatted graciously with her while the children played with Candy, and managed the whole affair—I thought—with English style and American vivacity. The next day as Candy and I were cleaning house (she always helped me by dragging the dust mop over the floor), the county animal-control officer appeared at the door.

"Understand you're harboring a wild animal here," he said as Candy peered around the corner at him. "I'll have to give you a citation. You have two weeks to get rid of the bear, or we'll have to impound her." I didn't hit him, either, but it was only because I couldn't move. I think I just sat and held Candy until Ted came over.

We decided to hide Candy at Peaceable Kingdom on the day that the officials were to return to inspect our premises. We had been told by an attorney that once they had checked to be certain the bear had been removed, it would be difficult for them to pursue that matter any further, unless the bear was reported a second time. I vowed that no one would ever set eyes on Candy again.

They appeared early in the afternoon with two dog-catcher units, a patrol car, and five Animal Control officers with nets and guns. I told the one with the 20-gauge shotgun that Candy weighed slightly more than nine pounds, but he only grew

redder in the face. I led them on a tour of our house and
grounds, while the entire neighborhood stood by, speculating
loudly as to just where the body was buried. The search took
the better part of an hour, ending at Candy's cage where, with
undeniably childish malice, I had enclosed Prissy, my pet
goat. She chewed her hay and stared placidly at the squad of
sweating, frustrated officers. Everything interested Prissy mildly.

"I don't think this can be the one you're looking for," I
said hesitantly. "I mean, they *sold* her to me as a goat or something. Are they illegal too?"

They packed up all their nets and guns and went away. I
was warned that they would be watching me, and that any
further reports would be dealt with harshly. Two or three weeks
went by without incident. I had fixed a hiding place for Candy
in the attic, and I kept a supply of fig newtons and bananas
(her favorite foods) on hand in case of a surprise visit. We
even held practice raids: Ted would ring the doorbell without
warning, and I would grab Candy, whisk her up to the attic,
stuff a banana into her mouth, and race down to the door. In
midseason form, we were doing it in two minutes flat.

Booper's friend, the old woman next door, was waiting for
me one day when I came home from shopping. "Them cops
was back here just now," she whispered dramatically. "They
went all around the house, checked the back field and everything. I asked what they wanted; they said they was looking
for you, be back in an hour or so. What are you gonna do?"

Suddenly I was frightened, and very unsure about the security of the attic. "If I put Candy in her little traveling cage,
will you hide her in your garage?"

"Sure will. But what do I do if she starts cutting up?"

"I'll give you a couple of packages of fig newtons. Do you
have a screwdriver? She loves to play with screwdrivers."

I ran indoors and loaded Candy into the cage. I had just
passed her over the fence when the Animal Control car arrived, accompanied by three crowded squad cars. We reen-

Candy, my little Himalayan bear, as a cub, chewing on her favorite screwdriver. She had the run of the house and followed me everywhere.

acted the same scene as before, and though the officers departed furious and empty-handed again, I was too depressed this time to take any pleasure in our small victory. Zoning laws could be outfoxed for a time, but not forever. I would wear down before they did.

"Maybe we should keep her out at the ranch," Ted suggested that evening. "You could visit her there every day, if you wanted."

Candy was playing on the floor with the old woman's screwdriver as we talked. In the course of the day's adventure, she had consumed six boxes of fig newtons, which had made her slightly less active than usual. But her eyes were bright and aware, and she gripped the screwdriver between her teeth like the bumbling pirate she was.

"I can't," I said. "Not this one. I'm not letting this one out of my sight for a minute. I'll have to move, that's all. I'll just go somewhere else with her."

We fought it out in a Macbeth and Lady Macbeth pattern that was already becoming familiar: me proposing some outrageous upheaval, Ted at first resisting with all his considerable power, and then invariably succumbing to the lure of demanding how I was going to set about it. Leopard and lion.

In the following months, we began looking for property in an area zoned for agriculture, where wild animals would be classed as pets and permitted. By great good luck, I managed to sell the Beachy Street place for enough money to buy a lovely two-story Victorian frame house on half an acre of land in Newhall, a small town not far from Peaceable Kingdom. The house had been used as a location for the original film of *The Virginian,* and the whole area was full of old movie sets. I moved in immediately with Candy, Prissy, Salomey the pig, the two dogs, and two horses. The old lady next door hugged Candy goodbye, and told her to behave.

5

Shortly after I had settled into the Newhall house—Candy had the run of the place, a barn to play in, and no need to practice being raided anymore—Ted came up with an offer for me from Jack Krebs. Would I be interested in working two or three hours a day at Peaceable Kingdom, caring for the baby animals? I was doing it at home, anyway, and I could certainly use even the little money that Jack would be paying me. The antique shop had gone under before I moved, never having recovered from my month's absence in Alaska. I could set my own hours, to make sure that the job didn't interfere with my nightclub work.

Surprisingly, perhaps, Ted was more enthusiastic about the offer than I was. I didn't think I had many illusions left concerning the nature of professional animal training; and I knew just enough about the work itself by now to understand that I might as well know nothing at all. But I still had unlimited faith in my capacity for learning new things, and I still believed that devotion and desire conquer all. *If I don't take the job, God knows who Jack's likely to hire. Let it at least be an idiot who loves them.*

On my first day at work, I was told to take over the care of two black fallow deer fawns who were being quartered at the Krebs' house. They were on a bottle four times a day, and Connie Krebs, Jack's wife, showed me how to make up their formula from goat's milk and water. She had taken the bottles out of the refrigerator, and I questioned her instinctively: should fawns that young be getting cold milk? Connie was certain and reassuring, and I accepted her word.

In addition to the fawns, I had two wolf cubs, a young cougar, and a bear cub in my care. My kitchen was one of the several small trailers which were used for offices on the ranch, this particular one equipped with a tiny hot plate. The two hours a day rapidly expanded to eight, or even longer. I would arrive home at night just in time to make dinner, change my clothes, and go to work, returning from the nightclub at 3:00 A.M., at the earliest. I had no help, no one but a frantically busy Ted to advise me, for the other keepers were as ignorant as I, and far more wary of showing it. Nobody volunteered opinions at Peaceable Kingdom.

The fawns worried me. They seemed very weak, and they both had continual diarrhea. I always began my working day by giving them their morning bottle, but one morning I arrived at the Krebs' house to find their pen empty. Connie apologized: "Oh, Pat, didn't anybody tell you? I sent the deer over to the ranch. They're so messy in the house, with all that loose stool."

"Where did they put them?" It was the middle of February and very cold. The fawns weren't used to the outside temperature, and I knew they weren't well.

"I don't know. I think in the small-animal section."

I ran all the way to the ranch. The small-animal section was the hellhole of Peaceable Kingdom: cold and damp even in good weather, with cement floors and no shelter. As I approached, I saw two of the keepers standing by a pen littered with filthy straw. I knew what I was going to find before I got there. Both fawns were lying on their sides, thin necks stretched out and back like those of dying birds. The only sign of life was the faintest bubbling of mucus in their nostrils. I screamed at the keepers to get Jack, Ted, a vet, anybody, and I sat down in the straw hugging the fawns against me, trying to warm them with my body. They died in my arms within a few minutes.

Jack called me into his office that afternoon and told me to contact the man who had supplied us with the fallow deer and order two more. The dealer's name was Mr. Via, and when I telephoned him later that day he questioned me thoroughly about the death of the two fawns. "Did you make sure the temperature of the milk was extra hot? You know them deer need it even hotter than most babies; the mother's body temperature is higher. You want to make that milk plenty warm."

I started to cry. I told Mr. Via about the cold milk and explained that I hadn't known. Mr. Via was shocked and angry, and refused to sell any more deer to Peaceable Kingdom. "I told that feller that picked them up about the milk. I spent an hour showing him how to mix the bottles, and how long to heat it so it was just the right temperature. You mean to say he never told you?"

"I wasn't here when they delivered the fawns, Mr. Via. I started to work just after that. When I took over the feeding, that's what they were doing." I couldn't make myself tell him that I had always felt it to be wrong. "I know you shouldn't give cold food to any baby, but I thought these might be some special type of deer."

"Fallow deer come from Europe," Mr. Via said. "They're special, all right—nicest little deer you'd ever want to see." He began to talk about them, telling me more than I thought it was possible to know about a single species: diet, mating habits, social relationships, illnesses, parasites, color phases. He was one of the very few dealers I had ever spoken to who knew or cared anything about the animals they sold. I copied down everything he said on bits of wrapping paper.

When he paused, I asked, "Mr. Via, could I come out there some day and learn a little about deer, and whatever else you have? I'm trying to take care of all these young animals, and I don't know where to ask or what to believe. I'd be willing to pay you for your time. I just don't want to kill any more of them."

"Young lady, if you want to learn about deer and birds, you come on out here any time." He was silent for a moment. "I guess maybe I'd better let your boss have them two other deer. If he doesn't get them from me, he'll go and buy them somewhere else, and they won't be healthy. But you tell that fool about the milk. Like to kick somebody's tail about that." Mr. Via hung up.

Jack was charmingly philosophical. "Pat, you've got to learn not to take these things too seriously. I'm glad you care so much, because it means the next pair of deer won't die. But you just have to learn to face it, these things happen sometimes."

"But it was so stupid. It wasn't an act of God, it was plain dumbness, a waste. Can't you tell the men to write their instructions down when they pick up the animals?"

He chuckled and patted my hand. "Guys just get careless. Listen, I'll tell you what—you take the truck and pick up this new pair yourself. No middlemen involved that way, right?"

"All right," I said. "No middlemen. Not just with the deer, but with all the babies. I don't want anybody handling them but me. And I don't want any of them kept in that small-animal pit. I'll keep them at my house if Connie can't stand the mess. I'll be responsible. Somebody has to be."

My relationship with the Krebses, and with everyone else who worked at Peaceable Kingdom—excluding Ted—deteriorated steadily after the death of the fawns. I'm no fuzzy duckling to live with at the best times, and I seemed to be perpetually tired and bitter and full of contempt, defending my babies ferociously, taking nobody's word for anything, looking for trouble. But it was that or the ostrich state again—there was no middle ground for me there. Jack would have fired me a dozen times, I think, except that he couldn't have found anyone who came as cheap and worked as hard. And after all, he had my number; he knew where I was vulnerable. He could afford to put up with my scenes.

When my body finally forced me to choose between the animals and the nightclubs, it was the clubs that went. I was now subsisting entirely on the salary I earned at the ranch, and on occasional casual dates as an entertainer. Ted, however, also got some stunt work doubling for actors when he did studio calls with animals. He took me with him on one of those calls once.

They were working cougars at Universal Studios for some Western series. I knew and loved both of the cats: a dignified old male who had suffered from rickets as a cub, and a beautiful, sweet-tempered female to double for him. The scene required a cougar to run among some rocks and leap off the top of an embankment. There were four trainers, counting Ted, each one with a CO_2 gun. They would place the male cougar in position on a rock, and then everyone would yell and scream and pop the CO_2 cartridges, so that he would run out in terror. When he ran to a wrong corner, they would spook him out with more noise and confusion. They were forced to do this repeatedly, as the cougar in his bewilderment would frequently run in the wrong direction. It went on and on, until the cougar was so tired that he refused to budge, whatever they did. At that point, they put him in his cage and continued with the female.

When I left the studio, no usable footage had yet been shot, and both cougars were hysterical with exhaustion. The female had to be dragged back to the van, and it took all four men to get the chain off her. I tried to help, because we were friends, but she would have killed me or anyone else who came within range. This was the cat who purred like a giant kazoo whenever she saw someone coming toward her cage at the ranch. It was a week before I could approach either her or the old male again.

"I know," Ted said that night, over and over. "Pat, I know, I don't like it any more than you do. But it's a business, we have to get the job done. At least we don't beat them, like some of the trainers at the other places do. We just get it done the best way we can."

"What do you think that excuses? How can you say you love those animals, and then do what I saw you do to them?" That hurt him, and I was instantly sorry, but I couldn't stop. "I wouldn't let you work Candy after seeing you there. I'll never let anybody work her, not if we were starving."

"All studio work isn't that rough," he said. "Cougars are always trouble, because they don't like to walk on leashes and you have to drag them to get them into place, and they're never that hungry so that you can work them to food. Lions are a lot easier, and the bears really like to work because we feed them up so much. You just caught one of the bad days."

"It's so *dumb,* Ted. All the time they waste, all that film they shot for nothing. What kind of a business is that? Just from the point of view of economics, there must be a better way of doing it."

Ted nodded grudgingly. "I think about it. I try things out sometimes, when I'm by myself. But there's just never enough time at the studios, and I'm always with the other guys. And wild animals aren't like dogs and cats—you can't teach them tricks and make them understand what you're doing. You know that."

"Then why can't the studios film them when they're all relaxed, and use whatever they get that way?"

"Because—Pat, for Christ's sake, because they have a script to follow, and the director has a set pattern he wants to see.

You can't tell them to wait for the animal. Look, let's drop it, I don't want to talk about it anymore. Just stay away from the studios, if the work gets you that upset."

A few days later, I was sent to pick up the fallow deer that we had ordered from Mr. Via. His farm was about two hours' drive from Newhall: twenty acres of green fields with deer, swans, Australian wallaroos and wallabies, and all manner of unfamiliar birds wandering freely everywhere. Compared to Peaceable Kingdom, it was the Isles of the Blessed; and Mr. Via had to come out of his house and introduce himself to me. I was standing at the fence offering a handful of grass to a tiny Asian barking deer.

Mr. Via turned out to be a round, brown-eyed man whose real business was raising turkeys. "My wife and I, we just liked having the little marsupials around because they were all so pretty and friendly. Not much like turkeys. Then, the way it happens, somebody gave us a couple of deer—Axis deer, they were, those bright spotted ones over there, *chitals* they call them in India. And we liked them too, and the first thing you know, we've got all these deer. And then I always did love birds. Come on, we'll go for a walk."

He took me through the fields, happily pointing out flights and gardens of flamingoes, crested cranes, Victoria crowned pigeons, and many rare varieties of ducks. Besides the deer I had already seen, there were African bushbuck, blowing away from me when I came too near like bits of paper, burned to lace, swooping up the chimney. We talked mostly about hoofed animals that day, and when I asked how he could possibly know deer so well, not being a professional zoologist, he looked at me with something like Grizzly Pete's dour amusement, but without the bitterness.

"You never asked me what I know about turkeys. Now, I don't love turkeys. I don't think I ever met a man who could love a turkey. But I know turkeys." He let it go at that.

I stayed for hours, asking questions and watching Mr. Via with the deer and the wallabies and the birds. His wife, as round and gentle as he, brought out the two fallow deer fawns to me. "They're two days old," she said. Only the fawns' eyes moved as she held them—they were keeping as still as they would have in the wild with lean danger gliding by. I remember that their hooves were as precise and delicate as frost crystals, and that I have never been more frightened in the presence of an animal.

"Keep them warm," Mrs. Via said. "Feed them every four hours, if you can. If these two die, I don't know if we could sell you any more."

She put the fawns into my arms. I said, "If they die, I'd never be able to come back here. And I want to come back."

"Both of you quit talking like that," Mr. Via ordered. "You come back. Whether they live or die, you come back."

The fawns didn't die, and I stayed friends with Mr. and Mrs. Via.

Ted took the back seat out of my station wagon and replaced it with a large, hay-filled box for the fawns to ride in as I drove back and forth between Newhall and Peaceable Kingdom. He also built a cage in the back for Candy, who was passionately eager to play with the new babies. I think the remodeling of the station wagon was a gesture of husbandly pride on Ted's part—he expresses himself most truly with his hands—and I occasionally heard him defending my truculent craziness even to Jack Krebs himself.

At that time Ted was working at Universal on a movie called *Fluffy,* starring Tony Randall and Shirley Jones. It was the story of a professor who had a pet lion, and since the lion's role was a big one, Universal was using two of Jack's full-grown males in the part. I don't think they were father and son, but they were named Zamba and Zamba, Jr. Zamba, the lead cat, was a normally gregarious lion who hated Ted savagely, for no reason that we could ever discover. Some ranch employee resembling Ted must have teased him at one time or another, and whenever Zamba was working, Ted would have to go off and hide. It hurt Ted's feelings beyond any disguising. He especially wanted to be liked by lions.

Because he was never able to work with Zamba, Ted devoted a great deal of time to the understudy, Junior, who was bigger and handsomer than Zamba, with a reputation for being difficult. ("Difficult," to an animal trainer, most often means growling when kicked.) He would take Junior out under a tree on the set every day, and they would sit quietly together watching the filming. Everyone on the picture became aware of the rapport that was developing between the two of them. It was a very new experience for Ted, and he seemed almost afraid of it at times.

"You know, I can sit there with him and know exactly what he's thinking. I feel everything he does. Every time he moves an ear or his eyes dilate, I know why it happened."

"It's the way I feel when I'm with Candy," I said. "With the fawns. I'm sure Candy thinks I'm her mother, and I can feel what she wants almost the way a mother bear would. A lion would know what Junior's feeling." I spoke cautiously because Ted had understandably come to shy away from discussing training techniques with me. "You might try working him like that sometime. Lion to lion."

I wasn't too sure I knew what I meant myself, and Ted changed the subject as quickly as he usually did. But in the next few weeks he continued to spend as much time with Junior as he could, even going out to the studio on days when there was no call for him. One evening he was more elated than I had ever seen him. He was trembling a little, and his voice was hoarse as he told me about the day.

"The way it turned out, we had to use Junior all the time, because Zamba just didn't feel like working. Acted exactly like he had a migraine. I wonder if lions do get headaches?—I've seen them act like that before. Anyway, we had to use my boy, and I asked if I could work him, and they let me. Pat, he worked all day just to me, never got upset, we never had to spook him, and he was beautiful. I'd find out what they wanted him to do, and then I'd set it up, try to figure out what would make this lion want to do that. You know, like if he had to walk somewhere, I'd call him, and he came to me, Pat—he came every time. And when he started to get tired of that, I'd let him rest in the shade until they wanted him to move. Then I'd get them to shine a reflector in his direction, and he'd move, just as calmly, out of the light and right into the shade again. I always placed the shade in the area they wanted him to move to. I wish you could have been there, Pat. This one you would have loved."

We began to stay up late every night, discussing the problems that Ted had encountered during the day's shooting. He would observe the tactics that were used to make Zamba work, and we would try to imagine ways of getting the same result without hurting, frightening, or degrading the lion. Junior continued to work so much better with Ted than Zamba did for his troop of yelling, pot-banging trainers that the two of them kept getting other film jobs after *Fluffy* was finished. Junior was always the star lion's understudy, but he generally wound up with more footage than the lead cat. He was a lovely, calm lion, and he made Ted calm too.

My own practical education progressed by hiccups and lurches and skids. One of my tasks at the ranch was to feed a gang of spider monkeys and clean out their cage. I am not crazy about monkeys even now, especially spider monkeys— apes are different, behaving less like men—and I was utterly terrified of this lot. They knew it the first time I entered the cage (monkeys are nearly as quick as human children to sense whom they may torture); and they pulled my hair, rode my back, bit me when they dared, threw their feces at me, and never failed to have me bawling helplessly as I mopped the floor every day. They used to line the front of the cage, watching me as I went about my other chores, waiting for me.

One of the trainers advised me, "They'll kill you if you don't get after that big male." He pointed out the oversized beast who was always my chief tormentor. "He's the head man, the king. You kick his ass and they'll leave you alone." But when I was in with the monkeys, I was too paralyzed by the swarming malice and the hateful chittering even to think of fighting back. And I had never yet struck any animal.

But there came an afternoon when something snapped. It had been a wretched day, anyway, full of sick babies, separate fights with both Krebses, and a bear who had given up and wouldn't last the night. I had put off cleaning the spider monkey's cage as long as I could, and they were all over me before I was quite through the door, with the big male in the lead. He clawed my face, almost daintily, and set his teeth in my forearm.

"God damn it, all right!" I screamed. I hit the monkey backhanded, as hard as I could. He flew all the way across the cage, slammed into the bars and dropped to the floor, momentarily stunned. I stood over him, howling like a madwoman. "Is that it? Is that what I'm supposed to do, you bloody, stinking misery? Does that make me the head monkey now?"

The other monkeys had scattered to their perches and branches and rings, for all the world like panicked birds. They were absolutely silent, looking from me to their leader, who got up slowly, whimpering. "Come on," I said. When the monkey's eyes focused on me, he covered his head with both arms. I wanted to pick him up, but I cleaned out the cage and left. I never had any more trouble with the spider monkeys.

The situation at Peaceable Kingdom, however, got worse every day. There was, somehow, always enough money to buy more animals; but there was what I considered a meager budget for food, and seldom enough money to build larger, warmer facilities, or to hire good keepers and trainers. The cages were sometimes filthy, and even the healthiest animals often suffered from all sorts of internal and external parasites.

It was no secret that Jack Krebs was trying to sell the ranch. Matters had reached the point where he had hocked Margie the elephant, putting her up as collateral for a loan from another animal outfit. We were forever having to hide Margie from Jack's creditors on very short notice. Anyone with a savings account who showed the remotest interest in animals was given the red-carpet tour of Peaceable Kingdom and offered everything but physical violence to part him from his money. But no deal ever seemed to get beyond a good look at the ranch. A red carpet covers only so much.

One day, however, the Krebses called a staff meeting and announced triumphantly that the wealthy film producer Ivan Tors had bought an interest in Peaceable Kingdom, which would be renamed from that moment forth. The new name was something else but I'll call it Animals, Inc. Not only would there now be money to expand the ranch and entirely remodel all the facilities, but Tors intended to use it as a base for his movie and television productions, among them *Daktari, Cowboy in Africa,* and *Gentle Ben.* The atmosphere was as though Robin Hood had arrived, bankrolled by Cinderella's godmother.

Ted and I were overjoyed—how could conditions help but improve for the animals now?

6

In an odd way, there's something to be said for the time before Ivan Tors bought into Peaceable Kingdom and made it Animals, Inc. Ted and I were so poor that we had finally become liberated from worrying about money, or even thinking about it very much. We didn't have any real hopes or ambitions—we were too tired for that—but we were more fearless and inventive than we may ever have been again. There was absolutely nothing for us to lose by doing what was important to us.

Maybe Freddie the Freeloader epitomizes that time of our lives as well as anything else. Freddie was a two-year-old lion with the most endearing face that I have ever known on any animal. His adolescent mane stuck straight up from his forehead in a wispy topknot, and he had huge brown eyes with long, delicate eyelashes that would have been normal for an elephant, but looked outrageously Hollywood on a lion. Both eyes were so crossed that Freddie literally couldn't see straight: he had no depth perception at all, and would miss by three or four feet when he tried to jump up on a picnic bench or into the back of a truck. He fell out of trees. We never laughed at him—lions can't endure being laughed at. (Cougars don't care, and leopards never liked your voice much anyway.)

Freddie was Ted's baby, more so even than Junior. No one else at the ranch wanted anything to do with him; what was the point of paying attention to Freddie? He'd never work, he'd never be good for anything but finding his way to his food dish, and he could hardly even do that. Jack Krebs was forever trying to sell or trade off his cross-eyed misfit, but each time Ted somehow talked him out of it. Ted would take Freddie on long walks every day, and spend hours with him, trying to find out who he was, what he liked and didn't like, and how he seemed to respond to our tentative new ideas of training. There was no studio work coming in, and nothing much to do but our regular chores. For once we had plenty of time simply to be with animals.

Then Ivan came and there was a new manager, and for the next few months all was swirling, energetic confusion, and a ceaseless parade of new typewriters arriving in the office. Sound stages and new buildings were going up everywhere; strange people were running around waving leather-bound clipboards and shouting incomprehensible orders that never seemed to be heeded (they themselves were usually never seen again); all the trucks were painted with zebra stripes (it had something to do with Ivan's movie *Rhino*).

Ivan Tors himself was very visible, most often coming out to the ranch with his wife, the actress Constance Dowling. Ivan is a kind, sweet man who truly cares about animals, and truly does believe that the lion and the lamb can lie down together. Everyone at the ranch encouraged him and Constance in the belief that they were picnicking in a kind of Elysium where such things happened all the time, and where the animals' welfare and happiness was the single concern of every employee. The question of how much fresh fruit, vitamins, and medical attention Ivan's money was actually buying couldn't be expected to come up in such surroundings.

Ivan was neither a fool nor inattentive, however. On his first visit to Animals, Inc., he walked all over the ranch, inspecting every area, including my makeshift kitchen. When he arrived I was struggling with the hot plate, trying to heat the fawns' bottles and prepare oatmeal for a sick chimpanzee. Ivan was very gracious to me, but I heard him talking sharply to the manager when they left the trailer; and the next day I was told to start buying supplies for the new kitchen and dispensary. Ivan saw other things beside visions.

Heaven knows what he must have thought of me in those days. I was more than ever the scroungy outlaw of the ranch: troublemaking, belligerent, unable to get through a day without fighting with someone over my babies' care or condition; granted a kind of royal fool's freedom, because nobody could manage me, but with no more influence than any such jester on the things that happened. For my point of view, the office equipment at Animals, Inc., might have changed hands, but the nature of the ranch itself remained the same, always. All that mattered with animals was to acquire them, like typewriters.

One afternoon I was in the midst of furnishing the new kitchen when the manager stopped by for a moment to tell me that there would be two young gorillas arriving within the next few days, and that they would have to be kept in their shipping crates until a cage could be built for them. He warned me to be careful with the older one, as she had attacked her previous keeper, and suggested as he left, "Be a good idea to read up a lot on gorillas, Pat. You know—what they eat, and so on."

In the following days I called every major zoo in the country, begging for any information that they could give me on the care of gorillas. I purchased George Schaller's book, *The Year of the Gorilla*—then the only study easily available—and I wrote urgently to Dr. Dietz, one of the foremost authorities on primate behavior. He rushed a great deal of data and practical advice to me, and I was up most of one night reading it all. But I became, rather than confident, increasingly angry and frightened, not of the gorillas, but *for* them—if one fact stood out of all I read, it was that neither I nor anyone else at Animals, Inc., had any business handling such beautiful and complex animals. I thought of them being somewhere in the night, in the baggage compartment of some plane or van, on their way to hell, and I vowed desperately to be their friend and fight for them, and I knew it wouldn't help.

They arrived the next day, and the two huge shipping crates were deposited in my trailer kitchen for warmth, as the new kitchen was not yet completed and it was the middle of winter. There was no other place on the entire ranch to leave them. I walked around the crates as they rocked and shifted on the floor, shaking the trailer. I could see the gorillas' eyes through the wooden slats, and I tried to talk soothingly to them, but there was nothing I could say.

They smelled wonderful. Nothing smells as sweet as a gorilla, though bears smell as good in their own harsher way. It's a slightly musty kind of sweetness, a little like the smell of grapes in the sun. I would know it anywhere. If innocence had a smell, it would smell like a gorilla.

Ted tied the crates down to keep the gorillas from moving them all around the trailer. "The cage'll be ready pretty quickly," he assured me. "They'll be all right till then, don't worry about it."

"Don't worry! Dr. Dietz says they have to eat twice a day, and they shouldn't ever have any mess in their quarters. How do you think I'm going to feed them and keep them clean while they're in those boxes?"

"You'll just have to do the best you can until they've got the cage ready. It'll be all right, Pat—they'll adjust." The phrase was the manager's favorite.

The gorillas were in the shipping crates for more than two weeks. I fed them by pouring their liquid formula through a tiny airhole, using a watering can with a long funnel. I pushed cut-up fruits and vegetables and pieces of whole-wheat bread through the same holes. Eventually I found a way of hosing out the crates, letting them drain through other holes that I had cut in the bottoms. Even so, the stench of the crates spread out from the trailer kitchen to other ranch facilities, and many employees began to complain about it.

I thought often of opening the crates and letting the gorillas out. I didn't do it, because I was afraid of their being hurt, or hurting themselves; but sometimes I still wish, very seriously, that I had.

They never stopped smelling like gorillas. Forcing a man to live in his own excrement until his mind and all his senses are drowned in foulness—and the average gorilla is considerably cleaner about his person than the average human being—is an approved traditional method of breaking him, of reducing him to an animal, as we say. The two great animals shut up in boxes in my trailer, crouching alone in darkness and filth, never gave in, never went mad, never diminished for an instant from what they were. Edging around the crates a hundred times a day, lugging my eternal buckets and bottles of baby-animal formula, or pressed close against them crooning pitiful, hopeless lies into the reek, I could still smell their old sweetness of dark grapes and attic sachets.

The cage was no improvement on the crates when it was completed at last. Gorilla cages, Dr. Dietz had written to me, need to be warm, easily cleaned, and properly drained, to keep the animals from catching cold. The new cage was none of the above: the gorillas' usual choice was to be indoors, immured in their own feces, or to go out into the cold wind and the pools of stagnating water. I cleaned the cage myself, and I increased their medication until half their formula must have been pure Terramycin. I was sick with the certainty that they were going to die. In their privacy and dignity, it seemed the only thing for them to do.

They were both females, and their names were Shamba and Wog. Wog was only three—still a baby, really—but Shamba was six years old, with a gentle, wondering face and an incredibly delicate manner of touching everything. I can still feel the petal grace of her inch-thick fingers on my cheek, where she used to touch me through the bars. The manager had seriously instructed me to feed her with a long spoon—as though I were supping with the devil—but I gave her her bananas and lettuce and melons by hand, and we would stand looking at each other. Gorillas like to look straight at you. She would turn her back to me, which is a gorilla's way of displaying trust, formally making herself vulnerable to a friend. Elephants do that, too. Sometimes I'd reach in and tickle her, and she always laughed.

Oh, they are so lovely. There is an indomitable, unbetrayable goodness about gorillas; and if I am committing the behaviorists' deadly sin of attributing human virtues and emotions to a lower animal, let them bloody well strip off my buttons. The fact is that gorillas practice every one of the virtues that we claim as uniquely our own and mount in the echoing museums of our souls. They are brave and loyal, they help each other, they rival elephants as parents and whales for gentleness; they play and they have humor, and they harm nothing. They are what we should be. I don't know if we'll ever get there.

Shamba and Wog were eventually sold. I heard that they were to go to the Dallas Zoo. I was glad of it, for their sakes. On the day of their departure, I was asked to come out to the ranch and help get Shamba into the van that was to take her to the Los Angeles Airport. She was making trouble about it, and nobody wanted to go near her.

When she saw me she called out and came to me, and she followed me unquestioningly into the van. We sat in the dark together all the way to the airport, and we held hands and cried. I kept telling her earnestly, "Shamba, it's all right, it'll be wonderful, I promise you. You'll be warm all the time, and there won't be water in your cage anymore, ever. And there'll be lots of good food, and you'll have a boy gorilla to play with —oh, it'll be so good, so much better than here, truly." Then

I'd start to cry again, and Shamba would touch my face and feel the tears and cry too. She knew as well as I did that we would never see each other again.

My daily routine at Animals, Inc., had been established long before Ivan's arrival, and it changed very little in the bustling weeks that followed. All animals are creatures of habit, and it's rather necessary to become one yourself to understand them and care for them properly. I usually began at six-thirty or seven every morning by walking over the entire compound with a notepad, checking as best I could on the condition of all the animals. I would talk to them and try to get them moving around, in order to study the look of their coats, the brightness or dullness of their eyes (this is still the truest indicator of an animal's health that I know), and the way they held themselves. The cages wouldn't have been washed down yet, and I was slowly learning to read an animal's stool for signs of parasites or dietary deficiencies. It was the most important part of any day, that first cold, silent hour.

Honey the tigress was a good example of my daily concerns. Honey suffered from renal rickets, which is common among cage-bred big cats: in this form, the anal passage doesn't develop fully, and the animal suffers agonies of blockage when given things like chicken necks to eat. I watched singlemindedly over Honey's diet, making certain that she always had a great deal of oil in her food, and that she was given only what her crippled intestines could handle. She was eventually sold to some little traveling circus, where she was fed on chicken necks like all the other carnivores, and died of it.

(Honey and her sister Princess appeared in a Disney movie called *Tiger Walks,* which I remember particularly because the script also called for a pair of tiger cubs, as well as the grown animals. Not having any cubs handy, they took two baby cougars that I was then raising at home, and painted stripes on them. The film was made like that, which tells you something about the way these things are done.)

One result of those early mornings is that to this day I can't walk past a cage—at a zoo, or at any other sort of animal compound, including my own—without stopping to see if it's clean, and if the animal inside has food and water and seems in good shape. It's automatic even to notice whether there's something like straw or earth on the floor to keep their feet from the cold stone. I don't think you can be an animal person without this reflex.

Then it would be time to go back to my kitchen and take the bushbaby out of the oven. The bushbaby, a small African lemur, is a nocturnal creature, and he would carom around the kitchen all night long, usually curling up in the oven toward dawn. I would put him back into his sleeping cage and begin preparing everybody's formula. This always took a good deal of time, partly because of the large quantities involved, and partly because of the precision with which the blending had to be done. Too little butterfat, and most of my nursing babies became badly constipated; too much, and they got diarrhea. The mixture for Cyrano and Beatrice, the giant anteaters, had to contain not only ground round, egg yolk, cottage cheese, vitamins, and calcium, but also exact amounts of formic acid, to give it the proper ant flavor. The anteaters lived in the kitchen, and Cyrano would generally be trying to climb my leg as I worked, pinching it with oversized front claws made to tear open termite hills and fight off jaguars. Giant anteaters don't look real, and they are awesomely messy and smelly to keep in a kitchen, but they like to be hugged, though they aren't built for it.

The bulk of my morning would be spent in carrying the big bottles of formula on foot to cages located all over the ranch. There would usually be a suggestion of sunlight in the early afternoon, and I would try to have some of the babies outside during those hours—in particular the tropical ones, such as

Most people wouldn't think anteaters to be capable of affection, but Cyrano, in his own way, was a lover.

Cyrano and Beatrice. Anteaters, who walk on their knuckles with the great sickle-shaped claws awkwardly turned under and in, need very much to be on earth and leaves—they suffer, and can in time become crippled, on concrete floors like the ones provided at Animals, Inc. I bought a playpen, removed the flimsy flooring, and set it up in the sun most afternoons, lugging the anteaters out to it, one under each arm. (I was stronger in those days: Beatrice was petite, but Cyrano weighed a good forty-five pounds.) Our favorite park was a certain well-kept lawn, which was used as one of the regular sets for *Daktari*. We were in continual trouble over that lawn, because Cyrano and Beatrice always dug holes in it, grubbing ecstatically in the good warm dirt. Their happiness at once comforted and saddened me. They asked for so little, and so rarely got even that.

I cleaned cages and went over my medical records while the baby animals were outside, and brought them in again when the grayness and the wind crept back. Then it would be time to prepare dinner for those animals who were fed more than once a day: the gorillas, the fawns, the bears. I would be able to be with each of them for at least a little while, talking to them, brushing them, even singing sometimes, and sometimes not doing anything at all. Perhaps the most important thing I learned during my apprenticeship at the ranch had to do with the power of being still with an animal: not talking then, not staring, but sitting quite still every day until—in a month, in a year, in two years—you know what that animal is, because you are the same thing. It takes times and silence, but it happens.

Something else I was learning every day was that animal work tends to attract a high proportion of sadistic psychotics, on the one hand, and sentimental incompetents on the other. We had both sorts at Animals, Inc. For instance, there was a girl whom we shall call Faye who used to beat the bears with a rubber hose to make them work. She's still around, one of the most successful studio trainers in the business. And I remember two wild-caught baboons whom I pitied and feared and loved to look at, because the male was so good to the female, and so protective of her. When two keepers entered the cage one day—the older man showing the younger how you handled the big monkeys—the male thought they had come to harm his mate, and immediately flew at them. The first keeper hit him on the head with a club and killed him.

They are so much frailer than they look, those big monkeys, and all the other big animals who arouse the worst possible combinations of terror, egotism and power-hunger among the people who work with them. *"Ah, it's just a hot-shot, just getting his attention." "You got to clout a chimp up, let him know who's boss." "Hell, you can't hurt a bear hitting him in the head."* But you can—you can kill them in an instant—and it happens all the time, in the studios, on the animal ranches, everywhere. I've always suspected that that's how poor Freddie the Freeloader died, after he had become a star as Clarence the Cross-Eyed Lion. Some human being's fear killed him.

It was Ivan Tors who, having become aware of Freddie's unique charm, changed his name and introduced him as a regular character on *Daktari*. Overnight, in the best theatrical tradition, our useless little outcast was the center of attention, the head lion at Animals, Inc. He even got fan mail, like Marshall Thompson, Cheryl Miller, and Judy the chimpanzee. Nothing was too good for Clarence, and Ted and I went around like parents with a boy in Harvard Law School. *My son, the lion.*

This was four or five months after Ivan's arrival, and just before he and his brother-in-law, Lenny Kaufman, produced their promotional film on Animals, Inc. The idea of the movie was to show the personnel of the ranch in their daily jobs, in loving company with as many animals as possible. I was shown feeding and caring for some of my babies; Charley Franks, an old trainer who was one of my few friends at the ranch, exercised his elephant, Sonita (it was his and his wife's greatest fear that they might die and leave Sonita with no one to care for her); people like Faye were all very affectionate with their particular charges, and so on. Even the secretaries appeared with chimpanzees sitting beside them, presumably helping. It was a successful film of its kind. I've seen it many times.

Clarence is in the promotional film, of course, but not with Ted. The manager had his foreman appear with Clarence, since, after all, Clarence was the new treasure of the ranch. I don't think that I have ever seen Ted so hurt, and I shrink inside myself, writing about it, to remember his pain. It wasn't that he had tamed Clarence, who was born as gentle as he looked, or that he had trained him to do any tricks; but that he had taught that half-blind, utterly uncoordinated lion how to play, and how to wrestle, and how to have fun. He was proud of Clarence for it, not of himself, and he really wanted people to see his son, the lion, at his best. I remember that he was too bewildered at the manager's decision even to be angry.

I'm sure the manager never had any idea that Ted felt badly about it. There was no malice to the manager's choice of the foreman—it was just the way the manager was. People like Ted, who were loyal to him, got used like paper towels.

Ivan's *Daktari* series began to be filmed at Animals, Inc., at about that time. I liked most of the people who were involved with the show—Marshall Thompson was friendly and easy-going, and there was a delightful succession of English character actors doing minor roles who brought back my Sussex accent for a few moments, and my awareness of a world beyond Sand Canyon. And Judy—the chimpanzee star—used to come down with the crew in the morning and have coffee and doughnuts with them. She was a courteous and extremely intelligent chimpanzee, and a very neat dunker.

The action sequences on shows like *Daktari,* as most people know by now, are almost always filled with professional trainers and stuntmen doubling for the lead actors. Ted was Marshall Thompson's regular double, but Marshall always wanted to do his own stunt work, and once in a while he insisted on it. In one episode he was supposed to be fighting with a leopard in a pit, and chose to do it himself instead of letting Ted stage the scene. The leopard, to whom Marshall was a complete stranger, became frightened and bit him badly several times before they could be separated. You can still see that particular episode rerunning on daytime television. The fight photographed beautifully, and Ivan just left it in.

My own action sequence for *Daktari* was never filmed, but I never can watch the show's standard opening shot—a smiling Cheryl Miller riding a lion straight into the camera—without remembering it. When that shot was decided on as the one over which the show's main credits would appear, Ted pointed out that it would take several weeks of pretraining before any lion at Animals, Inc., would be ready to carry someone on his back. He recommended that we experiment with several different lions —Junior, Zamba, Clarence, perhaps a handsome, black-maned cat named Romeo—and added, "Of course, we couldn't take chances with Cheryl during the pretraining. We'd have to use Pat." The odd part is that I seem to have taken my expendability almost entirely for granted. I might argue training technique with Ted, but when it came down to the actual work— and when it came to me—I always went along.

At that time, the only lions I knew much about were Zamba and Clarence, and my only working experience had been with Zamba, when he and another lion were part of a Roman-gladiator float in the Rose Bowl Parade. During the freezing predawn hours while we waited for the parade to begin, Zamba thoughtfully ate all the rose petals on his side of the float. Lions like flowers. I've seen them go out of their way to find a flowerbed to lie down in, where they either roll like puppies or just sprawl looking blissful. It's one of their most appealing qualities.

It's also a tipoff to one of the qualities that can make lions troublesome to work with. They're the most sensual of the big cats, and they quite often react sexually to their trainers and keepers—Balzac's story *A Passion in the Desert* has more truth in it than he probably knew. I remember one occasion when a television commercial was being filmed with a lion and a young model. The manager made a point of asking the girl whether she were menstruating; as it happened, she was, but she wanted the job and said no. When the shooting began, the lion, excited by her smell, pounced on her and held her down, not hurting her, but rumbling and snarling and rubbing his four-hundred-pound self against her, as lions do with lionesses. Whenever anyone came near, he gripped the girl harder, making a rescue attempt almost certainly fatal. Eventually the manager had to lean as close as he dared and whisper what she would have to do to escape.

What she had to do was fondle the lion to a climax. It reads like a gruesome dirty joke, but it worked, and it probably saved her life. The manager spoke from experience, having been in much the same situation himself. A horny lion respects neither age, sex, nor species.

Ted and I conducted our pretraining sessions with the various lions according to the most fundamental rule of animal work, which is that animals only think about one thing at a time. Put a lion, for instance, in unfamiliar surroundings, and he'll be so curious, so distracted by the new smells and sights, and by the need to remain cautious until he knows about this place, that he wouldn't notice if you set an infant, a woman, or an anchovy pizza on his back. It's one of the very few edges that an animal trainer has—or a parent, for that matter.

One morning Ted took Romeo—so far, our most promising student—down to an enclosed arena that was occasionally used for this sort of work. He left him there and started back to find me; unfortunately, he got shanghaied into a staff meeting, which could happen to you two and three times a day at the ranch then, if you weren't careful. It was nearly two hours before we could get back to the arena to work with Romeo.

By that time, Romeo knew everything about that arena.

There wasn't an interesting inch of it that he hadn't sniffed, rolled on, pawed up, urinated on, or just generally made his own. His smell was on everything, and the enclosure had become his turf. Two hours is a long time for a lion, and Romeo was ready for some fun.

I'm small. I know now that to many large animals my size is often a piquant sort of thing, making me a potential rag doll or catnip mouse. Even then, there was something in Romeo's bright, expectant air that made me a bit hesitant about going into the arena with him. But Ted said it was all right, and I went in.

The usual procedure was for me to kneel beside Romeo, stroking him, talking to him, brushing his mane, and then gradually to slide onto his back while his attention continued to be diverted by the strange things around him. The first part went admirably: Romeo bumbled and moaned with pleasure, I relaxed considerably, and Ted said, "Well, as long as he's being that good, we ought to get a picture of it. Stay like that a minute."

I'm sure the click of the camera didn't have anything to do with it; but with no transition at all, I was off the ground in Romeo's mouth. Two fangs were pressing into my stomach, two into the small of my back. Romeo continued to make deep, happy noises.

Time slows down at such moments, and a strange, almost pensive calmness often takes over. I remember thinking very carefully, *if he closes his mouth, I'm dead,* and then wondering why Romeo wasn't closing his mouth. In fact, he was holding me as gently as he possibly could, everything considered. He didn't want to eat me or hurt me; he only wanted to play with me, and was thinking about how to begin. Something in me knew that, as ignorant of lions as I was, and I'm sure that I could have escaped without a scratch, if that dazed detachment had only endured a little longer.

The trouble is that I have terrible claustrophobia. I think

it dates from a swimming episode just after my father's death, when I came very near drowning. I can't bear to be restrained, especially when I feel that I can't get away; even now, it takes an instant of concentrated effort for me to let Neena wrap me in her trunk and hook a foreleg around me, or the bears pull me close to wrestle. Instead of keeping still, I went into the blindest possible fit of terror, crying and struggling between Romeo's jaws. That made me even more interesting, and Romeo gripped me tighter than before. He hadn't ever had a toy that put on this kind of a show, and he wasn't about to let it get away now.

I heard Ted shouting, "Leave it, *leave* it!" and suddenly I was spilled to the ground at Romeo's feet. Romeo understood about *leave it*—he even sat back and put a paw over his nose momentarily, because if he didn't leave it when told he usually got batted on the nose. I could still have walked away unhurt if I'd held onto the slightest wisp of self-control, summoned up ten seconds' worth of common sense. But I scrambled to my feet, and I ran.

This is the snapshot Ted took just seconds before Romeo decided I was a rag doll and took me in his mouth—one of the worst injuries an animal has ever given me.

You mustn't ever do that with the cats. It's suicidally stupid, because it excites them, and it's pointless, because they catch you. I knew that, but just then I didn't know anything. I ran and screamed, and Romeo bounced along after me, having his nicest time in ages. He began to bite me then, still not meaning any harm, but just wanting to get a decent grip on me again. The bites came mostly on my back and shoulders. They were puncture wounds, not deep, but the power behind them kept knocking me down.

Ted did the best he could to rescue me, but he was dreadfully handicapped by my crazy panic. Every time he jumped between Romeo and me, waving his arms and roaring, the lion stopped in his tracks, having no desire at all to try the nice new game on Ted. But I was beyond realizing what Ted was trying to do, or taking advantage of any chances to escape. I bawled and bled and stumbled in circles, and Romeo would joyously veer around Ted and grab me again. I think he was still purring.

At last Ted got me onto his back and sidled out of the arena, leaving Romeo to wash his face and look put-upon. I was taken to the hospital with my back covered with blood from nearly a dozen bites. I came properly to myself in the emergency room, waiting for the wounds to be attended to. My head was very clear and quiet, and I lay on a cold table thinking about what had happened to me.

I learned everything I know about the dangerous part of work with animals on that morning. First came the utter chagrin and self-disgust at my hysteria. *Idiot, dummy, how could you have taken on like that, when you know so much better? You know better than to run.* But then I thought, *All right, I did everything wrong, and I didn't die. I got bitten by a lion, and I didn't die.* The wounds themselves hadn't hurt at the time, and they only began to pain me later, when they were cleaned and bandaged. I always faint at tetanus shots.

Sooner or later, everyone who works with wild animals has to get hurt. It's a professional necessity, in a way, if you're ever to overcome your fears of getting hurt. Sometimes you even have to be hurt quite badly, to learn, as I did, that you don't die. If you're occupied by fear, the animal always knows, and that becomes all there is between you. The cruelest trainers, almost without exception, are the ones who are most frightened and most desperate to conceal it; and they make the thing they dread happen, inevitably. You have to get it over with.

The truly painful thing that happened that morning was not the being hurt, not the humiliation of panicking, but the realization that it had been wrong for me to go into the arena. My instincts had warned me that Romeo was not at all distracted, but bored and ready to be entertained; but I was used to relying more on Ted's feelings about animals than on my own. I didn't want to give that dependence up. Even when it angered or hampered me, it was *there*—far more reassuring than the icy darkness of making my own decisions—and Ted's pride in it mattered to me. But I knew that I didn't have any choice in the matter anymore. From now on, there was nothing for it but to trust myself only to myself, whether I would or no.

I felt that Ted knew immediately. I didn't talk about it, but I'm not a good dissembler, and I think he was looking for the change, anyway. It did make a difference in the way we were with each other. Perhaps he knew what I didn't know then— that his scrapbook had been in that arena, being bounced around and chewed on by happy Romeo. My fault entirely: it had no business there.

7

As far as my interior life went, I have a clear memory of one moment that sums all that time up for me: a dusty, breathless noon, and me pausing on a rise of ground to set down my bottles of formula and push my sweaty hair back from my cracking skin. From where I stood, I could look down a little way and see the *Daktari* cast sitting in canvas chairs, having their lunch. Ted was sitting next to Cheryl Miller, the leading lady of *Daktari,* as he usually did, most likely talking about show business and passionately confiding his undying dream of making it as a singer. They looked cool and handsome together, and it struck me ironically that I sometimes doubled for Cheryl in the action sequences. She was uncomfortable around animals, and too valuable a property to risk damaging.

I didn't blame Ted for anything that might be going on between Cheryl and himself. At least they seemed to know, like everyone else around me, exactly who they were: a television actress and an animal trainer who wanted to be Elvis Presley. But I knew only what I'd been, and that was receding from me every second as I stood on that little hill. I wasn't a student, or even someone who read very much anymore; I wasn't any kind of an entertainer, but only somebody's bloody double; and I certainly wasn't the real trainer I'd hoped to become when I first came to work at Peaceable Kingdom. I was a cook, housekeeper, amateur nurse and ineffectual defender of twenty-two assorted baby animals, and that was the end of it. And no sign of any new beginning in sight.

That's how Taj, my baby elephant, found me when she came into my life, herself bellowing with loss and terror in a little crate in the Los Angeles air-freight terminal. I remember that she kept smashing against the sides of the crate, hurting herself almost deliberately, as frightened captive animals will, especially very young ones. I had never seen that pitch of anguish before, and I couldn't bear it. I wanted to get into the crate with her. Taj and I were equally hysterical by the time we got her home.

Yet within a few days she had accepted the situation entirely, adopting me forever as her mother. It created a number of new problems for me: in the first place, she was always a frail runt —at four months of age, she weighed slightly under two hundred pounds, which is about what most Indian elephants weigh at birth—and her precarious health kept me perpetually running between the Animals, Inc., veterinarian, the animal kitchen, and Taj's watery stools. In the second place, I was trying desperately at that point to draw back at least a little from loving the animals under my care. The gorillas were still in their shipping crates then, and I truly felt that I couldn't handle any more helpless empathy and doomed concern. I was beginning to learn what love meant, and it was wearing me out.

(I think it's extremely important to mention here that the female elephant carries her baby for twenty-two months; and that she always selects another female to be with her during her labor, and to act as a sort of aunt or second mother to the calf after its birth. Which is what makes the importation and exploitation of baby elephants so uniquely cruel. They need a great deal of love and constancy, and are born knowing that they should have it. Even at an enlightened place like the San

Diego Zoo, the girls who tend the elephants are changed around all the time. Elephants are not meant to understand faithlessness.)

In the third place, I was allergic to Taj. She had a habit of wrapping her trunk around my arm as I gave her her bottle. A few weeks of those bristles against my skin, and both arms were developing rashes that looked and felt like jellyfish stings. My arms grew more swollen and painful every day, but I wouldn't see a doctor. I was afraid of being told what I already knew, and of losing Taj to some high-school drudge who wouldn't remember to talk to her, or to make her wear the blanket she hated in cold weather. When I finally made myself go to a doctor, he laughed and gave me a shot to build up an immunity. I never had any more trouble with the allergy, but the slow fear of having Taj taken from me at even the whim of my own body never did go away. And yet I was happier than I'd been in all the time since I came to work at Peaceable Kingdom, and perhaps in a much longer time than that.

What patience I have—as distinguished from stubbornness— I learned from Taj. Elephants have to be taught by their mothers to use their trunks, and Taj had been taken from her real mother much too young. She would stand for hours trying to coordinate thousands of muscles well enough to pick up a bit of hay or grass, or a swallow of water, and she would tremble all over as she tried to bring the food all the long way to her mouth. Invariably she would falter and drop the hay—or spill the water over her forelegs—when it was only a few inches from its goal; and I'd go raging out of her pen in tears, wailing, "If only I had a trunk! Damn it, damn it, why don't I have a trunk?" But Taj, who fussed and grumbled about so many smaller matters, never complained or grew irritable: she merely began the whole wretched process over again, time after time, month after month, until she got it right. I learned more than patience from watching her, but it doesn't have any more of a name than that.

Lunchtime at the lake with Taj and Candy. Taj had just bellowed at Candy, and Candy had taken temporary refuge behind me.

We used to have our lunch with Candy, my Himalayan bear, down by a pond at the ranch. Candy would play with anything from a puppy or a colt to a lion cub, but Taj was closer to her size and bulk, and they were best friends almost immediately. Their regular routine was as choreographed as that of a pair of nightclub comics: Taj would dabble in the dirt with her trunk, elaborately paying no attention as Candy shuffled in on her, weaving like a drunk imitating a fighter and growling challenges to inconceivably horrible combat. Then, at the last possible moment, with Candy almost upon her, Taj would curl her tiny trunk, shake her head, flap her ears, and bellow shrilly as Candy sat plump down to stare at her with the affronted innocence that bears can do even better than cats. They never tired of their old number, and they never laid a glove on one another.

I spent as much time as I could with Taj in the evenings, usually in a kind of fury of love and fear. Her absolute trust in me made my awareness of my own ignorance almost unbearable. The medication I was giving her was still largely a matter of guesswork, and I knew that if she ever became really ill, I wouldn't know how to care for her. Charley Franks had patiently begun to teach me most of what I understand today about elephants, but it was a uniquely lonely time even so—exactly as vulnerable and trembling as it was joyous.

One of the actresses was afraid of Taj, and Taj disliked her with a bright maliciousness that she showed to no one else on the lot. She appeared to time her digestive tract so that the urge to mess always caught her in the middle of a scene with the actress—typically an intimate two-shot. Nothing in the world smells worse than the stool of a baby elephant who's being raised on a mixture of canned milk, rice, barley, dextrose, vitamins, and cooked vegetables. The actress never failed to respond with panicky screams for me to get this disgusting elephant away from her. The camera crew used to make book on it. Once Taj did it to the actress in a boat, and there wasn't a thing I could do about it.

The turning point, for good and ill, came when Taj and I were approached on our evening walk by Ivan Tors. He asked me a great many questions about Taj's disposition, health, habits, and various abilities, and ended by writing her into the script of a *Flipper* show, to be filmed in Miami, as they all were. I was sent with her—not as a trainer, of course, but as her nurse, with no more say-so than the right to fuss about her medical treatment and the temperature of her bottle. But I was with her.

Taj loved Florida. Elephants endure the cold far less well than the average parakeet does, and it was freezing in Los Angeles when we left for Miami. When I ceremoniously removed the hated blanket, she trumpeted ecstatically and ran back and forth, turning in circles in the sunlight like a child spinning round and round on tiptoe. I overstepped my authority on our first day by refusing to leave her in a Tobacco Road of an animal park where she was supposed to stay, and finagling a twenty-foot trailer for her on the *Flipper* lot. Within a week, every child in the area knew about Taj, and I felt like the Pied Piper whenever we went for our walks together. She was comfortable enough with the children, but they learned quickly never to block her way to me, as she would barrel right through them if we became separated.

My diary entry for January 2, 1964, is typical of my concerns: "She took ¾ gallon formula. I walked her for an hour. She seemed very warm, and her stool was not as firm as usual. I took her temperature—normal 101 degrees. I have asked to have a shelter built over her trailer to deflect the sun. 1:00 P.M.—One quart of tomato juice. She will not eat during the heat of the day, but enjoys the tomato juice. We walked and played for an hour. Nap time. 6:00 P.M.—½ gallon formula and 250 cc Cosa Terramycin. Stool still soft, but getting firmer. She seems happy, and is behaving like a doll."

The trainer who had been sent with me from Animals, Inc., was a wizened little man I'll call Lester, some way beyond middle age. (It's not an accident that so many people who work with elephants are small. I'm five foot two myself.) He was in charge of handling, not only Taj, but a young male chimpanzee whom the script required to be in several scenes with Taj, and even to ride her. The chimpanzee belonged to a Miami resident who kept him on rollerskates all the time, so that he couldn't run away. The poor animal was terrified of Taj, and would skate off, screaming and wetting himself, every time Lester dragged him close to her. Lester beat him and cursed him constantly, but to no avail. This put Lester considerably out of sorts—he had his professional standards and reputation to maintain, after all—and he was looking for trouble when it came time to shoot Taj's scenes.

On the first day of shooting, on the beach near the **Miami**

Seaquarium, he began by grabbing Taj—to whom he was a complete stranger—and snarling, "Come on, elephant, get your ass over here!" as he pulled her to the marks where he wanted her to stand. Taj was frightened, and utterly unused to being handled roughly. As soon as Lester let go of her, she turned and trotted back to stand by my side, looking at him in perfect security from under her absurdly long, curling eyelashes.

Lester turned a sort of washy maroon color with rage. He had a bullhook, which may be the most viciously efficient goad ever invented, and he caught Taj around the trunk with it and hauled her back toward him as I stood paralyzed with disbelief. Then he took hold of her with his hands, one hand behind each ear. There are big nerve centers there, and they make young elephants fairly easy to handle, if you don't mind hurting them. I didn't know that then. Taj screamed suddenly, in pain, and in a shock worse than any pain. Blood leaped from her ears.

I've been told more of what followed than I really remember at first hand. I don't recall knocking people down to get to Lester—like Taj shouldering children aside to reach me—but I know that I took the bullhook away from him and swung it at his head with all my strength. I was trying to kill him. He ducked and took off, running down the beach, and I went after him.

It's funny now. It would make a great shot for a Fellini movie: a scrawny gray man scuttling as fast as he can along a properly palm-fringed beach, with a red-haired girl close behind him, waving a bullhook and yelling for his blood. Then the camera pulls back, and there's this bawling baby elephant lumbering along, trying to keep up with the girl, and after the elephant a scrambling string of television actors and technicians, all of them floundering and falling down in the sand. It's funny, except that I meant to kill him.

Brian Kelly, the star of *Flipper,* and two other men caught me first. They carried me back to the set, more or less by my elbows and the back of my pants. I cooled down, once I was certain that Taj wasn't badly hurt, but Lester wouldn't come back. The director, behind schedule already, and realizing that Taj would work with no one but me, appointed me her acting trainer on the spot. So if there ever was an official beginning, I suppose that was it—that crazy, murderous afternoon that looks so funny now.

From that point, the shooting went far more easily than I had any right to expect. Taj had always been a natural actress, and she worked as hard as I would let her every day under the hot lights. She seemed forever to be having to walk down rickety gangplanks and into boats where I would hide under tarpaulins to calm her as the scene was being shot. She refused to remain anywhere unless I was hidden near her; and she frequently forgot where I was and stepped on me. One day she had to be led by an actor along a narrow walkway well out over the water. It was essential that he keep tension on the lead rope to prevent Taj's falling backward off the plank, and I cautioned him endlessly about this. At the crucial moment, he got into a furious argument with the director, and in his impassioned state completely forgot about Taj. The shows' three standby scuba divers were in the water almost before she was. So was I.

I can't swim. It seemed to take the divers an unconscionably long time to notice this, as intent as they were on rescuing Taj —who, like all elephants, was a born swimmer, and got back to shore perfectly well on her own. After they fished me out, she bellowed and scolded me, our mother-and-child relation-ship reversed for the moment. She was always fully aware when I had done a foolish thing.

When she wasn't working, I would sit under a tree, and she would grub about in the dirt, practicing with her trunk, or go to sleep with her head in my lap. One morning we went for a walk along the shore of a small lake where—unknown to either of us—the various dolphins who played Flipper were housed. Taj had never seen a dolphin, and when one of them suddenly broke water, leaping high in the air to survey us, she wheeled and ran, squealing like a puppy. She was back in a moment, however; and after a little while she became bold enough to dip her trunk in the water as the dolphin glided close to touch the trunk with its smooth, smiling beak. They were like that for a long time, the dolphin lying motionless in the water, and Taj occasionally shifting her feet but not making a sound.

I remember that one day she had to play a long scene in the midst of five actors, and that it went into take after take, because either an actor would blow a line or Taj would get restless and move off her marks. At my suggestion, she was given a pan of water to drink during the scene, both to occupy her and to keep her from getting overheated. That take went along beautifully, until Taj abruptly decided to give herself and the rest of the cast a bath. Within half a minute she had thoroughly sprayed everyone within range, and two cameras as well. I was rather proud of her—she'd never been able to control her trunk that well before. The director was less impressed. I noticed that the remainder of Taj's scenes were shot in the least possible number of takes.

Cheerful and sweet-tempered as she was, she continued to be underweight, whatever diet or medication I put her on; and as we neared the end of the shooting, she began to tire quickly during the day, even falling asleep on her feet in the rackety middle of a scene sometimes. The guard at the studio told me that she paced all night after I left her. Eventually I moved a cot into the trailer, and slept within arm's length of her every night. I would bring formula with me, and she wakened every hour to take her bottle. If I was dozing, she would nuzzle me with her trunk and make little chuckling sounds. At 3:00 A.M. I would get up and begin cooking rice, barley, and carrots for the six gallons of formula that she would need during the day.

After ten days of this arrangement, she looked pink and beautiful, while I resembled a middle-aged lady who had been on a three-week drunk. But at least it wasn't Taj who fell asleep during her scenes anymore.

I don't think I ever forgot that she belonged to Animals, Inc., not to me. I didn't forget that I wasn't her real trainer, either. It just didn't seem to matter.

Incidentally, when it became obvious that the roller-skating chimpanzee was never going to become even slightly relaxed around Taj, the director sent for Judy, the chimpanzee from *Daktari.* Judy was a complete professional, who had no trouble at all in getting along with elephants; but she had been given to Lester to handle, and he treated her as barbarously as he had treated Taj and the first chimpanzee. Judy loathed and feared him, which seemed to restore his self-esteem considerably. We had as little as possible to do with one another, but on one occasion he dragged Judy over to me and handed me her chain, indicating with a jerk of his head that he had to go to the bathroom. I accepted the chain in silence, not looking at him after the first glance.

Apart from mutual hatred, there was a specific reason for this dumb-show: a scene was being filmed with live sound, instead of having the dialogue dubbed in afterward, and everyone on the set was under instructions to keep absolutely still. The actors' term for this is "being on a bell," since a bell or a buzzer always sounds to announce the beginning and end of the silent period. We were already on the bell when Lester brought Judy to me.

Judy glowered after him until he was out of sight, and then gave me to understand that she wanted me to let go of the chain, so that she could go off and hide from Lester. I sympathized with her entirely, but I shook my head and motioned to her to sit down beside me. Without hesitating, Judy took my free hand gently between her teeth, not biting at all, but looking inquiringly across at me, grinning as chimpanzees do when they mean business. She knew what being on a bell meant as well as I did, and she never made a sound.

I was frightened, but I shook my head again and made myself tug slightly on the chain. Judy began to close her jaws harder, watching me all the time, increasing the pressure with delicate precision. When the first drops of blood sprang up, I reached over with the hand holding the chain and managed to get a strong grip on Judy's throat. She bit down fiercely then, and I squeezed as hard as I could—all in a perfect, dreamlike silence. At least fifty bystanders saw what was going on, but no one could come to help me, because of the bell. Judy was starting to strangle, but she wouldn't let go of my hand even to breathe, any more than I would have surrendered at this point if she had bitten the hand clean off. I don't know how long it went on.

Then the second bell sounded. Judy and I promptly screamed in anguish, let go of each other and lit out in opposite directions, me bleeding bountifully and Judy staggering and croaking for air. Everyone on the set now came stampeding to my rescue, and Judy almost escaped anyway in the ensuing pandemonium. She walked around with a stiff neck for as long as my hand was in bandages, but we were as good friends the next day as we ever had been. How could we not have been: equally pig-headed, equally professional?

When the shooting was over, everyone connected with *Flipper* had fallen in love with Taj, and there had begun to be serious talk about having her stay on as a regular member of the cast. That in turn would mean my remaining with her, whether they called me her trainer, nurse, companion, or bodyguard. I had a Florida tan, a few new friends, and a growing sense that I was someone who could learn whatever she had to learn about working with animals, and do whatever she had to do. We were all right, Taj and I. Us elephants.

But Ted was writing and telephoning from Los Angeles, say-ing, "When are you coming back? I miss you." Neither of us had ever said that to the other before. When I spoke of remaining, he grew more urgent, sounding hoarse and scared, and more concerned than I had ever heard him. "Look, I wish you'd come back. We could get married."

The plans to add a baby elephant to Flipper's social circle never quite materialized, though they might have if I had been surer in my own mind that I wanted to stay in Miami. So Taj and I went back to Los Angeles and Animals, Inc., where everything ended.

The manager gave her to Lester. He explained to me that it was time for Taj to be placed under the care of a proper trainer —that it would be easier to have her transfer her affection to an experienced professional while she was still less than two years old. I would, of course, have to refrain from seeing her, since it would obviously be painful and inconvenient for everyone otherwise. Until I die, I will see her looking back at me as Lester led her away. She didn't understand.

I resigned from Animals, Inc. I thought that the only way either of us was likely to survive would be if we never smelled or sensed or knew about each other again. Taj died a year later, of unknown causes.

I love you, elephant: teacher, trap, playmate, wound, old buddy, daughter.

8

I didn't quit Animals, Inc., solely because Taj had been taken away from me. During my absence in Miami, Cyrano and Beatrice, the giant anteaters, had been moved out of the kitchen because my replacement didn't like their smell. I found them in the small-animal section, where my first fallow-deer fawns had died. Cyrano had been dead for almost two days, and Beatrice was dying. She had burrowed under Cyrano's big body, trying to keep warm.

Judging by the accumulation of filth in the gorillas' cage, it might not have been cleaned once while I was away. Those animals who had been ill when I left seemed worse; several others had grown dull-eyed and unresponsive. It was long past time for me to leave—working there was turning me into a frantic, humorless near-paranoiac who was angry all the time —but I would have stayed on as long as there was Taj.

Leaving was made easier by my knowledge that a girl named Louise Gust would be taking over the care of my baby animals. Louise was a kind, responsible person, and a registered nurse, which put the babies in more competent hands than they had ever known in their lives. For my own part, I wanted to back away from my involvement with animals, at least for a while. I was tired of being the person I had become at Animals, Inc.— it was too painful, too bone-grim. I wanted to be a lot of other people.

I began taking acting classes again, and stayed with it seriously enough to try out for and land the leading role in *Born Yesterday,* which had a limited run at the El Rancho Playhouse in Hollywood. But I was still taking care of those baby animals that Ted brought me for one reason or another—Sonia Hyena, for instance. Except for the van Lawicks' book, *Innocent Killers,* hyenas have probably had the most peculiarly contemptuous press of any animal in the world. Most people still believe them to be what Ernest Hemingway called them: hideous, hermaphroditic cowards and carrion-eaters who sneak into huts at night to bite off children's faces. Hemingway killed them whenever he saw them, and was proud of it.

Sonia was a dear love. She made a wonderful little raspy shriek when she was excited about anything, and her ears would go in a circle. She used to bow to me, as young hyenas do to their mothers—it's their unique gesture of submissiveness. I never knew her to be anything but affectionate and adventurous. She was due for a distemper shot when Ted finally quit working for Jack Krebs and we had to take all the babies back to the ranch. It's difficult to get the proper distemper serum for hyenas. Whatever serum they gave Sonia, it was the wrong sort, and she died.

I also found myself with an eight-month-old lion on my hands. His name was Scoo, and he had been shipped to Animals, Inc., in a crate whose slats were far enough apart so that his feet had kept slipping between them and been badly smashed. Ted picked him up at the airport and started to take him out to the ranch; but Scoo was so terrified and hysterical that Ted simply brought him to me. A lion of that age is not quite a baby, and I had some three weeks of being all over bites and scratches before Scoo gentled down and began to

Sonia Hyena with Ted's boot. She never gnawed on it; she just carried it around.

follow me around, instead of charging at me all the time. Lions, as I must have made amply clear by now, are the hardest animals for a woman to handle. At Scoo's age, or thereabouts, the young lion invariably becomes aware that you're a female and that he's supposed to dominate you (although you get to do all the hunting), and after that it's a wearying go-round for a while. I'm sorry to undermine a popular epithet of our times, but lions are far more male-chauvinistic than pigs.

And where do you find your animals, Mrs. Derby? Scoo had been a mascot for some college football team back East; apparently the school always ordered baby lions for the team, and then just sold them off anywhere at all when they grew too big to be convenient. As far as I know, the practice is still going on.

Scoo had renal rickets, like Honey the tigress, and died of it on Christmas Day.

Things went along. Ted and I got married at Newhall, and

Jack and Connie Krebs stood up for us. Clarence's star continued to rise, and he won a "Patsy" award, which is the equivalent of an Oscar or a Tony for animal actors. It's worth saying something here about the Patsys, because in the last decade they've become astonishingly prestigious in the trade. The award ceremony gets more press and television coverage every year, and the campaigning that goes on is hardly different from the grotesque publicity battle for the Oscar. The difference, in theory, is that the Patsy promotes humane treatment for animals in show business, and encourages trainers to explore new working methods, based on affection and understanding. This is not true.

The Patsy had been a meaningless social event from its inception. I've always felt that the people who run it were never as concerned with animal welfare as with attracting as many movie stars as possible to the ceremony. I have been to several Patsy-award evenings—I turned one down for Chauncey last year, as loudly as I could—and, though many good trainers get awards, I have seen prizes given out to people like the trainer who burned his rabbits' haunches with turpentine, and to others whose animals I knew to be habitually quartered in cages where they couldn't stand up straight, without shelter from the sun and the wind, and usually without adequate food or water. But all the humans attending the award banquet are dressed to the teeth, and *TV Guide* runs a funny feature on the difficulties of getting all those chimps and rats and tarantulas to tolerate one another; and nobody knows about the real world of animal training—the dead baboons and bears with broken noses and a bunch of screaming rabbits.

It rained a lot that winter, far more than is normal for Southern California. One week it rained all day every day, and a dam broke. Animals, Inc., was built on both sides of an old flood channel, and the river tore through the ranch with power that seemed closer to an earthquake or a massive landslide.

Flash floods in the Southwest hit like that, but this went on and on all night long.

The rushing water undercut the cages, and one by one they began to topple into the river. To do the trainers justice, even the ones I hated most worked heroically trying to get chains on the trapped animals and pull them to safety. But most of the chains were stored in a building that was now cut off by the flood from half the ranch, and there was no crossing the river that night. We did stretch a rope from one bank to the other, and the foreman tried to haul himself across with a supply of chains wrapped around his waist. The current ripped him away from the rope, the chains kept him from swimming, and he very nearly drowned as we looked on.

Ted came close to death too, trying to save a half-wild lion named Cubby. The cage had already fallen over, but was still hanging just above the water, obviously the next to go under. Ted was balanced on it, straddling the open door. He had managed to get a chain around Cubby's neck, but the lion was dead weight, paralyzed with terror. Ted would have had to strangle him to drag him out of the cage. Yet he couldn't make himself abandon Cubby though the cage was shuddering and everyone was shouting for him to jump clear; he kept trying to call the lion to him until the cage did go at last, taking him down with it. Ted struggled to shore a few hundred yards down the river, but Cubby drowned in the open cage.

There were deputy sheriffs standing around with shotguns. They were there for one purpose: to shoot the wild-caught animals as their cages fell, lest they somehow escape to ravage the fields and citizenry of the area. Heaven knows, the deputies were all probably as frightened as poor Cubby; but human beings—especially deputized ones—relieve their fear by killing things. I was more afraid of them than of the flood.

For my own part, I tried to rescue those animals I could reach who knew me, and whose trust in me cast out their fear. I saved some, and I lost others. There was a family of five wolves whom I had raised in my house: half-grown now, and increasingly a closed, self-contained pack, they still thought of me as their mother, and they came to me when I opened their cage. I had no chains to lead them with, but they followed me up a hill away from the water—six wolves, for the moment, trotting in a line. Then I turned my head and saw the deputies aiming their shotguns.

I screamed, *"Don't, don't, they're tame!"* and I threw myself across the nearest wolf, who was startled and snarled wildly under me, and then licked my face as we lay there in the mud. She was my favorite, a runty female. I waited a terribly long time for the deputies to shoot, but they just stared at us and finally went away.

Animals, Inc., was lucky in some ways—the bear Gentle Ben, probably the most valuable animal of all, was missing for two weeks, but turned up unharmed; and the hippopotamuses calmly swam the river and were found the next day, twenty-five miles down the main road—but the ranch was almost totally destroyed. It was rebuilt in exactly the same place, and some time later a second flood tore it apart again.

It was at this time, through my theatrical work, that I met Bill Burrud, a Los Angeles television personality, who had his own show, *The Wonderful World of Women.* He got excited about the idea of doing a program on an actress who lived and worked with wild animals; and suddenly there were cameramen out at the house every day, filming me as I took care of the various babies, while others shot footage of me at the acting class and playing in *Born Yesterday.* I was happy about the whole fuss, hoping that it would lead to more stage jobs, and possibly boost Ted's stock at Animals, Inc. The show was to be done live, with the film clips inserted, and I intended to talk as much as I could about Ted's theories of animal training, and his work at the ranch.

But Animals, Inc., was going steadily and frighteningly downhill, primarily because of the people they were hiring. The manager had gone off to Africa to film some background footage for *Daktari,* leaving a lot of power in the hands of a man we'll call Curt. I don't want to talk about what Curt liked to do to animals. One of his ideas of a pleasant afternoon was to fire the tranquilizer gun that was such a Daktari trademark at random into a crowd of the ranch horses. Several of them injured themselves badly in their panic, and at least one died from the direct effect of the dart. It was a nightmare straight out of the terrible books I was always being given as a child, and nobody seemed to care.

Ted cared. Unfortunately, he also believed that the manager would set everything right on his return from Africa, like Richard the Lion-Hearted coming home. Ted complained to him about Curt's treatment of the animals; Jack staged a big, messy investigation, and the upshot was that Curt was somehow totally vindicated and Ted lost whatever official title he still had at the ranch.

I had been thinking for a long time about the possibility of our breaking totally away from Animals, Inc., and starting some sort of small animal ranch of our own. My temporary retreat into theatre had kept the idea more or less a casual daydream; now the manager's betrayal of Ted suddenly made it imperative to move, to try anything. Candy was the only animal at the house who actually belonged to us; but I had heard what amounted to a legend of an enormous Siberian tiger owned by a man named Bob Baudy in Florida. The Siberian tiger is all but extinct in the wild, and Baudy was then the only person successfully breeding them in captivity. On an impulse, I wrote to him, asking if the huge tiger I had heard about was for sale.

I found out that the tiger's name was Rijo, that at a year and a half he already weighed 375 pounds, and that he liked to play with the neighborhood children. Ted and I began negotiating with Baudy, which was a truly profound craziness, since we were then barely able to support ourselves and Candy.

Baudy's final price for Rijo was $3000. To our own utter amazement, we were able to borrow the money, and I asked Baudy to ship Rijo to us immediately. The Bill Burrud show was due to be broadcast in a week, and I had been seized by a child's determination to have the tiger on the program with me.

Rijo arrived on the day of the show, which also happened to be the day Ted finally resigned from Animals, Inc. He had had a big fight about animal treatment with several of the other trainers, and when the manager backed them up, it was abruptly too much even for Ted. We went on the Burrud show as sudden free-lancers, without the least idea of where the money was going to come from to care for the big young tiger we had just met a couple of hours before. I can best describe Rijo's disposition by saying that he stepped out of a box after a long and cramping journey, and almost immediately followed a couple of nervous total strangers into the hot lights and scurrying confusion of a large television studio. I love to remember him as he was that first evening: calm, patient, and amusedly magnificent. He seemed to regard us all as more of those neighborhood children.

So I didn't talk at all about Animals, Inc., on *The Wonderful World of Women*. I talked about Ted instead, and about Rijo and Candy and our hopes for success as independent animal trainers. We didn't look broke and desperate; we looked like what an old friend once described as "Mr. and Mrs. Cute," charmingly confident and primed to set up shop as potential competition for Animals, Inc. I'm sure it was Rijo's grand presence that gave us that air.

Oh, we were fairly launched, all right, with no jobs, no prospects and a debt as big as Rijo. On top of that, we had just acquired another vast mouth to feed: a year-old lion named Joe, given to us by people who had raised him as a family pet. They had fed him like the rest of the family, on mashed potatoes and gravy, and Joe's fur was literally falling off his body in fist-sized hunks as we stood and looked at him.

Miraculously, he had no trace of rickets, only a whopping vitamin deficiency. But he was too young to work, and for the time being he was simply another liability with an appetite. I didn't know what the hell we were going to do.

Somewhere in his memoirs, Charles Dickens says brightly of a similar situation, "Then I thought of Mr. Pickwick." The levels of creativity are hardly the same; but it was then, in the spring of 1966, that the Lincoln-Mercury division of Ford Motors decided to call their new luxury sedan the Cougar, and to use live cats in their television commercials. They held an open audition in Los Angeles, inviting anybody who had a cougar to bring it down and try out.

For all practical purposes, Ted and I knew nothing about cougars. I had raised a number of cougar kittens, and Ted had had his studio experiences of popping CO_2 cartridges at grown cats, but none of this was likely to see us through a television audition with a completely strange animal. Which it would certainly have to be, since Animals, Inc., seemed a dubious prospect to lend us any of their cats. We checked around frantically among our acquaintances: the proprietor of a pet shop in Hermosa Beach had a young male cougar named Pume; and Gordon Meredith, a good friend, had a female named Tanya. I favored her just because she was Gordon's cat, since Gordon is a blessed stumblebum who could fall flat on his face, as he often does, in a cageful of leopards, and have the cats leap to pick him up and dust him off. He is a classic proof of the fact that anybody can work successfully with a wild animal, if it happens to love you. Pume frightened me, but Tanya had to be an amiable cougar, and I was in great need of one of those.

To make matters worse, I was going to have to go to the audition alone, since Ted had to finish up his last week at Animals, Inc., with one more doubling job on *Daktari*. When I picked up Tanya at Gordon's house that morning, he advised me, "If you have a chance, let her get up on the hood of your car. She likes to do that—it makes her feel secure. And you'd better take her dog." I assumed that he meant a favorite stuffed toy, but he handed me a rather nondescript puppy, saying, "He's her friend, he always calms her down. You know, like goats with racehorses." I didn't know about goats and racehorses, but I took the puppy anyway. I definitely wanted Tanya to stay calm.

Ted had insisted that I take Pume along too; but the dealer had no handy pacifier for him, and no helpful advice for me. All he said when we had finally gotten Pume stowed in the car was, "Good luck." I kept Tanya's little dog up front with me during the drive to Los Angeles. I felt that I needed him more than she did.

The audition was held at the John Urie Studios, a tiny production house which was so packed with applicants and utterly confused people from Kenyon & Eckhardt—the advertising firm that still does the Lincoln-Mercury commercials—that the scores of cougars present had to be shown in a little back alley outside the sound stage. I drove around to the back of the studio, left Tanya, Pume, and the puppy in the car, walked inside, and with the audacity of any terrified idiot, buttonholed the first man I met, who turned out to be Lee Zimmerman, the head of production for Kenyon & Eckhardt. He came out to the car with me, nodded briefly at the two cougars, and said, "All right, get your cat out."

"What do you want it to do?" Ted had instructed me to ask that. Lee shrugged, looking a little embarrassed for the first time. "We don't really know yet," he said. "Right now, we just like to look at the cats."

I opened the car door and tugged very gently on Tanya's chain, asking her in a small voice if she would please be so gracious as to come out. Tanya was perfectly willing—she licked her puppy's nose for luck and bounced to the curb, where she stood wrinkling her nose at the smelly cacophony of Los Angeles traffic. Then a garbage truck came rumbling down the alley, and Tanya hissed and sprang up onto the hood of my car, as Gordon had said she might do. I pulled on the chain, trying to get her to come down.

But Lee cried, "That's it! *That's* what we want!" and his face was alight with the advertising man's equivalent of stout Cortez's wild surmise. Tanya, now feeling safe and at ease, turned her head to snarl at the garbage truck, and Lee shouted again, "That's it, that's perfect!" He grabbed my free hand and shook it. "Come down to Chatsworth tomorrow morning, we'll start shooting right away. Bring both cats, but I want to use *her*." I stood with my jaw hanging to my navel as he bent a melting look on Tanya that could have gotten him arrested in a lot of communities.

The hard part was getting her back in the car. It probably wouldn't have seemed so difficult, except that Lee hung around for the longest time mooning over Tanya, and I desperately didn't want him to see me struggling with her and perhaps realize my absolute lack of experience with cougars. I remember that the puppy jumped out of the car and started biting my heels, thinking that I was hurting Tanya. I drove to the nearest pay telephone and called Ted on the *Daktari* set. "We got the job. We have to start tomorrow. *Now* what do I do?"

Ted was more horrified than anything else by the news. He came home immediately, and we stayed up half the night devising wild ploys meant to conceal our ignorance of cougar behavior in general, and of Tanya and Pume in particular. But we found out when we met the Kenyon & Eckhardt company the next morning that compared to them we could pass as slick professionals, for a while at least. As Lee Zimmerman had implied, they had no real idea of what they wanted to do, and they were about to gamble a lucrative, prestigious account on the chance that they would somehow come up with something unique. They were far too busy shaking in their own boots to notice what was going on in ours.

In those days, all advertising writers seemed to believe that cougars lived exclusively on very hot rocks in the desert. The first Cougar commercial was shot in a place called Red Rock Canyon, which is the great landscape of American folklore. Most of the movie and television Westerns you ever saw were probably filmed around Red Rock Canyon: with its sagebrush floor and its high sky, and its buttes and mesas like old dinosaurs, it's the eternally perfect setting for a stagecoach ambush or a range war. But it's a dull and wearisome place to work—as early as we had arrived, the rocks and the sand were already so hot that the cougars could hardly walk there at all. Pume hated it on sight, and said so. Tanya purred and bided her time.

Today when we shoot a Lincoln-Mercury commercial, as we do twice a year, the operation is smooth and precise, with no waste motion. The director will tell me, "Okay, I want Christopher to walk from *here* to *there*," and Chrissie does it in one take, and that's it. But ten years ago in Red Rock Canyon, it would have been, "Well, I think it might be nice if the cougar were sort of ambling around over in that area." We were all having to learn everything at once—while concealing the necessity from one another as much as possible—and the atmosphere was one of groping experiment, utterly formless. I'm rather grateful now that the commercial evolved in that manner; but at the time I'd gladly have chanced exposing my own ignorance, just to meet one person who seemed to know what he was doing.

Tanya knew. We began by posing her on a high rock—*why not? let's see how it looks, anyway*—and she briskly took off, running in beautiful flying bounds directly away from the camera, so that we couldn't even get any footage of her departure. Gordon had neglected to tell me that what Tanya mostly did when not on her chain was escape. We ran after her, calling and tripping over famous rocks, until she disappeared behind a sandstone outcropping from which Bob Steele occasionally used to pounce on John Wayne, or the other way around. The next two weeks were all like that.

There was no catching Tanya, and we could only leave chicken necks out as a lure and hope that she would wander back during the course of the day. We had to use Pume in the meantime: he turned out to be comparatively cooperative, except that he hated the sound of the camera and refused to work at all when it approached past a certain point. It was a godawful day. I don't think the company got any usable footage out of it at all.

Tanya had not returned at sunset. Gordon had come out to the set by then, and I have a haunting little memory of him wading through the sagebrush and trudging up and down those irritatingly legendary hills in the twilight, calling, "Tanya, Tanya!" He spent that night, and the next, in Red Rock Canyon.

We blundered along, working with Pume and a cougar named Vercingetorix, who belonged to Bill Engler, an old trainer. Vercingetorix had been both declawed and defanged, but he was unquestionably capable of killing any of us with his gums, and he appeared to spend a lot of time considering the idea.

Ted and I with Pume during the filming of one of our early Lincoln-Mercury commercials in Red Rock Canyon. Pume had already done the scene once and was reluctant to return to the same spot for a retake. Normally, if you lift up on a cougar's tail as you pull on his leash, he'll go right along. But not Pume. (Photo by Don Lewis)

He was one of the very few truly terrifying cougars I have ever known. I was afraid to go near him, though I did; and even after Tanya turned up on the third day—over in Aguadulce Canyon, only a few miles away—and we slowly began to build up a small stock of reasonably atmospheric shots, it seemed to me that I was hot and tired and frightened all the time, spending twelve to fourteen hours a day running after equally scared and exhausted cougars. It was no different from ordinary studio work, and I couldn't quite remember why I had expected it to be different.

I used to leave the set at night thinking, *I wish we had a cat who loved us so much that he'd just come to us when we turned him loose. What they want the cougars to do is always so simple, but the cats don't like anybody enough to have any reason to do it. We have to start with our own animals, when this is over.*

Later on, the company moved to the beaches just north of Malibu, because it seemed like a good idea to get some footage of the cougars running in the sand, with the Pacific surf dramatically in the background. (If they weren't desert creatures, maybe they all really lived at the seashore.) The cougars mistrusted the crash of the waves, and they hated running in the sand. They were also at one point required to race through smoke across a surface of raised letters that spelled out *Lincoln-Mercury*. It was long ago, and nobody knew any better, except the cougars.

By then we had temporarily acquired a fourth cougar named Diablo, whose snarl is the one you still actually hear in the commercials. Diablo would make that sound if you so much as looked sideways at him, and he meant what he said. He was as frightening an animal as Vercingetorix, and could be made to work only in the traditional manner, by spooking him with CO_2 cartridges. Ted had to do that part—whether through shame or simple klutziness, I almost invariably pop those things in my own face. My detestation for all the dirty little gadgets of fear doesn't arise from the fact that I usually can't make them go.

Apart from matters of morality and actual efficiency, there is a dangerous built-in limitation to the practical use of fear-training. In the cats, it happens most often with older males, like Diablo, who suddenly say to themselves—beyond reason, beyond a wretched lifetime of conditioning, beyond the knowledge of consequences—"The hell with this. I am going to eat that noisy little dingus and the fellow waving it around, or I am going to get killed."

I saw it happen for the first time with Diablo on the beach. Between one instant and the next, he had at last had it with human beings, and he flew right past a barrage of CO_2 shells straight for Ted's throat. Ted dropped to the ground, curled up into a ball and escaped with miraculously little damage; but I knew what I had seen. I was terrified for Ted, but somewhere in myself, even then, I couldn't help finding it glorious. I never can.

It was a grueling, frenetic time, made scary by everyone's ignorance. Little by little, we all taught ourselves what we had to know. I was wearily chasing down Pume one afternoon, with all work on the set halted once more until I could get him back on the chain, when he abruptly turned at what he decided was bay and charged me. Pume was no Diablo, but he hated being caught, and he had nothing much against taking my head off. I stepped back as he sprang, tripped over my own feet, and fell into some sort of crackly bush. Comfortingly normal. I said *ow*, or *eep*, or possibly *help* in a loud squeak—and to my astonishment, Pume stopped in midcharge, almost falling down himself. He stared puzzledly at me for a long moment; then shook himself all over, seeming to say very clearly, "Oh, well, if you feel *that* way about it . . ." I went up to him and put the chain around his neck, and he walked serenely away with me, back to the set.

It's my only weapon—in a sense, it's the one trick I really know, like the cat in the fable. *Change his mind.* I had learned something about the virtues of distraction when Ted and I worked with Romeo and the other lions for *Daktari*; but it was after the brush with Pume that I began taking it seriously, both as a means of protecting myself and as a possible aid in training. Dancing, for instance, has continually gotten me out of trouble that whips and guns would have turned into the end of the world. To this day I'm in the habit of breaking into an odd little soft-shoe shuffle whenever I see someone about to be in a bad place with a wild animal, and it remains the most effective gambit I ever found. I don't know anything else that works all the time.

When the shooting was over, we slept for three days straight, and then we sat up and began to consider things. This first job had paid most of our bills and still left us with more money than we had seen since I quit full-time nightclub work. Lee Zimmerman was happy with the film, and said that as far as he was concerned, we had first call on any future Cougar commercials. The logical step now seemed to be to start looking for a few cougars of our own—possibly a leopard, as well, and maybe another bear. We were absurdly sure of ourselves all at once, confident that we knew enough now to make even full-grown animals workable by our methods—though it would be nice to have the time to raise them from the beginning—and that with the Lincoln-Mercury credit behind us, we were already established as successful free-lancers. Shows how much we knew.

9

I know an animal dealer who once sold a full-grown cobra to a twelve-year-old boy. As I remember it, the transaction was hastily annulled by the boy's parents; but the incident provides as good an illustration as any of the morality of the world which Ted and I entered when we began to look for animals of our own. *If it's alive, and someone wants to buy it, sell it. Don't ask questions. Move the merchandise.* Actually, by the standards of the animal dealer's world, that dealer was practically St. Francis of Assisi. His cobra was in excellent health, which is not usual.

We wanted to buy Pume, both of us having gradually become very attached to the temperamental young cougar. The dealer let us keep Pume at the house, but he was very reluctant to sell him, reasoning logically that there was bound to be more money in renting the cat to us every time we needed him. But he did give us the name of a local trainer who had said something to somebody about wanting to get rid of a cougar.

The cougar's name was Bud. He wasn't very old, but he had already been declawed, defanged, castrated, and blinded in one eye. When we saw Bud first, he was chained outside in a desert heat of over 100 degrees, with no water and no shade. In his effort to find some shelter from the sun, he had dug a shallow hole in the sand and was lying in it, barely conscious. I started to cry when I saw him, and the big St. Bernard dog near him, who was in the same condition. The trainer said that they enjoyed the heat, and were just asleep.

We knew at a glance that Bud would never be able to work; but I also knew that I wasn't walking away from that place without taking both him and the dog with me. Ted eventually argued the trainer down to a price of $500, which included Bud, the St. Bernard, and the cage-trailer in which Bud was sometimes kept. We did use the trailer from time to time, for taking animals on location.

At this writing, Bud is fourteen years old. His grave sweetness to everyone has always broken my heart, and sometimes still outrages me: he has every right in the world to eat any human being he wants to. The trainer won an award a while ago, by the way.

That's one way of finding exotics, as they call them in the trade. We bought most of our animals from dealers in the early years. Not all the purchases were premeditated, however— in those days, I had the classic inability to keep from buying every baby animal I saw in a pet shop. I don't mention this to call attention to my goodheartedness, but to my self-indulgent ignorance, and that of other people like me. It is no kindness, as I know now, to rescue that forlorn little ocelot or fox cub: in the first place, you probably don't know how to care for it; in the second, you have just encouraged the dealer to rush out and get hold of four or five more babies. When I bought Mandy, an adorable Malayan bear cub, the dealer had four Malayans in the store a couple of weeks later, where there had only been one before. I may have done Mandy a service, but I did nothing for the species. I stay out of pet shops altogether now.

Yet there is a sadder way to acquire animals, and one that makes the cash-register callousness of dealers look almost admirable by comparison. A Mandy, or a Murgatroyd—an American black bear cub whom we also bought from a dealer at about that time—may have been robbed of their mothers and their natural lives, but at least we betrayed them no further, and we tried to give them our own lives in some poor exchange. A Banté is another story. There is nothing you can do for a Banté.

Banté was a South American cougar who had lived with a wealthy young couple for all but the first two months of his five years of life. They had treated him well, and he was a magnificient creature, weighing close to 180 pounds. Whenever they had company, Banté was the favorite entertainment for their guests. I can't say they didn't love him.

We met them through a friend of ours, who knew that we were looking for cougars, and had heard that they wanted to sell Banté. It had been a kick and a conversation piece all these years to have a cougar as a housecat; but now the kick was travel, and they couldn't very well take such a big animal around the world with them. They brought Banté to our home on a Friday afternoon.

Ted and I had scheduled our time so that we could spend the next twenty-four hours with him, getting him accustomed to his new surroundings. He was quite placid and docile when we took him inside, and he lay down gracefully on the cool tile floor of our upstairs bathroom. The couple said goodbye to him, and Banté lay there staring straight ahead.

We sat with him on that bathroom floor for twelve hours, stroking him, talking to him, offering him things to eat, and he never moved or made a sound. I don't think he ever really saw us. Only two human beings had ever existed for Banté, and they had left him here and would never come back. We called them the next day. They were busy that weekend, but assured us that they would try to come by on Monday. Although Ted and I tried to explain what was happening to Banté, they were noncommittal about his condition. He had ceased to amuse them.

A cougar as large and healthy as Banté can normally survive for ten days or more without food; but Banté was becoming visibly weaker every hour as we sat helplessly beside him. The veterinarian who came out late on Saturday to give him intravenous feedings said when he left, "There's nothing wrong with him, he just wants out. I've seen it before."

At four o'clock on Sunday morning, Banté rolled over on his side and looked at us for the first time. He heaved a great sigh and quietly died.

I can't say they don't love them, those people I meet who have monkeys in their bedrooms, wolves in the backyard, full-grown lions in the garage. Their eyes fill with tears as they tell me how much their pets mean to them, and I don't think they're lying. But I no longer believe that the word *love* excuses stupidity in the slightest, or that it alters the fact that the animal is almost always kept around as a projection of its owner's ego. It's a useless, meaningless kind of love that feeds a lion on mashed potatoes and gravy; that can't be bothered to clean up an animal's droppings; that can't—or doesn't dare—conceive of a nonhuman creature choosing to die rather than soullessly adjusting to the fact of his abandonment. Poor Banté. He thought the couple he lived with were like him. He never understood that they were only human beings.

No, I'll take the dealers, if I have to choose. At least they never say *love*.

Another couple came to us with Clyde, a seven-month-old jaguar, whom they had bought as a very young cub. They loved Clyde too, but they were afraid that he was turning mean—*doesn't that happen with them sometimes? don't they revert?* He broke things, and he was starting to play *very* roughly and growl at people, and he had backslid terribly about his potty-training. *I guess they just revert after a while.*

Ted roughhousing with Clyde. With most jaguars, if they have part of you in their mouth, forget it. But Clyde never put a mark on Ted. He was all play.

No, dear sir or madam, they don't revert. On the contrary, they go straight ahead, as they should, becoming what they are, Clyde had just discovered that he was a jaguar, and that jaguars do not normally concern themselves with catboxes, or with the fragility of bric-a-brac from Niagara Falls. Their nature is a jaguar's nature, which is very much like a leopard's: bright, high-strung, utterly fearless, capable of magicking a brief, devastating firestorm up out of some darkness of survival where only those two spotted cats seem to have to go. They are supposed to be like that.

You have to love them for what they are, as you must take all animals for what they are, or leave them the hell alone. I sometimes think that I unintentionally mislead people when I talk about affection-training. Perhaps it leaves them thinking, "Oh, well, it's a leopard, but if I raise it with love, then it won't grow up to eat the furniture, because it won't have any frame of reference about such things." Leopards are born knowing how to eat the furniture. They don't have to be taught. You cannot improve on a leopard.

I do like to remember the old, old man who gave us Pumpkin. Pumpkin was an Indian rock python, slightly over eleven feet in length. She had lived with the old man almost since her birth, along with a rosy boa constrictor whose name I can't recall, though he gave her to us as well. He adored those snakes and treated them wonderfully, not only letting them be free in his house, but playing with them and bathing them— snakes in general like water, and the big ones need to bathe often, to keep their skins supple. He even used to exercise them, after a fashion, by lifting them up and carrying them around, making them use their strength against him. I think they must have been the happiest, most secure snakes in the world, though it's hard to tell.

Then he had a heart attack and couldn't lift the snakes anymore, or really take care of them very well. He was terribly concerned for them, and gave them to us only after satisfying himself that we could be trusted with his friends. We kept them in our guest bedroom upstairs, and let them out every evening. If we forgot to put them back (the old man had built them a beautiful sleeping box, with a heat light), they'd often head for our room and slide into bed with us, for the warmth and the companionship. I slid out of bed rather abruptly the first time; but eventually I came to respect and like Pumpkin and the boa for themselves, exactly as I respect Neena the elephant or Rijo. They were used to being handled, and their need for contact and affection may not have been the same as a gorilla's, but it was a need. Nor could they give us back what a gorilla gives, because they were snakes, but I never doubted the reality of what they gave us. It's language that falls short, not feelings.

Mr. Via, kindest of dealers, gave us Thumper the baby wallaroo. We hadn't come out to his ranch looking for a wallaroo, but for a pair of Virginia white-tailed deer fawns. Thumper was in the kitchen, having fallen out of his mother's pouch that same day. He was only a few months old, and Mr. Via doubted that he could live without his mother at that age.

But he gave us a formula that "might keep him alive, might not, I don't know. Always worth a try."

Thumper made it. I improvised a pouch for him by folding up the corners of an apron and fastening them with safety pins. He had to have his formula several times a day, so I took him everywhere with me, even walking into restaurants and movies with him in my purse. At home he hopped around freely, and if anything frightened him he'd come running to dive headfirst into the apron-pouch. I used to dust and vacuum the house with

I loved having Thumper the wallaroo in the house, but he kept dropping little pellets all over the place. Diapers didn't work. Then one day I got an inspiration: Jockey shorts, turned around. They worked fine, and Thumper enjoyed wearing them.

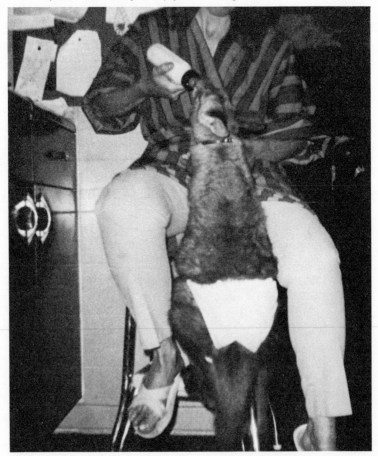

Thumper's little back legs hanging out of my apron. Mailmen and Avon ladies never got used to it.

We had stayed in touch with Bob Baudy in Florida, and one day he called to let us know that he had come across a leopard and a black bear, if we were still interested. Neither one sounded like a promising subject for novice trainers: the leopard was six years old, and had never been handled in his life; and the bear was a circus animal whose training had amounted to scientific semi-starvation and having had his nose broken four times. (Your truly professional bear-trainer always goes for the nose.) His name was Willy, and he was about to be shot as incorrigibly vicious, because his trainer had finally come one step too close while beating him. We told Baudy that we would take both animals, and set about trying to find a cheap way to get them across country. The Cougar commercial money was running out fast, and we'd had no other work yet.

We had recently become friends with an older couple named Ora and Jean Johnson, who lived in Saugus. Ora was a Ford motor mechanic, and Jean was then working in a local dynamite factory. I think we met because Ted had been looking for a second-hand tractor, and Ora had one. The Johnsons were gentle, patient people, with a gift for contentment and for loyalty, as they still are. They were very different from anyone else we knew in our world of dealers and trainers and television people. I liked being with them.

The Johnsons' older son, Johnny, volunteered to drive a truck to Florida for us to pick up the bear and the leopard and bring them back. Johnny was nineteen years old, and he didn't know anything at all about animals, but he did like to drive. He made it to Bob Baudy's without incident, and he and Baudy wired off individual compartments for the two animals in the back of the truck. Then Johnny started back for Newhall, separated from Willy and—let's get it over with—Spot by two feet of space and one very thin partition.

Bears and leopards are not normally compatible types, and

Willy and Spot were so frightened of each other that they immediately set to work trying to rip their way out of the truck. Johnny could hear the wire starting to go as he drove, and the different sounds that blunt and sharp claws make on wooden paneling. He drove day and night, calling us several times a day to report on the animals' progress in remodeling their quarters. His voice was higher and shakier with each call. We huddled around the telephone, hardly daring to look at Ora and Jean, until the truck finally rolled into the yard and Johnny fell out of the cab, saying faintly but quite clearly, "I'm leaving, I am going away. The bear's halfway out."

So he was, but we decided to take the leopard out first, hoping that his absence might calm Willy a little. We contemplated him for a lengthening while—a hundred pounds of splendid, hissing, mad-eyed power—until Ted muttered, "Well, he's probably never had a chain on him even once, but let's try." The Johnsons watched from the front window as he stepped quickly into the wrecked wire compartment and snapped the chain around Spot's neck.

Spot left the truck at forty miles an hour, hitting the end of the chain so hard that he popped Ted like a whip-tassel, snapping him off his feet and dragging him across the yard. He was like a great fish, a marlin, leaping and leaping at the end of a quarter-mile of line: he walked up the air, swam on his back, flickered like a spinning dime; he filled the sky. Ted clung to the chain, skidding on his knees and elbows and chest, until Spot went under a cage-trailer and lay there, seemingly playing like a kitten with one of the heavy tires. The tire came apart in rags in his claws, as you see them shred themselves at high speed on a freeway, and the trailer fell on Spot. The end of the chain dropped from Ted's fingers as we stood there.

But Spot came boiling out from under the trailer and made for the barn, with the chain rattling behind him. We ran in after him, in time to see him bounce twelve feet straight up into the rafters. Now he was over us, a full-grown leopard frightened out of his mind. Yet never once during the whole fracas did he attempt to harm us in the least. It would have taken him ten seconds in the confines of the barn to unravel us both as he had the trailer tire—but by the kind of miracle that is supposed to attend fools, and usually doesn't, Spot simply isn't that sort of a leopard. Ted got hold of the dangling chain and managed to pull him down from the rafters and get him into a cage.

Willy the bear proved somewhat less troublesome, in one sense (Ted backed the truck up to his cage, and then herded him into it down an impromptu tunnel of plywood boards); but in another, he was the most unyieldingly difficult animal we had ever had to deal with. Spot, having announced himself, turned out to be almost appallingly affectionate, as he has remained ever since. He is still a leopard, and he still doesn't care for loud voices or crowds of strangers; beyond that, he's a disgrace to the species. In the wild, he would probably have nuzzled antelope to death.

But Spot had little to forgive human beings. Spot had never had to learn to sit in a rocking chair, roll barrels, and walk on his hind legs, waltzing and doing pirouettes, to keep from being beaten; never had to sacrifice every scrap of his dignity in order to survive. Willy had retreated from a lifetime of pain into the safety of hardly existing at all. I have never seen an animal who said so clearly, "Don't touch me. Don't touch me." Candy and Mugatroyd and little Mandy splashed in their tubs and played with their truck tires; but Willy stayed in the same corner of his cage all the time, and stared at the same place in the air. He refused to accept food from us, and would eat only at night when everyone was out of his area. I have always believed that he had come to associate food entirely with performing, and that he had decided that man expected too much for a few crumbs. I think he would have starved, rather than survive on those terms ever again.

Spot disliked the camera and snarled, but the nice thing was that he didn't want to take it out on me. Leopards are like dynamite—they sit there and sit there and suddenly they go off—but Spot never hurt anybody.

I changed his name. I thought he must feel the same way about the sound of *Willy,* so we began calling him Sweet William. It didn't seem to make any difference. He had been with us for several months with no apparent change, except that his health had improved and he was definitely gaining weight. Ted and I had almost decided that we would have to settle for that, and be glad of it. Happiness is a learned thing, and many people and animals come to the knowledge too late.

He liked fig newtons and Hostess Twinky cupcakes, so I began to make a point of bringing some to him daily, as separate treats from his regular meals. I would stand at his cage for an hour or more at a time, day after day, offering him the cookies. The moment when he finally came out of his corner and warily took one fig newton from my hand is one of those that I will carry with me to whatever comes after this world. Death has no power over the feeling of Sweet William's breath on my fingers.

But that was all the giving and taking he could manage for over a year: the little acceptance of sweetness from me, and later from Ted. He never showed any desire to join in when we played with Joe the lion or Candy or Rijo on the grass, and we never dared to force our affection upon him. Then one morning I was out in the yard with Candy when I looked up to see Sweet William solemnly walking around the cage on his hind legs, with a tire draped over his front paw. He looked exactly like a lady carrying a large pocketbook. As I stared, he carefully placed the tire in his bathtub and got in, sitting down with the tire as a pillow. I ran into the house, calling for Ted.

When we came out, Sweet William was still sitting in the bathtub with his feet propped up on the edge and his back resting against the tire. He licked his lips, as contented bears do, as he calmly surveyed his surroundings. Ted and I approached the cage cautiously, but Sweet William showed no inclination to retreat to his corner, as he had always done be-

Sweet William in his bathtub. At this point he was still withdrawn and suspicious, but he was coming out of it.

fore. We began talking to him in high, soft voices, telling him how good he was. Sweet William scrambled out of the tub and began to run about the cage again, bouncing his tire.

"I'm going in with him," Ted said abruptly. "If I can get him to play, we've got ourselves a new bear. If he grabs me, you start yelling, bang on the bars with a stick or something." He was unlocking the cage door as he spoke.

Walking in, he crouched low, trying to look smaller and less of a threat. (Sweet William's circus trainer had been a tall, powerful man, like Ted.) He talked continuously in a babyish chirp. "Nice William. Sweet William, he's a good boy, a good William." Sweet William had dropped his tire and backed away, making the little moaning sound which indicated that he was growing fearful. I stopped breathing as Ted crawled across the cage on his hands and knees. When he reached Sweet William's corner he lowered his head and crouched there beside him. "Sweet William. Hey, what a good William."

The moaning stopped. With the gentlest, saddest movement I have even seen, Sweet William reached out a huge paw and pushed at Ted's shoulder. Bears do that to one another.

"Good boy, William!" we squeaked together. "Oh, good *boy*!"

For the first time, surely, Sweet William had touched a human being and not been beaten. We saw his whole life break open inside him. He picked Ted up in his arms and literally carried him around the cage. They wrestled together like bears, and Sweet William took Ted's entire head carefully between his great jaws. After ten or fifteen minutes of play, Ted eased himself out of the cage, and we fed Sweet William fig newtons and told him he was the best and most loved bear in the world. When we left I saw him take his tire back into the bathtub and sit down placidly, watching the other animals.

As Ted had said, he was a new bear. We started taking him out for walks every day, and he learned to play with Candy

When Sweet William opened up and learned to trust me, he became so exuberant that he wanted to play all the time. Ted would wrestle him but, because Willie had never played before, he played too rough. So we let him play with Candy, who, as you can see, sometimes got the worst of it but was always eager for more.

when Ted was too tired for roughhousing. He was still afraid of other people, however, and would stop playing the minute company arrived.

In what was to become our normal cliffhanging pattern, we landed our first television job since the Cougar commercial just as I was beginning to sell my furniture again. The show was a good one called *The Monroes,* dealing with the adventures of four young orphans trying to survive on a frontier ranch. Michael Anderson played the older boy, and Barbara Hershey was one of the two girls. I remember her as an innocent, sweetly out-of-it person who liked animals.

One of the *Monroes* scripts called for a grown bear and a cub to appear as mother and son in a few short scenes. We talked about it for a long time, and decided to try working Sweet William with Mandy, who was the only cub we had. (The idea of a male American black bear playing the mother of a Malayan does indicate something basic about television standards of accuracy.) The cast and crew were warned over and over to be quiet during Sweet William's scenes, and not to make any sudden movements or noises that might frighten him. He worked all day out in a field, eating grass and rolling seriously through the woods. He was actually enjoying his day out, and I think everyone in the company fell in love with him.

When the shooting was finished for the day, the little girl who played the youngest Monroe asked us if she might pet Sweet William. He had never taken food from anyone but us, but we gave her a fig newton and she went up to him saying, "Here, bear." Sweet William unhesitatingly nibbled the cookie out of her fingers, and then carefully sniffed her hands and face as she stood beside him. The other children approached and he did the same with all of them, although it was apparent that he preferred the smallest child. There was no slightest indication of nervousness or fear about him. Almost by accident, we had discovered that Sweet William loved children.

At home he began to hold court in his cage, sitting in the tub with his arms resting formally on the sides, as the neighborhood children filed in in groups of three and four, all of them holding fig newtons between their lips. Sweet William would incline his head graciously and take the cookies from them with perfect delicacy. We learned after a while that he was becoming known among them as the "Kissing Bear."

His experience with *The Monroes* had been so rewarding that we never hesitated when a call came from the show *Land of the Giants*. This was a downright silly one about space travelers stranded on a planet whose inhabitants were all gigantic. Sweet William was to be a giant bear, and we were told that all he would have to do was to walk through a scene on his hind legs. It seemed simple enough, and we agreed to be at the studio with him the next morning.

We had hoped to get there early, to let Sweet William get the feel of the area where he would be performing; but as soon as we arrived, the director rushed up and told us that it was time for the bear's scene. We walked Sweet William out to the lighted set, and on cue Ted released his collar as I called softly to him. Sweet William rose up on his back feet and started to move toward me.

Suddenly a huge man, dressed in gypsy clothes and carrying a small whip, came striding into the scene, shouting gruffly, "Up, Willy! Turn, Willy!" As Ted and I gaped, Sweet William bellowed in utter panic and despair, unquestionably seeing the terrible circus finding him again, trampling down his fragile new life. He dropped to all fours and took off, knocking over lights and reflectors, tearing down scenery as he raced about trying to find a safe place to hide. The actors and the crew scattered in all directions, though we tried frantically to get everyone to stand still, so that Sweet William could see us and hear us calling to him. But the more they all ran and yelled, the more terrified he became.

Finally Sweet William ran up a ladder and climbed onto a scaffolding high above the crowd. He huddled there, waiting to be beaten and muzzled again. The big actor, who knew only that he was supposed to do a bit as a bear-trainer, was genuinely wretched; the director—who was hiding behind a candy machine—apologized profusely for not having told us that there would be a strange man in the scene. He hadn't thought it would matter.

Ted told him to clear everyone off the set, and to send for five pounds of fig newtons and Hostess Twinkies. We climbed up to the scaffolding where Sweet William crouched and sat near him, not yet daring to touch him, but crooning softly and comfortingly, telling him again and again that he was with us for always, that the other was the bad dream. By the time the cookies arrived, he had become somewhat calmer, and we coaxed him down the ladder with a fig newton for every rung. It took us over an hour.

Once he was on the ground again, we led him over to the spot where he had been standing when the actor frightened him, and stayed there, stroking him now. When he seemed almost himself, we sent for the actor and had him talk gently to Sweet William and feed him cookies. It was close to another hour before Sweet William would accept the food from him; but when the filming resumed, the actor went through his role with his pockets loaded with sweets, and by the end of the day the two of them were old army buddies. I saw them leaning together, sharing a Twinky, with Sweet William already pawing his new friend's pockets for more. The actor was scratching that four-times broken nose.

As long as it lasted, *The Monroes* represented our first real security. Animal sequences were written in for us as a regular thing, and working on the show took up most of our time. We used to get up in the morning at three or three-thirty in order to clean all the cages and take care of those animals who needed a morning feeding. We would usually be filming until seven or eight at night; then we still had to drive home and do our evening feedings before we finally got to bed around midnight. This happened five days a week.

Ted was Michael Anderson's regular stand-in, as he had doubled for Marshall Thompson on *Daktari*. In one show the script required a cougar to leap from a high rock onto Ted, and the two of them then to tumble into a freezing river. We borrowed another of Bill Engler's cats, Laeti (all of Bill's cougars had Roman names), who turned out to have no interest in jumping off rocks on people, and too much sense to chance falling into any river at all. Bill and another trainer actually had to throw her down on top of Ted, and when they hit the water, Laeti went into shock from the cold. It doesn't show on the film. We got her out, and everyone swarmed to cover her with blankets, give her brandy, and turn on car heaters full blast to warm her. It was ten minutes before the crew nurse even noticed poor Ted, who was standing around soaked blue, in near-shock himself. Both he and Laeti survived, but it was Ted who had two cups of coffee and went back to work.

For another show, we bought two young cougars from the Dallas Zoo. One was Chauncey, the other his sister Cassandra. We sold Cassandra after the episode was filmed, since we only wanted to be raising one cougar at a time.

I tell these stories very deliberately. It seems to me that my stories up to now have been making us look too good, and I don't want there to be any misunderstanding about this time in our lives. In the little while since we had gone into business on our own, we had already begun to do most of the dumb, bad things for which I detested other trainers. We hustled and conned people, we took on animals we didn't understand and agreed to push them through stunts and sequences that were not natural or pleasurable for them, as with Laeti. (For Mandy's show, I even covered her chest with hairspray every morning to hide the telltale Malayan V.) Our animals were well-fed and decently kept, and never intentionally hurt; but we had almost no time anymore to be with them for no purpose, to do things with them that had nothing to do with work, or getting work. In many ways, at that time, you could hardly have told us from Animals, Inc.

I can't claim that I didn't know what we were doing. It's the old means-and-ends business—you have to believe that evil isn't evil when it's your side doing it. We had never sold an animal before Cassandra. I knew it was wrong then, though she went to kind people, for the same reasons that I know it to be wrong now. Wild animals are not meant to be owned, any more than human beings are. No one has the right to pass a cougar or a gorilla from hand to hand, not for the purest of motives. I couldn't be sorry to have rescued a Bud, a Willy, but I knew even then what it made me to own them. All I can say in honesty is that I learn slowly, and only by doing all the possible wrong things first.

10

When it became dangerously insane—even by our standards—
to keep doing *The Monroes* on three hours' sleep, we finally
hired an Animals, Inc., acquaintance named Tom to clean
cages and feed the animals. Tom was a decent, unassuming fellow, and I've never been able to imagine why Rijo hated him
on sight: genial, expansive Rijo, who liked everybody. It was
like Ted and Zamba—a matter of chemistry. Frightening Tom
became Rijo's hobby. He gave it a lot of serious thought, and
got very good at it.

Tigers are astonishingly vocal, by far the most so of the big
cats. The Indian belief that the tiger can make his voice seem
to come from all points of the compass at once, so that his
prey often flees straight toward him, is essentially true, as is the
belief that tigers can twitter like birds. Their greeting to each
other, and to human friends as well, is a curious puffing sound
which I learned to duplicate by blowing through my closed lips
—like giving a raspberry. It is necessary to master this sound
in order to become friends with a tiger. I suppose Tom never
really got it right.

They have another greeting-call—a sort of nasal, elongated

ma-oow—which is generally employed to gain attention. Rijo was quite capable of keeping that one up all night, until the whole house thrummed with it, if he happened to want company. There is also a low rumble of utter contentment, not a purr, exactly, but different; and then there is the bark. Tigers don't roar like lions: they give a short, compact bark, which could be used for dynamiting tree stumps or blowing bank vaults open. I've always found it much more chilling than the roar.

The bark comes with adolescence. Rijo barked for the first time in his life within a few days of Tom's arrival, and from that time it became the chief weapon in his psychological guerrilla campaign. Tom was a creature of habit: arriving at seven every morning, he would have hosed and scrubbed his way to Rijo's cage, which lay hidden around a little bend in the path, exactly at ten sharp. Rijo was always ready, and Tom never, never was.

Tom almost quit on the spot when Sugar Baby showed up. Sugar Baby was a full-grown Bengal tiger whom we had agreed to board for the middle-aged couple who owned her. She adjusted well enough to her new home, though it was soon apparent that she was definitely not tame, and probably never would be. It alway saddened me to compare her jumpy aloofness with Rijo's delighted puffing and calling whenever he saw a familiar face. I have seen so many animals like her since, neither properly wild nor ever trusting, accustomed neither to cruelty nor to loving, never given anything but food. They are worse off than Sweet William, in a way, the ones who have to live like that.

Sometime shortly after Sugar Baby had come to live with us, I had to drive Ted and Clyde the jaguar to the airport. They were going to Florida for three weeks to work in a Disney film. I drove home in a leisurely manner, feeling almost relaxed, almost secure for a change, looking forward to spending the day with Sweet William. Turning into the driveway, I had time, as

I pressed the automatic gate-opener button, to marvel at my newly planted primroses, just now reaching their full bloom, and at the forsythia bushes brimming with golden life, and also at the beautiful tiger sauntering down the gravel path toward me.

If that tiger—I took it for Rijo then—got out onto the road, Ted and I would be displaced persons by tea-time. I hit the button again, simultaneously trying to herd the tiger away from the gate with my car. The gate did not close, it being a variant of Murphy's Law that in moments of extreme crisis nothing mechanical ever works properly. I also realized at that moment that the tiger was not Rijo, who could have been led back to his cage with a hair-ribbon, but Sugar Baby, who couldn't; and all my instincts told me to stay inside the car and pray a lot. I kept pushing the button, silently encouraging Sugar Baby to bolt out of the gate and disappear forever, as I busily concocted a perfectly logical story to tell the neighbors. It was built around the repeated phrase, "*What* tiger?"

My luck was definitely not in that day. The gate suddenly lurched shut, cutting off Sugar Baby's escape route and making her my responsibility. I stopped the car and sat looking through the window at her, still vaguely hopeful that she might fly away, or dissolve in the sunlight. For her part, Sugar Baby seemed unsure of what to do next, and sat waiting for me to make an interesting move. We might have remained that way forever, had not Tessa Parsons come walking down the road.

Tessa was one of the least enthusiastic animal lovers in the area, and I was well aware that the slightest incident would send her over the edge of tolerance and out into the neighborhood with a petition. Sugar Baby was unquestionably the lesser of the two evils. I jumped out of the car and ran to the barn, where we kept all our leashes and chains for exercising the animals. Sugar Baby was watching me with suspicion, but the sight of Tessa bearing down on us made me fearless. I could put up with being killed, but I wasn't about to move.

○

By then I knew something at least of the uses of surprise; and besides, I was trying to look brisk and decisive for Tessa, as well as for Sugar Baby. The tiger's mouth literally gaped open as I walked up to her and threw the chain around her neck. She sprang straight into the air and took off running the moment her feet hit the ground. It was Ted and Spot all over again, except that Sugar Baby was more than three times Spot's size, and I was half Ted's. I can only compare it to the experience of a bedbug trapped in a Waring blender.

Tessa stared in fascination as we caromed around the yard. She finally called cautiously, "Are you in trouble? Do you need help?" I forced my petrified lips into what had better be a lighthearted smile, bracing my back against whiplash and answering between bounces, "Oh, no—just giving Sugar Baby— little exercise—she loves it, we do this every day—having wonderful time . . ." Tessa hurried off, stopping occasionally to turn and look back at us as Sugar Baby continued her Canadian Air Force workout.

When Tessa disappeared, I began to fight Sugar Baby's course, trying vainly to get her tacking toward her cage. But that meant passing a row of other animals, all of whom she hated, and so she buckjumped and zigzagged more frantically than ever each time we drew close to that area. I hadn't meant to spend the rest of my life quite like this, but was resigning myself to tossed salads and very long drinking straws, when Sugar Baby ran around a cottonwood tree and got her chain caught in the branches. The more she fought, the more entangled she became, and I took advantage of her temporary restraint to catch my breath and change strategy. As I stood there panting, eyes popping from the exertion, I realized that I need only tie off the chain to have her pinned to the tree, if she didn't shrug her shoulders and rip it out by the roots. At that moment, I truly expected to see her do it.

When I was certain that she couldn't escape for the moment, I raced into the barn and got another chain. With a highly unlikely expertise, I threw it over her head, made it fast, and stood back to survey my handiwork. She wasn't about to go anywhere now, but I wasn't much better off, as I knew she couldn't really stay chained to that tree for three weeks. I sat down on the porch steps, considering the situation and hoping for bill-collectors, or a visit from the Jehovah's Witnesses.

It occurred to me for the first time that Tom, who should still have been at his chores, was nowhere in sight. Sugar Baby gasped and snarled under the tree, glaring at me. *Dear God, where was Tom?* I heard a shuffling sound above me, looked up and saw him standing on the upstairs balcony. The house was equipped with an outside staircase which connected the back kitchen with the upstairs bedroom. Tom was standing at the top of the stairs, hidden behind the bedroom door. He was clutching the telephone and staring at me with unseeing eyes.

"Tom, have you been up there all this time? You might at least have tried to help me."

He slowly turned his head and finally focused on me. "No sense both of us getting killed. I was gonna call somebody."

Hard to argue. I walked up the stairs and pried the telephone out of his tightly clenched fist. I then proceeded to call Bill Engler, Gordon Meredith, Charley Franks, and everyone else I knew who had any experience with tigers, yelling for advice, assistance, and company. When I hung up for the last time, Tom was still standing in the same spot. It was obvious that he had no intention of moving until Sugar Baby was safely back in her cage. I agreed with him profoundly; but she no longer looked as well-secured as she had a few moments before, and I knew I'd never be able to make myself go after her if she got loose again. And Tessa might return any minute with a bunch of deputy sheriffs.

I went back to the barn once more and brought out all the chains, ropes, and chain collars that we possessed. Measuring the distance from the tree to Sugar Baby's cage, I was delighted to find that I had slightly more chain than I needed to anchor to the bars and gradually reel her in. It took another half hour of patiently gaining ground and instantly losing it all to a single shake of her head; but mercifully she was almost as tired as I was, and the security of her cage must have been a welcome prospect at that point. When the cars began to arrive, I was standing there looking in at her: sweating and shaking uncontrollably, but grinning like an idiot.

"Better take those chains off her," Gordon Meredith suggested. "She could choke herself if she gets to moving around later."

I couldn't understand for the longest time why everybody laughed so hard when I asked humbly, "Gordon, could you or somebody do that for me? I really am scared to death of that cat."

The Monroes was bread and butter while it lasted, which unfortunately wasn't very long. By the time the program was canceled, however, Ted and I had begun to get calls for free-lance work on other shows, and were managing fairly well by comparison with our time at Animals, Inc. In addition to *Land of the Giants,* we did a *Daniel Boone* episode, and a Canada Dry commercial with a camel. When it came time to film a second Lincoln-Mercury commercial, we returned to Red Rock Canyon feeling aggressively competent and very much in charge. Other people might have their own professional problems, but we knew *our* business.

Tanya escaped on the first day, exactly as she had done before. As before, she was gone for two days, while I took desperate ads in *Lost & Found* columns and called every radio and television station where I knew someone who might ask listeners to watch for Tanya. On the second night, the telephone rang as I was going to bed, an old woman's voice asked hesitantly, "Are you the lady who lost a cougar? Well, I think we might have it, my husband and I. I think it must be the same one."

"You do? Where? Where do you live?" I was trying to scramble back into my clothes one-handed, almost gibbering with hope and relief. "Is she all right? Where do you have her? What's she doing?"

The gracious old voice faltered only slightly. "Well, right *now* she's on our kitchen table, eating the Kentucky Fried Chicken."

I jumped into the car and tore off to the address she gave me: Aguadulce Canyon again. When I reached the house, I found all three of them—Tanya, the old woman, and her husband—sitting in the living room watching the late news. Tanya was nudging her head against the old man's shoe, purring politely.

Tanya always knew what was the best thing for Tanya at any given moment. Finding herself hungry, lonely, and rather bored with escaping, she had simply scratched on the door of the first house she came to, and walked in when it opened. "She's really been very sweet," the old woman said. "She played with my husband all evening, on the floor, the two of them. Only I *did* wish we'd had more Kentucky Fried Chicken to give her when she was up on the table. You give her some when you get her home."

Chauncey had nothing to do with the Cougar commercials in those days, and there seemed very little likelihood that he ever would. Some months before, home on a day off from *The Monroes,* I had looked out into the yard where he was playing with Joe the lion to see him dragging his hindquarters like two sprawled corpses: dead weight, suddenly as unrelated to the rest of his body as though every nerve had been severed. It was a paralysis caused by a calcium deficiency—under X-rays, Chauncey's bones looked almost transparent. We were advised by veterinarians to have him put to sleep. As far as *The Monroes* was concerned, ironically, he had become the perfect television cougar, since he would stay where he was put for filming.

Chauncey as a cub, in an installment of "The Monroes," sitting still not in obedience but because he couldn't walk.

Chauncey's show-business career really began after his paralysis.

We kept him in the house with us, and we took him outside every day to exercise. What a forlorn, grotesque little procession we must have looked, walking around and around the yard, with Ted leading Chauncey on a rope and me holding his helpless back legs off the ground, so that the muscles would try to work and perhaps be kept from atrophying. As ridiculous an effort as it seemed, even to us, in seven or eight months Chauncey was walking again, with the hauntingly stately gait that marked him ever after. It was the pace of someone who couldn't take being here for granted.

The jaguarlike massiveness of his chest and forepaws dated from that time, as did the famous video snarl. Many cougar cubs have a natural bluffing snarl, which they use to warn playmates, mothers, bugs, dead leaves, and water dishes of their power and menace; but as they mature, it becomes something they do only when they are seriously angry. Chauncey needed his snarl to keep the other animals from jumping him, since he couldn't roughhouse with them as he used to do. Ted and I encouraged it—as we encouraged any show of spirit and resistance in him—by waving sticks before him, and then praising and caressing him when he snarled at the sticks. It still worked when he was grown, even though he knew perfectly well that it's just the old game we'd played forever. But he purred all the time, even under the snarl. Chauncey was never not purring.

(Since the stick trick won't work with other cougars, we learned to get what looks like the same result by putting some strong perfume on our hands and letting the cats smell it. All cats test foreign smells by filling their nostrils with the odor, and then throwing their heads back and breathing rapidly several times. On camera, it comes across as a fine, defiant snarl.)

Then suddenly there wasn't any work, and we weren't established trainers after all. I wonder now how much difference —if any—it would have made if I'd known that this was to be our regular cycle, as it still is mine today. The good little run, with bills almost paid, the animals eating well, the temptation to feel that this time it might be all right to breathe deeply, to let your stomach relax; and then, for no reason that can ever be explained to you, the telephone isn't ringing, and you know, as surely as people used to believe in heaven, that it never will again. Free-lancing in most fields is like that; and in this work, at least, the chances are very good that anyone with a savings account acquired it by short-changing the animals. I don't say that out of envy. I wish it weren't true.

For myself, I had never minded the lack of security, having been accustomed to that way of life since I was fifteen. You learn to forage and gamble: actresses try new agents, dancers take whatever bit turns up, even if it means doing a *pas de deux* with a huge can of floor wax; all show-business people know the tricks of not eating. But having the animals made it dreadfully different now. From being a profound sleeper, I fell into dozing shallowly and precariously, waking long before dawn in the increasingly familiar, almost friendly, panic of wondering where I could possibly scavenge for oats, hay, chicken necks, and horsemeat today. Live like that long enough, and I doubt that coming into a fortune would ever have you sleeping through the night again. After a time, your back begins to carry its own wall with it, always.

At last we got a job doing a dog-food commercial, for which we worked with a pack of bloodhounds belonging to a San Diego man named Bert Webb. (We always *said* we had whatever animals the show or the commercial required; once the job was safely ours, it became a matter of staying up all night calling people—in this case, every search-and-rescue team we could find.) I remember the job now not because of the money, which we needed so desperately then, but because at the end of it Bert Webb gave us Belvedere. Money is all alike, but Belvedere was special.

He was five months old; but no bloodhound is ever really a puppy. They seem to be born with an aching need for responsibility, and I think that the reason they seek out strayed infants, lost backpackers, and escaped convicts with impartial enthusiasm is so that they can round them all up and take care of them. Bloodhounds would watch over every living thing in the world if they were allowed to; and they ought to be, for our sake, if not for theirs. In no time at all, Belvedere had become the chief moral influence in our house. He took it upon himself to babysit for all the other animals, of whatever age or species: when several of them were out in the yard, playing and dozing and playing again, Belvedere would wear himself to exhaustion running from one to the other, making sure that everyone was all right, and that no animal was either getting hurt or getting lonely. In the end, he would fall off to sleep himself, usually curled next to Murgatroyd, with the little black bear sucking peacefully at his ear.

Bloodhounds are strange dogs. Their vision is literally dangerous to them, since, like Clarence, they have no depth per-

Belvedere the bloodhound, whose affection for every creature we owned extended even to a bumptious raccoon named Winnie.

ception, and no sense at all about heights. On Belvedere's first night with us, put outside on the balcony when he asked to go out, he hurled himself down the flight of outside stairs in a single crashing leap, apparently never understanding that he was high off the ground. Perhaps for that reason, bloodhounds often seem very wary of the betraying ground itself, and unfamiliar terrain can paralyze them with terror. To his dying day, Belvedere never came to terms with the waxed wooden floors of our house, but walked them—or any other suspicious surface, for that matter—as though they were minefields, sometimes taking five minutes to cross a room. It was the purest possible act of love for him to come to us across the living-room floor, but he always came.

The dog-food commercial didn't mean much safety by itself, but it kept us breathing a little longer, until the offer from *Lassie* came out of nowhere. *Lassie* and Lincoln-Mercury were our lifeline for years, our fingernail-hold on a crumbling overhang. There were long, long stretches of time when we had no other work, and managed to feed the animals only because of them. It crosses my mind occasionally to dedicate this book in all seriousness to an automobile and a collie.

We got the *Lassie* job, ironically, because Bill Beaudine, the producer, had had a falling-out with Animals, Inc., who had been doing all of the show's animal work until then. I liked *Lassie* as a show. The stories were gentle, the acting level higher than is usual for a children's program, and there was a genuine family feeling among the cast, which did come across on screen. The first *Lassie* episode we ever did was also the one time Bud ever worked—he played a pregnant female cougar; the fact is that poor Bud *looks* like a pregnant female—and I've always remembered how kind and affectionate everyone was to him. Granted, if you want to warp my artistic judgment, that's the way to do it, but *Lassie* really was a surprisingly enjoyable show.

I was honestly starstruck when I met Lassie himself, which has never been something that happens to me. Lassie was always very friendly and courteous; and by *always,* in this case, I mean whichever Lassie it happened to be over the years. There were usually at least three of them at once: a main, or public Lassie; a stand-in Lassie, who would be younger and would eventually take over the lead role in his turn; and a stunt Lassie, who did all the fight scenes and leaps for life. They were all males, invariably—most people know that by now, but I hadn't, and I was truly a little disappointed at first. But the males are generally stronger and more outgoing; they like to perform, and they get excited about doing it. The females don't seem to care about show business, which tells you something.

Rudd Weatherwax, the head trainer, never minded people knowing that Lassie was a male, but he used to make an odd point of insisting publicly that there was only one Lassie at a time. I never understood why he bothered so about it, especially since on an eight-to-twelve-hour-a-day shooting schedule, with Lassie in almost every sequence, it would have been utterly cruel not to have stand-in dogs. Rudd is a complex man, crusty and irascible, but devoted to his dogs, and certainly one of the best trainers in the business. He truly deserves his honors and his influence.

I respect Rudd for a couple of reasons, apart from his skills, which may both look a little strange in print. For one thing, he trains only dogs, where most professional trainers—including us, in those days—diversify to a point where they're working with all sorts of animals they don't know anything about. In the second place, his dogs live in the house with him and his wife. That may not sound like anything special, but it's almost never done in this trade. Other trainers' dogs are no more like real dogs than those poor, bloated monsters living under fluorescent lights in egg factories are really chickens. They are either in a kennel or they're working; they may be fed and exercised well enough, but they never get to wash a face or jump up on a bed. I like Rudd for that, and I think it's a main reason why his Lassies are always unique, however many of them there are.

It's one of the few black marks I have against *Lassie* that perhaps the worst trainer I ever met also worked that show occasionally. I mention him only for this reason: that although everyone connected with *Lassie* despised him, he was still called on whenever a scene needed his special talents. There was always a representative of the American Humane Association on the set, as is required by law; but somehow the one on *Lassie* would have been sent off to get coffee for the cast when this trainer worked. Even the most decent and enlightened people still seem to place their deepest trust in the torturer.

But it was the best job we'd ever had, in terms of working conditions for ourselves and the animals. From Bill Beaudine on down, the basic concern was for the animals' needs, and whatever we asked for them was hardly ever questioned. Chauncey became a special favorite among the actors and the crew alike; and the writers, who used to come out to Newhall to pick our brains for story possibilities, would find excuses to sneak him into the scripts. The only difficulty we ever had—and it was certainly not confined to *Lassie*—was with directors who found it hard to understand that wild animals, unlike trained dogs and actors, will not work on cue. I fought the same skirmishes over and over: no, the fawns will not hold still until I call them; no, the cougar is not about to run anywhere for your cameraman, not in this noon heat—he'll only walk, and only to shade. But it was a long way from the rage and terror of the old days, watching animals die in the cold, gray wind.

What I loved best was going on location. Very simply, the only times when I have felt truly secure and taken care of, in the last twelve or thirteen years, have been when I was off somewhere in the wilderness with a show like *Lassie*. Companies on location, from television Westerns to Molière's and Shakespeare's traveling players, tend to draw very close together, excluding the outside world entirely. For two or three weeks, nothing exists but that show, good or awful, and all of you making it. Waiting back at Newhall for me might be bills, summonses, eviction notices, gangs of aroused neighbors with deputy sheriffs, bad news from my mother in England, perhaps even a catastrophic flood of my very own. But just then, all I had to worry about was the mental chess game of keeping the animals and the director happy— the rest of it was serenest, blandest Utopia, with wine at dinner, until I got home. I slept through the night only when I was on location.

Shortly after Ted and I had begun working for *Lassie,* I was contacted by a wealthy matron—I knew very few matrons in those days, but I knew right away that she was one—who had seen me with Thumper on some local television show. She called me immediately, introducing herself as a fellow animal-lover who also happened to have a wallaroo. On this basis, aided by the almost-innocent *chutzpah* of the very rich, she began coming out frequently to visit us at Newhall. We'll call her Mrs. Burchard.

God, she was an obnoxious woman! We were obnoxious too, of course, balancing her sad hunger to be important to wild animals against our eternal need for money. She had a crush on Clyde—or on being with Clyde, which isn't the same thing—and Ted used to take her into the jaguar's cage, much against my wishes. I was genuinely afraid for her safety, because she was one of those people who naturally do everything wrong around animals. The voice too shrill, the movements too quick and aggressive, the absolute lack of understanding that leopards want you to be quiet, and that even the best-natured cougar would rather you didn't press so close on first acquaintance —it's a small miracle to me that she didn't get hurt or killed. She was tone-deaf to animals, as some people are to music, or to the use of language.

I can't say she didn't love them; but as I've implied, that careless, misplaced, scatterbrained kind of love is possibly the most terrible danger that wild animals in captivity have to face. For example, she let her wallaroo thump around in the yard unattended, and one day he thumped over the low, decorative fence and thumped down the driveway into the road, where he was killed by a car. If she had had a lion or a tiger, it would have gotten loose too, and probably been shot down in some neighbor's garage. I know that love.

When another such matron asked us to take part in a charity fashion show she was organizing, I'd probably have said no—even though it meant a little money—except for the gown she wanted me to model while walking Rijo. It was long and green and magnificent, the kind of gown I'd dreamed about wearing to balls when I was little, and I think she offered it to me deliberately, knowing that I wouldn't be able to resist wearing it, even for an hour. The show was staged at a mansion, and the matron really had lined up an astonishing number of big names to serve as models. All that I recall about it is the green gown, and meeting my idol, the actress Colin Wilcox, and her husband Geoffrey Horne; and the English actor Michael Rennie.

Michael had agreed to be the narrator and master of ceremonies for the fashion show. When the show was over, he introduced himself to Ted and me—and to Rijo, in exactly the right sort of way—asking me if he might visit us sometime and take pictures of our animals. I remember that he didn't say that he loved animals, but only that he liked to take pictures.

He came out on the following weekend, and on the weekend after that, to show us the film he had taken with the Super-8 camera he was so proud of. The custom was born then: when Michael was in town and not working, he would come to visit one Saturday to film the animals, and return on the next to screen his new movie for us. It became a cherished ceremony of friendship and continued through the few years of him that we had.

After my father, he was the nicest, kindest man I've ever known. I suppose a Freudian psychiatrist would have no trouble at all interpreting the fact that my closest and most supportive male friends have almost always been old enough to be my father. Michael was fifty-seven or so when we met; white-haired, slender, bigger than he looked on screen; effortlessly elegant, even in blue jeans, flannel shirt, and ascot tie. He looked at least ten years younger than his age, and was in wonderful physical condition, except for the lung ailment that never bothered him dramatically, but never would quite go away.

With the animals, he was the exact opposite of all the poor Mrs. Burchards, doing the right things instinctively. He fell in love with Joe, the young lion, and Joe doted shamelessly on him in return. Michael, immaculately dressed, as always, would take Joe out of his cage, and the two of them would promptly tumble over each other in the nearest patch of mud or wet grass. I can still see them: Michael laughing and spluttering, hanging on with his arms around Joe's neck as Joe licked him and mouthed him and dragged him around by his sleeve or his collar. He met the lion on a lion's terms, and he never got hurt, even accidentally. Joe would never have hurt Michael.

I remember how distressed he was when Ted and I fell on

bad times again, out of money and needing to find a new place to live within a matter of days. I was growing reasonably used to this regular cycle of survival between disasters, but it upset Michael terribly. In spite of his star billing, and a career stretching back over thirty-five years, he had almost no money of his own at the time we knew him. As a British citizen living and working in the United States, his financial problems began with double taxation and took off from there. He worked incessantly, taking any acting job that came up—even going to Italy to perform in Grade Z costume and gangster epics—and existing on a kind of lunch-money dole, very much as we did. "The one time in my life I've ever found something to love, and I can't be any help," he said once, very softly. "I suppose it figures."

It's been five years, and I still can't believe he's dead. I cared for him so much.

11

"It's in the walls, all right," Bill Engler said. "I thought maybe it was under the house, but it's right up there in the walls."

"I've been hearing it for two days," I told him. "Ted keeps saying it's just a mother cat with a litter, but I never hear any other kittens. This one cries all the time, all night long, and today it sounds so much weaker, and I don't know what to do, Bill. It's starving all alone in my house, and I can't find it."

Bill cocked his head even farther to the side, like a shrewd old starling listening to the ground. "Ah, can't have that," he said. He was a singlehearted cat-lover, who lived in a strange, musky house with his cougars and his ancient mother, and he used to come to dinner often when we still lived in Newhall. Abruptly he pushed back his chair and got up from his half-eaten meal, saying, "Ted, my boy, I need a ladder. Got to take the front of your house off."

He did, too—it cost us a hundred dollars we didn't have to put the house back together—and that was how we found Thing that night, before we finished dinner. She was barely conscious when Bill reached her, but still trying to cry: she looked and felt like the limp, slimy clump of hair that you dredge up out of the bathtub drain. There were no traces of a mother cat, or of any other kittens. Thing had somehow been born and abandoned in the wall.

Cleaned up, she wasn't black, like Poe's walled-up cat, but a washed-out gray and white. I raised her on an eyedropper, as I had done with countless animals before, though never one so nearly not here at all. For the first week, she could have been breathed out like a match at any moment; then one morning she sneezed and grabbed my hand and yelled for me to bring the eyedropper back or she'd bite my ears off. The reign of Queen Thing the Terrible had definitely begun.

Thing ruled by stark terror. Her first playmate was a wolf cub named Woofie, and while he grew faster and bigger than she did, Thing could send him scurrying with a growl or a look any time she chose. Woofie got his turn at the food dish when Thing was good and ready, and so would have Rijo or Spot if the matter had ever come up. For all her eating, she was never much more than a scrawny piebald rag of a cat, but she feared nothing in this world, or in the next, having already seen them both.

In due course, Thing herself went into heat, became pregnant, and very professionally delivered an incredible litter of ten kittens. My pride in her turned to a fascinated horror within a few days, as she calmly began killing them at the rate of one a day. There was no way of keeping her from it: the one little blind corpse would continue to turn up, maybe in the linen closet, maybe shoved down between two sofa cushions, however much I scolded and spied on her. She killed all of her kittens but one—a gray-and-white wisp who looked exactly like her. I have always believed that she was in some way reenacting her own birth and her mother's desertion, and that that lone surviving kitten was truly Thing herself. She guarded it like some unsleeping creature out of legend—three-headed, hundred-eyed—and heaven help the animal who dared even to pass the door of the room where Thing's baby slept. Thing had no more mercy or moderation than she had fear.

One afternoon, when the kitten was three or four weeks old, I was sitting on the porch steps reading over my small role in a television play (I still took the rare acting jobs that came along, if I could fit them into our regular working schedule), while Joe, Clyde, Sweet William, Murgatroyd, and Mandy played in the yard. Certain species are simply not meant to live at close quarters, and they always know it—and I had given up my earlier fantasies and come to realize it too—but it made me happy to look up now and then and see Joe and Murgatroyd romping together, and Belvedere the bloodhound bumblingly vigilant, looking out for everybody.

His nursery charges abruptly increased by one as Thing's kitten wobbled from under the steps and made her tottery way into the yard. Like a lot of overprotected children, she was already beginning to rebel in small ways, and I often saw her exploring the world on her own, having apparently escaped her mother's fanatic watchfulness for the moment. Now, sparring with the sunlight and falling over tufts of dry grass, she wandered closer and closer to Sugar Baby's cottonwood tree, under which Clyde the jaguar lay tethered, his eyes almost closed, waiting for her.

There was nothing of the schemer about Clyde. If the kitten came close enough to be grabbed, that was fine, and if she didn't, life was just like that. He let her tumble almost between his outstretched forepaws before he struck.

Belvedere was on his way over there even before Clyde's jaws had closed, or the kitten dangling between them had caught her breath to squall. Seeing him coming, Clyde dropped the kitten immediately and lay down again, sublimely and sleepily innocent. He was in the habit of giving in to Belvedere.

The kitten was yelling her offended head off, and she didn't stop when Belvedere picked her up to take her somewhere safe from jaguars. He was plodding back across the yard with her, the incarnation of sober, selfless virtue, when Thing hit him like a hand grenade. She had come tearing around the corner of the house in response to the kitten's cries, and she never hesitated for a second, but flew through the air to land stiff-legged on Belvedere's back with all her claws working. It was the nearest thing I have ever seen to a bolt from heaven, and about as well-aimed as they usually seem to be.

I dropped my script and ran to rescue Belvedere, who, with Thing riding his back and raking him pitilessly from end to end, was racing up and down the yard, bellowing at least as much in utter outrage as in pain. The other animals stared and rumbled and flung themselves out of the way; and Joe almost stepped on the screaming kitten, who was toddling toward him now. When I picked her up and turned to flag down Belvedere this next time around the yard, I caught sight of Clyde sitting attentively under the cottonwood tree. His tail was curled around his hind feet, and his eyes were still half-closed, but he was smiling. I know Clyde's normal saturnine expression, and no one will ever convince me that that wasn't a smile I saw. Dogs can't deal with injustice, but all cats are born understanding its uses.

The only other of our animals besides Chauncey ever to become a national advertising symbol was Rijo, who was Enco's Tiger in Your Tank while that gimmick lasted. We learned of Enco's desire to experiment with a big-cat commercial of its own from an itinerant dealer who used to drive around in a truck with various animals crammed into the tiniest cages I had ever seen, like a grotesque parody of the Good Humor Man. He was clever at getting jobs—the last I heard, he had made a fortune from a movie about wolves—and he got the Enco contract by virtue of having a tiger already: my poor old friend Honey, from Animals, Inc. Honey proved impossible to work, and the dealer came to us with an offer of $300 to use

Rijo for a day's shooting. Ted was doing a *Monroes* episode that day, so I went along to be with Rijo. Even in those times, I never let our animals go out alone with any trainer.

We went up to San Bernardino to film, because the director wanted a background of hills. It was very much like doing the first Lincoln-Mercury commercial: the director thought that he might perhaps like to have Rijo start at the foot of a hill and walk straight away from it towards a stationary camera, *just see how it looks*. The dealer's method of achieving this was simply to release Rijo at the agree-upon spot and tell the director to start shooting. It's probably the most common technique of all—turn the animal loose and grab whatever you can grab. I had seen it done dozens of times.

The trouble was that the location was uniquely ill-chosen for the shot. Most animals tend to walk uphill, given the choice, and to come downhill reluctantly, as you know if you've ever chased a horse. All the cameraman got was Rijo's elegant rear ascending sedately out of range, and I had to run after him and bring him back down. As incredibly stupid as it must seem to read, that was what we did, over and over, for the next two or three hours, and nobody suggested that we try anything different, including me. I had no particular regard for the dealer, but I left the actual filming entirely to him, as was my habit with Ted. I was just there for Rijo.

Siberian tigers suffer greatly in the heat, and by noon Rijo was blowing and laboring so badly that I insisted on stopping the shooting to give him at least an hour's rest. The crew broke for lunch—without a foot of usable film in the camera—and left me sitting on the hill with Rijo, thinking dully, "I've got to do something. That dealer doesn't know what to do—he'll just kill Rijo this way, and never get any film at all. So it's me. I have to figure out something, for Rijo's sake."

When everyone came back, I spoke to the director for the first time that day, asking him to tell me exactly what scenes he wanted in the commercial. By then he was beginning to

think that it might be better to have the tiger run down a
straight stretch of road and—he didn't know for sure—just *do*
a few things. I put Rijo in the truck and went off looking for a
straight stretch of road.

Having found a suitable location, I walked a few hundred
yards down the road and stood there calling to Rijo when the
dealer released him. A camera car traveled alongside as he
came toward me. When he was near enough, I turned and
began to run, because Rijo—like Chauncey—loved to chase
me. Romeo had taught me in a matter of seconds that this is
not the proper thing to do with a big cat; but Rijo's chasing
was always play, and I felt sure of myself with him. He lolloped
along after me, rumbling with amusement, letting me keep
ahead of him, and the camera car got all the film the director
could possibly use. It was that easy.

If that hardly sounds like radical thinking, all I can say is
that people gaped and carried on as though I had invented
scrambled eggs. In the world of the animal trainer—as in
others—elementary common sense arrives like witchcraft. I
was vain of that utterly obvious maneuver for days, myself.

Another example of the creative uses of idiotic simplicity
came during the third Cougar commercial, which was the most
elaborate and trying one so far. It was filmed in three sections:
the first in Acton, where Tanya promptly vanished for her
usual two days; the second in a nightmarish place called the
Valley of Fire. The temperature was 115 degrees in the shade—
if you dropped any metal object, you didn't dare to pick it up—
and the atmosphere was composed entirely of burning red grit.
Ted and I were supposed to induce six cougars to race across
the desert (they hadn't given up on that shot yet) and leap into
a big tractor-trailer truck. I wouldn't have gone near an animal
crazy enough to do something like that.

The hellish circumstances themselves suggested a way of
setting up the scene. We specified that the truck must be air-

The script for this commercial required six cougars to run together across the Valley of Fire, and here we are, trying to line them up, the nervous cougars up front, the bold ones behind to push the nervous ones forward. But it didn't work. Then we tried the air-conditioned truck. (Photo by Don Lewis)

conditioned, and we kept the cougars in it all morning until they were led out into the swirling dust. Turned loose, with the cameras going, all six of them headed straight back toward the truck at top speed, and piled into it like students into a telephone booth. Our only difficulty with that scene was in keeping members of the crew from fighting each other for the right to be cougar wranglers, just to be in the truck for a few minutes. Several of them volunteered to be extra cougars.

The survivors of the Valley of Fire got to drive up north to Fort Bragg, where the third section of the commercial was to be filmed. Ted and I camped for the night just outside Sausalito, sleeping in our station wagon, which was towing a cage-trailer full of cougars. We were awakened in the middle of the night by a state trooper, who wanted to know if those were our cougars back there. I had already played this particular scene a great many times, in one version or another, and was resigned to getting dressed and driving on; but the trooper only wanted to know if we might be interested in a jaguar. He and his wife had had one for several years, and were afraid they couldn't keep her any longer. She was real tame, and her name was Princess.

We went with him that same night to meet his jaguar. She wasn't at all tame, but she was a beautiful animal even so, and Clyde was old enough now to be interested in company. We picked her up on our way back from Fort Bragg, and brought her home with us.

As it happened, Clyde was then getting ready to make his debut on *Lassie*. A couple of the regular writers had always been fascinated by the way he played with Belvedere, raging and snarling as though he were busily tearing his friend to bloody bits, and somehow never so much as scratching one of the bloodhound's trailing ears. Belvedere was also buddies with Chauncey, who was getting around quite well now, and with whom he romped in a much gentler, almost kittenish manner. Starting from the relationship between the three of them, the writers concocted a pleasantly unlikely story in which a cougar rescues his bloodhound friend from the jaws of a killer jaguar. It was silly, but it did give us a chance to try Princess out as a double for Clyde. She seemed as good-natured as he, for all her wildness, but we still had no idea whether she could be worked. You can never assume anything with the spotted cats.

The director of that *Lassie* episode thought you could. We had a worrisome time with him, and with the crew, because none of them would take the jaguars seriously. Clyde and Princess were both friendly animals, and accustomed to people —which also implies that they had no slightest fear of them. They liked having their heads scratched, and they took food from any hands; and it was impossible to explain adequately that they were no less jaguars for that, with all their ancestors' knowledge of what constitutes an offense or a liberty to a jaguar. The crew treated them with great affection, but without respect, and we feared a disaster before the filming was completed.

At that time, we had two occasional assistants: Billy Red-lin, the young son of a Disney producer; and a used-car salesman named Eddie Steeples. Eddie knew nothing about animals, except that he liked them, and he wanted passionately to be a trainer. He was a decent, earnest man, and he fetched and carried tirelessly for us, just to be around the animals.

Most of the episode's wild-animal scenes were shot in the San Bernardino Mountains, as Rijo's Enco commercial had been. We worked the three cats, as always, to chicken necks, which were kept in a large pan with a sliding cover and lugged around everywhere by Eddie Steeples, and which he almost literally guarded with his life. At the director's request, Ted had lured Princess to a particular mountain outcrop one morning by the usual means of placing a chicken neck on it. Unfortunately, he had absent-mindedly set the pan itself down near the rock, and when Princess arrived she immediately pounced on it and took it over. Eddie promptly started forward to get it back. Ted and I both yelled, "*No!*" but Eddie didn't hear us.

Jaguars are extremely possessive animals; their whole disposition changes utterly when you try getting them away from something they've grabbed. Eddie never faltered: all he knew

Some of the cougars enjoying relief from the Valley of Fire in the air-conditioned truck. Having already been photographed running toward the truck, they were reluctant to leave it. The chains were not to keep them there but to keep them from arguing over which corner was whose territory. (Photo by Don Lewis)

was that he was in charge of the meat pan, and he marched straight up to Princess, who was so busy sniffing the pan and rubbing against it that she didn't notice him until he was perhaps five feet away. When she looked up, she didn't waste a moment in snarling or lashing her tail—she simply hurled herself at Eddie, hit him in the chest like a slamming door, and smashed him right off the mountain. Then she crouched on the meat pan again, trying to get the cover off.

We thought Eddie was dead. Billy Redlin ran down to him, while the director and the crew trampled frantically over one another to the safety of the company bus. Princess was growling now, whipping herself rapidly into a jaguar's paranoid rage of destruction. Ted said, "Get me something to get her mind off the pan with. Anything, get anything."

I scrambled down the mountainside, passing Eddie, who seemed bruised and half-stunned, but otherwise unhurt. I grabbed the first remotely useful object I could find—the big umbrella that covered the camera in hot weather—and ran back up to give it to Ted. He opened it and began walking into Princess, holding it out in front of him, trying to back her away from the meat pan.

Princess ate the umbrella. I don't mean merely that she destroyed it—as far as I'm concerned, she ate the thing like a potato chip, and sent Ted sprinting back to keep from going with it. He yelled, "Get me something else!" and I was off down the mountain again, hoping to find something in our station wagon. There were a couple of heavy canes, holdovers from Animals, Inc., that Ted could never quite bring himself to give up. I brought those to him, and he advanced on Princess with one in each hand, like a knife-fighter in a movie. Princess never gave back a step, but knocked one cane thirty feet away and ate the other. She was as ready to die for that meat pan as Eddie Steeples had been, and with a far better understanding of the situation.

"Get something else!" I lurched and fell back to the car, and found half a dozen CO_2 cartridges in a rear compartment. We never used them anymore; all but two felt empty. I walked up the mountain this time, carrying the one that I guessed was the more fully charged. I was sodden with sweat, and so dizzy that it made me feel sick to keep my eyes open. The popping CO_2 did finally back Princess off the meat pan, though it seemed to increase her fury. Ted followed her, taking one step for each step of hers, and the two of them disappeared around a huge boulder. I noticed that I was sitting down. I liked that.

From the far side of the boulder, Princess's roars doubled in volume and took on an extra edge of screaming insanity. Through her tumult and my own boneless daze, I could barely hear Ted shouting to me, "Pat, I'm running out of CO_2! Go get the other one, *quick!*"

Oh, right. Other one. Car. Better stand up first. I must have made it to the station wagon all right, because there I was tottering uphill, me and the second cartridge, collapsing to the rescue. The faces against the bus windows, and those of Eddie and Billy, were gray and red and wet, and horribly fascinated.

I didn't have to climb quite all the way back, because I met Ted coming down with Princess on a chain. They had backed one another so far from the meat pan that Princess had forgotten completely about chicken necks and the territorial imperative. She couldn't remember that she was angry at anyone —and if she had killed Ted, she wouldn't have remembered that, either—and so she lay down calmly and sweetly and let Ted snap the chain around her neck. Jaguars are like that.

In the midst of working on the *Lassie* show, we got a call from the Disney studios, asking if we had a bear who might be interested in riding in a Ferrari and eating sandwiches. It was for a movie called *The Love Bug,* about an emotional Volkswagen. Of the several trainers who had been called before us, none had even been able to get their bears into the Ferrari. Experiments with building a mockup car around a stationary bear had worked out poorly for everyone concerned.

We agreed to try doing the scene with Sweet William, but only under perfect conditions for him. There was to be shade over the entire car; the camera was to be hidden, since Sweet William feared them; we were to have plenty of time to work, and no one else on the set. As for the sandwiches, which the bear was supposed to discover in the car, I instructed a Disney aide to make them out of whipped cream, strawberry jam, and Hostess Twinkies, and to keep making them until Sweet William specifically told him to stop. That seemed like a bear's idea of conditions.

It worked beautifully. On the trail of a five-pound bag of Twinkies, and with Ted calling to him from off-camera, Sweet William lumbered dutifully out of the woods and climbed into the Ferrari without hesitating for a moment. The only awkwardness was that his prodigious bottom only went part of the way with him. It wasn't particularly awkward for Sweet William— he had found the sandwiches by then, and had nothing against eating while stuck in a door. Ted and I had to call time and run out to stuff him into the front seat, while he smacked and mumbled and wondered mildly what was going on. People who have forgotten the rest of the movie always seem to remember the bear in the sports car.

Sweet William was summoned back for one final scene on the same day that we were to stage the three-cornered battle between Clyde, Chauncey, and Belvedere for *Lassie*. Ted took him over to the Disney studios, leaving me to handle the fight sequences. I think of that as the day when I gained my spurs, or my buttons, or whatever it was that one earned on *Lassie*. The director was furious when he learned that Ted had gone off on another job, putting me in charge of the show's roughest shots, and I didn't blame him. To him, as to everyone we worked with, Ted was the trainer, the one who actually got things done, while my only real function was to coddle the

In this scene from the Disney film The Loner, *Sweet William was supposed to menace some sheep until defied by the little sheepdog. Willie was the least menacing bear I knew, but he brought it off credibly.*

animals a good deal too much. I still accepted that assessment myself, most of the time.

But it went almost as easily as Sweet William's sports car scene. I had to tranquilize Belvedere slightly—the cameras and the strange people made him nervous—and paint fake blood all over him; after that, he and the two big cats settled down to serious playing, accompanied by enough roaring, barking, and snarling for a crowd at a hockey game. The editing makes it look as though Clyde the villain is happily disemboweling poor Belvedere when Chauncey charges into him from the side, knocking him off the helpless bloodhound and raging at his throat. They had a wonderful time. When the shooting was over, they fell asleep together, in a spotted and brindled sprawl of understanding.

Ted and I had begun occasionally lecturing to local humane societies by then, and we always included a clip of that fight scene in our presentations. It wasn't meant to show off my directorial skills, but to illustrate our main point: that it is perfectly possible to work animals in a show without abusing them, simply by giving them enjoyable reasons for doing what you want them to do. Again, I hope this sounds like the most ridiculously elementary of discoveries. It's supposed to.

Then the same old Beachy Street troubles caught up with us again. An ordinance was abruptly passed stating that it was necessary to have a conditional use permit in order to keep wild animals in the Newhall area. Our application for a permit was refused without explanation, and we were given thirty days to move our dozen animals out of Newhall, or have them confiscated.

We confronted a competitor whose methods we had criticized, knowing the extent of his local influence, but he denied our accusations earnestly. "I swear I didn't have anything to do with that business, Ted. As much a surprise to me as it was to you. I mean, all right, I can be a bastard, but I wouldn't do anything like that. I really swear it."

"Can you help us?" Ted asked him. "Can you do anything about getting us a permit? You know all those people, supervisors, whatever—couldn't you talk to somebody?"

The man sighed and spread his hands. "I wish I could; I'd do it like that, right now. But I'm not that kind of a wheel, honestly

—I had a tough enough time getting my own use permit. If there were anything I could do, believe me."

There was no question of moving to a new home within thirty days; it would be a miracle if we could even find a temporary place for the animals. We had been talking with Bill Burrud about opening an animal park together, but he was too busy. Then Ora and Jean Johnson came to us, as casually and diffidently as always, and Ora said, "We been thinking about what to do. You know that piece of land of ours, up in Acton?"

I had entirely forgotten that they owned a few undeveloped acres there. I said, "Uncle Ory, it's wonderful of you, but we couldn't just take your land—"

Jean rode right over me. "Why, it's not doing us or anybody any good, just sitting there. It's real back country—nobody's likely to come around bothering the animals. And we could help to look after them, Ora and me and the boys. Taking turns."

I don't know if we earned the Johnsons. I think that they were rather, in Robert Frost's words, something we somehow hadn't to deserve. The location was an inconvenient one, as far as our work went, but we had no choice at all. We moved the animals to Acton, hired Eddie Steeples to stay up there with them, and once again began searching for a new place to live.

We were still looking a couple of months later when we met Roy Cabot, who owned Jungleland, the animal ranch from which I had stormed away with an unpaid-for Candy eating my arms. He suggested that we rent a large barn on his property and board the animals there, since we were hoping to find a home in the Thousand Oaks area, where Jungleland was located. I disliked the idea intensely, and said so to Ted. "It's like moving back to Animals, Inc. It feels just as though we were starting all over again, like a dream, where you run and run and keep losing ground."

"Well, it's still better than anything we could set up for them on the Johnsons' land," Ted argued. "And we'll be the only ones handling them—that's the big difference, that's what matters. Look, it'll just be for a little while, a month, maybe two months." We agreed to the arrangement, and chose a date to bring the animals down from Acton.

All of our friends, from Jerry Johnson to Michael Rennie, came to help us on the moving day. We loaded the animals into vans and trailers, then broke down their cages and stowed them aboard as well. I set out before the others were ready, driving Eddie Steeples's old station wagon in company with a Mexican gardener and odd-job man named José Ortega. He had no English at all, and I no confidence in my kitchen Spanish, but we were united today by a common nervousness and a desire to get the whole thing over with quickly. José's understandable jitters were due to the fact that we were towing a flimsy cage-wagon containing a large male lion; mine to the fact that the lion was Flap. José had the easier time.

Flap was a recent acquisition, the result of Ted's determination to own a full-grown male like Junior or Clarence. He was a huge, handsome creature, weighing over five hundred pounds, who had been raised from cubhood in the tiny British Columbia animal park where we found him. Like Sugar Baby and Princess, he was dangerously knowledgeable about human beings, and Ted handled him with great respect and an eye on the cage door at all times. Flap's particular hobby—as I knew, and José didn't—was eating trailers. The journey back from Canada had been a nightmarish race with his joyous appetite for wood and wire, and we very nearly came in second. My Spanish wasn't up to discussing the experience with José, and I didn't want to think about it much, anyway.

We had driven for perhaps twenty minutes on Highway 101, heading for Thousand Oaks, when I began to notice that many of the motorists who passed us were honking their horns and pointing back at the cage-wagon. I drove a bit faster, trying not to look in the rear-view mirror; but José peered out of the window, and looked ten years older when he pulled his head in again. *"Señora, mire, mire! El león—el león!"* I was afraid that I understood him perfectly.

Flap had eaten the side window out of the cage-wagon, and had forced some two-thirds of his body through the jagged hole. He was now hanging over the freeway at seventy miles an hour, with the wind blowing his mane straight out around his snarling head. It made him look like a terrible golden flower.

I don't remember how I got the car stopped on the shoulder of the freeway, where one is allowed Emergency Parking Only. We jumped out, and I tried frantically to communicate to José that he must search through the car—which was full of Eddie Steeples's household goods—for something that we could use to get *el león* back into the cage-wagon. Then I ran to wave my arms and yell, "No! Stay!" at Flap, hoping somehow to distract him from his delightful new project. I might as well have brandished pork chops at him. The last third of a lion is the skinniest part, and Flap was coming through.

José brought me an ironing board. He was one of the bravest men I ever met, if bravery means being terrified and going ahead anyway. Together we marched into Flap with the ironing board, clutching it by the folding legs to keep him from removing our hands when he struck at it. He was furious, but he was also somewhat taken aback, not having had much to do with ironing boards before. Roaring and lashing out, he retreated into the trailer, and we slammed the ironing board across the hole and threw our bodies against it. I heard horns and tires shrieking behind us on the freeway, but I never turned my head. I had my own troubles.

"José, a rope—we've got to have a rope!" My Spanish was becoming more fluent with terror, though I recall that I kept asking him to find some *ropa*, which means clothing. Mercifully, he didn't return with an armload of Eddie's Hawaiian shirts, but with a length of clothesline, which we managed to secure to the ironing board while Flap was smashing at it from the other side. Then José ran around and around the cage-wagon, paying out the clothesline and pulling it as tight as he could. He was on his second or third circuit before either of us noticed that he was tying me, as well as the ironing board, over the hole. Flap almost got out for good that time.

We'd never have made it to Thousand Oaks with a leopard or a jaguar in the cage-wagon. Princess's claws would have reduced the ironing board to filigreed kindling before I had shifted through the gears—if she had backed off at all—but a lion's true weapon is the power of his blow; and Flap was having a hard time keeping his balance and gaining enough leverage and elbow-room to strike with his full strength. Even so, he bounced that board against the clothesline all the way to Jungleland, and something would have given within the next few miles. He was a very upset lion.

For some reason, there was no one available to help us at Jungleland, and no empty cage to put Flap into temporarily. José and I leaned our backs against the ironing board for half an hour, until Ted and the others arrived, feeling it split still further every time a somewhat-wearying Flap took another swing at it. During those last absurd, endless few minutes, too frightened to register fright, or anything much besides a dull headache and a need to go to the bathroom, I discovered that I knew quite enough Spanish to explain carefully to José why one should never look back when transporting a lion somewhere. No experience is entirely wasted or unrewarding.

12

Jungleland was a mess, but it was a mess with tradition. That didn't mean anything to the animals who had to be there, but it meant a good deal to old-movie buffs. The compound was to wild-animal movies what Red Rock Canyon was to Westerns: the Tarzan films of the 1930s and 1940s were shot at Jungleland, and so were things like the *Bomba the Jungle Boy* and *Jungle Jim* serials. The sense of being in a sort of museum of B- and C-movie history was heightened by the fact that Jungleland was always full of people out of that time, that world. There was Mel Koonz, for instance, the man who had trained the MGM lion; and Mabel Stark, an incredible seventy-five-year-old who had had both breasts torn off by tigers, but was still working big cats, cursing them savagely at the top of her voice all the while. I liked and respected a lot of those old circus and carnival people, even while I hated the way some of them were with animals and made certain that they never came near ours. Like leopards, like jaguars, people just are what they are.

At the time we were there, Jungleland was enjoying a short-lived reprieve from imminent bankruptcy, having done all the animal work for the film *Dr. Dolittle*. (They won a Patsy award for that movie, incidentally, and were simultaneously cited by the local Humane Society on several counts of animal abuse.) Roy Cabot was a decent man who was very good to Ted and me—he genuinely liked the way we worked with our animals—but his ranch was a sad, crumbling shambles. The barn was impossible to keep clean or properly drained, and the animals got even less fresh air and sunlight than they would have had at Animals, Inc. We could hardly ever take them outside, for there were always groups of tourists wandering around, and dogs and horses everywhere being exercised, trained, treated, or born. Eddie Steeples, who lived in a trailer he had parked next to the barn, did the best anyone could have done for the animals; but I came to hate going into the barn because of the guilt and despair that being there made me feel. The fact that we could have found no other place to keep them didn't help at all.

By then we had given up fighting the zoning laws of Los Angeles County, and were looking for land in the Santa Barbara area. With Michael Rennie's aid, we found a house in Montecito, directly on the coast, overlooking the ocean. The lot was far too small for us to keep the animals there, but we had hopes of being able to buy a few acres in Carpinteria, only five miles away. We felt increasingly pressed and jittery as it became daily more obvious that Jungleland was going under. It was very much like living an endless Eliza-crossing-the-ice scene, except that we were carrying lions and tigers and bears in our arms, and the hounds wore business suits, flourished legal papers, and were only following orders. And the ice floes were more like cakes of soap.

Rijo's Enco commercial had been successful enough that the advertising company, McCann-Erickson, wanted to film another—this one to be much more elaborate, with location shots of the tiger running on beaches, in snow, down country roads again, stopping short and wheeling to face the camera, and so on. I'd quit trying to make sense of copywriters' animal fantasies by then, and was just grateful that they seemed to have forgotten about deserts. Because it was such a big job filming, the company decided to split the work between us and Animals, Inc., since they had some twenty tigers to our one. Rijo remained the official Enco tiger, however, and as such was required this time to come leaping through the oval logo, much as the car splashes through the Shell Oil emblem. It's easier with cars.

The manager of Animals, Inc., said that it was impossible with tigers. He pointed out an elementary truth of animal psychology to the McCann & Erickson people: a tiger can be induced to jump through a circus trainer's ring of fire, because he can see his way to the other side, but he's no more likely than you are to charge blindly into what looks like a solid wall. The manager suggested blandly that they try dropping Rijo down a chute, so that he'd flop through the oval like a sack of laundry. We said that we thought we knew a better way, and the company granted us six weeks in which to train Rijo for the stunt.

We began in that dank, foul Jungleland barn, teaching Rijo to jump through a wooden framework with a few fluttery strips of paper hanging down from the crossbar. Ted would run slowly toward the frame, with Rijo loping amiably behind him, and fall away to the side at the last moment, calling, "*Up!*" Rijo knew the command, and he could see me just beyond the bits of paper, waiting to catch him and play with him. He caught onto the game immediately; nor did he balk when we replaced the strips with solid paper, leaving a hole in the center for him to see through. Over the weeks we made the hole smaller and smaller, until one morning it had vanished altogether. Rijo went at the blank surface with almost no hesitation, trusting Ted and knowing that I was still waiting for him on the other side. He was frightened the first time, and struggled through in some disarray, but I held him and loved him, and that was all right. I remember how strangely frightened I was, holding him, by the immense fact of his trust in us.

The Jungleland trainers used to come to the barn every day to watch us working with Rijo. I remember that very clearly, too: the ring of knobby, scarred circus faces, with their bright bird-eyes flicking to follow Rijo's moves. They usually said very little. I don't think they especially wanted us to fail, but I'm sure most of them thought we would. What we were doing with Rijo was in violation of all their grim old experience: wild animals don't play games—they do tricks, and not because they want to. They smoked and shrugged and looked sideways at one another.

We were working on a snow sequence as well, using a second young Siberian tiger named Boris, whom we had just bought from Bob Baudy in Florida. Boris was nearly as big as Rijo, with the same overwhelming serenity, and they promptly became playmates and best friends. Inviting Boris to run after us proved more hazardous than playing that game with Rijo, however, since Rijo didn't particularly care whether he caught us or not, while Boris thought that was the whole point of things. He never meant to hurt us—he'd simply jump on us and *sit,* looking as pleased as though he'd just scored some kind of grand slam. Ted had to resort to leading him on a little Honda motorcycle, trying to stay just out of his reach. It was a precarious business to begin with, and it almost ended for good on the day that Boris put on an extra burst of speed and caught the motorcycle too. He was a bit sulky about getting off Ted that time. I think he expected to be awarded permanent possession.

We filmed the snow scenes in Squaw Valley, where the drifts were five to six feet deep, making it impossible to use the motorcycle with Boris. "Actually, this makes things a lot simpler," Ted assured me. "He's a big heavy animal—he's got no chance at all of catching you in this snow. Over a short

Ted and I with our two Siberian tigers, Boris and Rijo, at the ranch in Buellton. Boris, being young and brash, took a poke at Rijo. But when Rijo stood up, the game was over. Rijo is the tiger on the cover of this book.

course." I gave myself a hundred-yard head start, signaled to Ted to turn Boris loose, and took off, running on a slight downhill slant as fast as I could go. I was very pleased with the way the sequence was working out, and just hoped that Boris wouldn't flounder too much in the snow and mess up the shot.

When Ted shouted, "*Look out!*" I had just time to turn and see Boris coming at me like a feather, gliding silently over the drifts almost without leaving footprints, as any card-carrying Siberian tiger can do. Those huge, fur-padded feet spread out and act like snowshoes, distributing the tiger's weight perfectly for the thin surface crust. It is truly beautiful to see, and I would have liked to have watched it longer; but Boris sprang at that moment, as I stood there giggling protestingly. He sailed high over me—a magic carpet, hiding the sun, floating slowly down —and he hit me like a safe dropped out of a window. I'm told that I simply disappeared.

The camera kept cranking, for the hell of it, and I've seen the film of Boris sitting on a smashed snowdrift, out of which my feet and one of my hands are waving dispiritedly. Boris looks calmly pleased with himself, because he won the game, but he also looks a little puzzled, because he can't find me. If I had to choose one shot to epitomize the daily life of an animal trainer, nothing else would be even close.

The Animals, Inc., group filmed the beach sequences for the commercial. Their method of getting their tigers to run in the sand of Pismo Beach was to tie several live chickens to a kind of fishing-pole arrangement and drag them just ahead of the tigers, like lures. They towed those chickens back and forth through the hot sand all day, and finally gave them to the tigers when the shooting was completed. It filmed just as well as our sequences, I suppose.

We were extremely jumpy when the day arrived to introduce Rijo's new stunt with the Enco logo. As we did whenever Sweet William worked, we requested total silence and a closed set. It was the first time we had needed to do this with Rijo, but over the last couple of months he had been growing into a proper adult male tiger: far less promiscuously friendly, increasingly more easily spooked, and almost as moodily unpredictable as a leopard. It's something that happens frequently as tigers reach maturity—it's almost as though they exchange one entire nervous system for another, and it obviously has great survival value in the wild. Rijo was still as puffingly loving as ever with Ted and me, but we no longer felt easy about letting strangers be near him. We even pulled his cage-wagon in behind the sound stage, rather than lead him into the studio past the director and the cameramen.

At that time, Enco Oil operated under the name of Humble in the Midwestern states, and Esso on the East Coast. (Now it's all Exxon.) Rijo would have to jump through each of the three signs a minimum of three times apiece. The director candidly doubted that we'd get all that shooting done in one day. I bet him a bottle of champagne against every time that Rijo either made the jump properly or messed it up. The cameras started rolling, and Ted led Rijo onto the set.

He did it perfectly every time. We hadn't been expecting

that any more than the director had, and we fell into a kind of hypnotic working rhythm that we didn't dare to break: Ted jogging ahead of him toward the sign, then ducking away as Rijo sprang; me hurrying around from the side to catch him after he came through, lead him immediately back to the cage wagon and reward him with loving and a chicken neck. He seemed to be having such a good time that the director went on to shoot the jump over and over, covering himself every way from Sunday. By noon, when we were finished, I had twenty-two bottles of champagne, and the director filmed me leaping through one last Enco oval with a bottle in each hand. I didn't do it nearly as elegantly as Rijo.

But I sat that night holding my tiger in my arms, with the other animals near in the darkness, knowing that those old Jungleland trainers had been right, in a way—that no tiger has any business doing what Rijo had done for us, out of love. I said aloud to him, to them all, "You don't know me—I'm no place at all for you to put your faith. I get frightened and angry easily, and I can't sleep at night for worrying if I'm taking the right care of you, and some days I'd be profoundly delighted to abandon you all and run away to Sweden. I don't know what the hell I'm doing, so much of the time, and I probably *am* a little crazy, as people tell me. If you knew who I was, you wouldn't trust me like that, not the way you do."

And yet I understood then that they did know who I was, better than anyone else ever had known, or ever would. A mixed blessing for everyone, surely, but a blessing.

A strange man named Pete Batten gave us our first lion cub. I think of Pete often, though it's been a long time since I saw him last, and I don't suppose we parted friends. He was the director of the San Jose Zoo when Ted and I first knew him, and while he was there it was a model zoo for its size: beautifully designed and kept up, and so obviously run entirely for the animals' benefit that Pete seemed annoyed when people came in at all. That was probably one of the reasons that he quarreled with the board of trustees and left the zoo, but there must have been others in any case. Pete quarreled with everyone, sooner or later. He knew as much about animals as anyone I've ever met, and he taught me a great deal, but his love for animals was the other side of a strong dislike for human beings. I've sometimes been afraid of becoming like that myself, but I think it's different with me. I just like animals better.

Anyway, Pete gave us Heathcliff, and in so doing brought the sunshine back into what had become a rather empty life for Belvedere. Belvedere had been pining for his friends ever since we moved everyone but Thumper to Jungleland, and even though we often brought him with us to visit them, it wasn't like old times. Murgatroyd had grown too big to sleep sucking on his ear, and Joe, Clyde, Candy, and even Chauncey were all past the point where Belvedere could mother them comfortably. But he had his own lion cub to cherish now, and he had a purpose again. It amazes me that Heathcliff actually grew up to be a lion, and not a kindhearted, slightly bewildered bloodhound. His earliest influences were all against it.

But he was Belvedere's lion, always, and they continued to romp together as though they expected to remain the same size forever. I came out of the house one day in time to see a 400-pound Heathcliff rear and come down on Belvedere with his full weight, knocking him silly. I was sure that he had broken Belvedere's back; and though Belvedere was quickly up and dizzily ready to play some more, I began keeping them apart after that. *Let him play with cougars and jaguars, like any normal dog.*

Belvedere understood very quickly that he had deliberately been separated from his huge puppy. His countermeasures took the form of lying by Heathcliff's cage most of the day, every day, howling his head off. He won, and Heathcliff was so glad to be with him again that he sent him spinning and yelping across the yard with his first joyous charge. He never hurt

Cougar cubs Herman, Harold, and Joyce were all born at the ranch. I got good at feeding two at once, but never three. There was always one waiting.

Belvedere seriously, as I had feared; but if he had, it would have been Belvedere's choice, as I choose to go on playing with bears. Love is big and dangerous, and you take your chances.

Bucky and Baby, the two white-tailed deer we had bought from Mr. Via, were old enough to work now, as much as you can work deer. The hoofed animals are far more difficult to train than any tiger—they aren't very bright, and everything in the world spooks them. Bucky and Baby were absolute geniuses, by deer standards, which means that they would stand over a heap of grain long enough to be filmed, and would always come to me when I stuck my head out from behind a tree and called to them. I wonder about that a little, since deer apparently don't see color, and I can't even be sure whether they associated me that clearly with food, affection, protection, or something that would only make sense to a deer. But they always came.

We did a *Lassie* show with them, which was shot mostly at the Big Bear ski-resort area. As I remember it, we spent almost all of our time getting the deer up and down the ski slopes, and one of my nicest recollections is of going up in the chair lift with Bucky, who loved to be held, draped across my lap. He was getting a good set of antlers, and I suppose that he might have been taken for a trophy, except that now and then he'd raise his head and gaze interestedly at the skiers piling into each other as they passed us staring back at him. We never managed the ascent without causing some kind of minor disaster on the slopes.

By that time we had established a pattern of going from a *Lassie* show to a Cougar commercial, to one or two odd jobs, and then straight down into abject poverty until the next call from *Lassie*. The trouble was that the destitute part of the cycle generally lasted the longest of all; nor did we ever have any guarantee of rising to the surface one more time. During the winter of 1967–68, when we were living in Montecito, commuting to Jungleland almost daily, and doggedly trying to find land in Carpinteria, we probably hit bottom. Michael Rennie took to visiting us, not merely with his Super-8 camera, but with great cartons of food, which we referred to as "Michael's CARE packages." It wasn't a joke. If it hadn't been for Michael, the Johnsons, and a number of other good friends, I don't know how we'd have gotten all the way through that winter.

We couldn't afford to pay what Jungleland charged us to feed the animals, so in desperation we made a deal with a meat-packing house in Saticoy, near Ventura. We used to go out there at least once a week, with as many big barrels as we could carry, and load up on trimmings from the carcasses—cheeks, lips, ears and so on. For me, raised a vegetarian, to walk into a slaughterhouse—breathing blood, hearing the animals bawling, seeing the raw, split carcasses trundling overhead on chains of hooks—was my first real experience of doing permanent violence to myself. I suppose I'd been lucky. The worst part was not going in at all, but sitting in the car and looking out at the fields where the cattle who were going to be killed next grazed and slept and swished their tails. Leopards and all, I wonder now if I have ever empathized with any living thing as much as I did with those cattle.

It rained on Christmas Eve, and we had $35 in the bank, after paying for another load of meat. Ted was inside the slaughterhouse filling one more barrel with guts and jowls, and I was waiting in the car, making myself think about Christmases in England. I heard a cow lowing nearby and turned to look, knowing that I shouldn't. She had just given birth to a scrawny, feeble calf that struggled in the rain, rubbery black, striped with bright blood. I ran over to where they lay, trying to keep the calf from being trampled by the other cows pressing closely around them. We huddled together while the rain came down, and I cried, and the cow blatted and licked her baby, and the calf tried to get up and couldn't.

"What are you going to do with it?" Ted asked the man we knew there. He shrugged. "Knock it in the head, like always. They can't live without the mother, anyway." We paid him $30 and took the calf home with us.

It didn't live, of course. I sat with it all Christmas Day, but it died that night.

Oh, that was a bad winter. Phyllis, my old German shepherd, died too, and our neighbors in Montecito began complaining about living next to a dangerous wild lion like Heathcliff. Our hopes of finding land in the area had fallen through completely, and the situation was serious now because Jungleland had finally gone bankrupt. The creditors permitted us to continue keeping our animals there until the land was sold, which was bound to happen soon. I put up the last of my antiques for sale, and spent the months after Christmas watching dealers and collectors prowling through the house, pawing over my parents' sixteenth-century Delft, Leeds pottery, and early Fulham ware. It was like seeing one more animal die; but this death seemed to have been going on for a terribly long time without my knowing. I was desperately, shabbily grateful when it was over.

A friend suggested that we try doing a live presentation with some of our animals. I resisted the idea intensely at first: no matter how badly off we were, we surely couldn't have fallen to the level of a traveling show, exhibiting half-dead lions and bears in shopping-center parking lots. But in time we evolved the rough beginnings of a kind of non-show, in which we would demonstrate a few of the training techniques that the animals themselves had taught us in our film and television work. There were to be no tricks or performances, as such, and we would only use animals like Joe, Murgatroyd and Chauncey, who didn't mind crows of strangers looking at them. If nothing else, it should at least pay for a slightly better grade of meat at the slaughterhouse.

Michael Rennie and Bill Burrud narrated the show when we

put it on at the Earl Warren Showgrounds in Santa Barbara. It went much better than we had expected: the animals enjoyed themselves, and the audience seemed geniunely receptive and interested in learning what makes working in a movie fun for a bear, and why a lion behaves somewhat differently in his cage than out of it. The only bad part was that the day was cold and damp, with a vicious wind blowing from the ocean. Michael was having trouble breathing when the show was over. And I wound up in the hospital, having cortisone injected directly into a nerve in my back, because I fell off Murgatroyd, the black bear. He took it into his head to stand straight up on his hind legs while I was riding him, and it was thought for a while that I had suffered a crushed spinal disc. I hadn't, but my back has never really been right since then.

It's odd—barring the incident with Romeo the lion, I have been seriously injured only by bears. I still love them, and I still work with them, so it will probably go on like that.

We had begun looking for land farther north, in the low live-oak hills of the Santa Ynez Valley. It's ranch country, in the main, but there are a few strange little tourist towns, such as Solvang, which was founded by Danish immigrants and is now a sort of pastry imitation of a Hans Christian Andersen fairytale village. A few miles west is Buellton, which exists only because of a huge restaurant and gift shop called "Pea Soup Andersen's." Andersen's is the landmark of the region, certainly the largest employer, and dominates Buellton like the medieval castle it almost resembles. The pea soup itself is quite good.

A man who owned a well-drilling concern in Buellton offered to lease us a bit of land behind an old warehouse, just off the main highway. The ground was paved with macadam, which would be good for setting up the cages, and be easy to keep clean. We agreed to lease the front part of the warehouse as well, since I wanted to try setting up a small African-oriented gift shop there. Our new quarters were too cramped to be more than temporary, but we had no choice and no time. The Jungle-land sale was imminent, and we were still gambling that we could get a permit to keep our animals in Buellton.

That part went as well as anything like that had ever gone for us, but it went cripplingly slowly. By the time we had gotten through a preliminary hearing of the county planning commission, Jungleland had already been sold. We were assured by the commissioners that we would definitely be granted our zoning; but there was a final hearing coming up in three days— a rubber-stamp approval, nothing more, but unavoidable. Meanwhile, Jungleland's new owners had given us twenty-four hours to move our animals off the property.

I still don't see what we could have done but what we did. The friends who had helped us move to Jungleland came again with their cars and trucks and trailers, their clotheslines and ironing boards, and we formed the same peculiar caravan as before. It was a longer haul this time, with a few more animals and a few less people, so the whole swarming actually took two days and a night. The weather was freezing grayness all the way through, and Joe got loose in the middle of everything, and nobody slept for thirty-six hours. We all lived on Andersen's pea soup.

When the cages had all been set up behind the warehouse, at midnight of the second day, Ted and I sent our friends staggering home, neither of us having the gall even to mention the remaining task in their presence. There had been no time at all to enclose the cage area with a chain-link fence before we moved; and, exhausted as we were, we knew better than to chance the animals' safety, or the dubious tolerance of our new neighbors, even for one night. So we put up the entire fence together, the two of us, digging postholes and twisting wire clips with hands as cold as the steel links themselves. It took us until 10:00 A.M.

Eddie Steeples, who had gone home to sleep, returned to look after things in the morning, and Ted and I drove directly to the planning hearing in Santa Barbara, where we were given final permission to put our animals where they already were. Then we took Boris and set off for Hollywood, because he and I had a date that same day to do our first film job in a grimly long time. I sang and told jokes to Boris all the way there, to keep myself awake, and I laughed at his jokes too.

It was a Dracula movie, but I don't remember which one. Boris played Dracula's pet and enjoyed himself immensely drinking beef blood and padding through the spooky corridors of a haunted mansion at Dracula's side. I wore a huge fall of hair and doubled for one of an assortment of vampire ladies, and I got killed by the tiger at the end of the job. When Boris sprang at me out of an old elevator, joyous at being allowed to knock me down and drag me around, I went to sleep. However well or badly that scene went, the direction was entirely Boris's, because I was gone. I never saw the movie, but I've been told that my horrible death filmed very realistically, what with Boris pulling my fall off and everything.

We got home to Montecito a little before midnight, slept until dawn, and then drove on to Buellton. The fence was still standing, which impressed me considerably. Ted and Eddie went to get breakfast for us; and I was drifting around the warehouse, almost as muzzy as though I hadn't slept at all, trying to hold myself together long enough to see the possible outlines of the African gift shop, when I heard the animals stirring restlessly outside. Rijo was making the sound that he makes for strangers.

There were two of them peering over the fence: county planning officials whom I had seen at the hearing the morning before. They looked perfectly furious, and they were writing in black notebooks like a pair of Recording Angels. I went up to them, knowing that there was no point in lying—we couldn't possibly have moved in *that* fast since yesterday—but with no faith at all in the truth. My favorite position.

The elder of the two let me have it as soon as I was within range. "Mrs. Derby, you are in *very* bad trouble." Then they were both at me, blowing me out of the water with salvos of righteous reminders—*"tried to help . . ." "stuck our necks out . . ." "a number of our colleagues were opposed . . ." "bent over backwards because you seemed . . ."* I never had a chance to say more than, "If you'd like to come in and have some coffee—" They ended by announcing that they were going to have the zoning decision reversed immediately, and getting into their equally indignant-looking county car to drive away.

I ran after them and jumped on the car, somehow clinging to the window frame and the side mirror as they backed up to turn around. I was wailing, "Please, please—this is my *life*—please believe me!" This part is very dreamlike, but I remember that it wasn't a matter either of hysteria or conscious control. Something ridiculously dangerous—something leopardish—rose up and took me over, something that was going to make absolutely certain that those two men didn't get away from there. I may have been crying, but I was also trying to scramble up onto the hood of the car, to cover the windshield with my body so that they couldn't see to drive.

They stopped the car, of course, and I knew I'd won before anyone said a word. The poor men were stricken, as apologetic and guilty as they had been in the right a moment before. "Don't," one of them said helplessly. "Don't be so upset, Mrs. Derby—we won't say anything to the planning commission. Really we won't." The other added, "We'll come back another time, maybe in a few days. It'll just be as though we'd never been here at all."

It's entirely possible that they thought I was crazy, and feared that I might do something incomprehensibly dreadful if they took away our zoning. But the truth is that I may never have been saner than in that moment, hanging onto that car door. Faced with the end of your world, may you also turn out to have a cold, wise animal inside you that tells you what to do.

13

It was like any other roadside zoo. We sold our pet items and African imports in the gift shop, and then the customers would go out in back and look at the animals. It rather embarrasses me to talk about that time; but at least the animals were comfortable and well-fed, and we truly had no other way of earning money then. *Lassie* was on its regular hiatus between seasons, and we had lost the Lincoln-Mercury commercial. Animals, Inc., had underbid us for the job. We were on our last legs there in Buellton, with no resiliency left, and no other place in the world to go.

The local people were very good to us—many of them used to come by regularly with loads of fruit and vegetables for the animals. The blessed Johnsons would come up every weekend to run the gift shop, while we put on live shows in a little arena that we had built for training and exercise. The shows ran about an hour, and were similar to the one we had given at the Earl Warren Showgrounds. Sweet William's solemn ceremony of taking cookies from between the lips of all the children in the audience was always the star turn, and Rijo had only to walk into the arena and stand there for people to stop breathing; but the most impressive animal in the shows, in many ways was probably Nehani.

Nehani was a Canadian timber wolf, wild-born, but raised for most of his life in the British Columbia pet park were we had found Flap, the lion who ate trailers. He was full-grown when he came to us: a magnificent creature, far bigger than the average wolf at two hundred pounds, with eyes like long diamonds and the grinning exuberance of Snoopy playing at being the Big Man on Campus. Nehani was a natural show-business personality, and he had the distinction of being the only working wolf in the trade, until he married and settled down to the serious business of raising his own pack. After that, he lost interest in frivolous matters, as wolves with families always do.

In the shows, we used to demonstrate our method of working Nehani to a system of buzzers. Ninety per cent of our work in films and television—as you must have noticed by now —simply has to do with getting an animal to go from one place to another. How you manage that depends on the animal's own nature: a cougar who likes you will come when called, while even the friendliest wolf almost never will. By the same token, although wolves and coyotes can be conditioned, like Nehani, to run to the spot where they have heard a buzzer sound, knowing that there will be food waiting for them, that system doesn't work nearly as well with a fox. Foxes are so nervous and high-strung that they can easily become too distraught to respond to food at all. Nehani worked for chicken necks and the fun of the thing. He had all the scene-stealing, upstaging instincts of an old summer-stock hand. I'll always believe that he knew perfectly well which was his best profile.

We could set up a remarkable number of dramatic situations using various combinations of the buzzers. If we wanted Nehani to go somewhere, halt, and then come on again, we'd

I raised Nehani, a Canadian timber wolf, and he would never hurt me. This kiss is the same greeting he would give to a female wolf. Behind us, the ranch house.

bury a buzzer in the ground without the chicken neck that usually accompanied it. Nehani would nose around the spot, and then look up in a mild puzzlement that always filmed as cunning ferocity. At that point we'd press another buzzer hidden in whatever further direction we wanted him to go— usually baited with two chicken necks, to make up for the earlier disappointment. He was so naturally photogenic and moved with such swashbuckling zest that everything he did looked good on film. Rijo was like a mountain, a redwood tree, a river, but Nehani had style.

He did a lot of work on *Lassie;* and he did one wonderful *Gunsmoke* episode, in which he was the last wolf in the country, hunted by the last of the oldtime wolf-killers, a Captain Ahab with a somewhat more limited vocabulary. They ended by killing each other. Nehani was marvelous in the show.

His first scene called for a shot of him sitting up on a rock, howling. Strangely enough, considering how often you've seen similar shots in Westerns and wilderness movies, real wolves are almost never used, though an actual wolf howl may be dubbed in. Wolves don't howl on cue, so what you usually get is a German shepherd with a tight rubber band around his tail, to make it lie down flat, like a wolf's tail, and rubber bands somehow arranged around his fangs to make the facial muscles contract dramatically. The poor creatures look like nothing so much as German shepherds who are going to sneeze in a moment.

For Nehani's scene, Ted and I set him on the rock, with a few chicken necks to keep him there, and then looked dubiously at each other. "I still wish we had some kind of alternative idea," I whispered. "Just in case."

Ted was very calm. "Don't worry about it. If we blow this one, they'll probably laugh us right out of the studio, anyway. Come on, Nehani's getting restless, let's go." And we dashed around behind the rock and began howling ourselves, as mournfully and quaveringly as we could manage. The director and the camera crew did indeed break up laughing, and almost forgot to start filming the scene at all.

Wolves are extremely social animals—the cubs I raised in the Beachy Street house had shown me that one of their first instincts is to sing with their friends and relations. On hearing our efforts, Nehani delightedly tilted his muzzle toward the sound stage ceiling and took the tenor harmony. We dropped out, once he was properly started, but Nehani went on alone for quite a while, like one of those people at parties who's been lurking around the piano all evening. It is that easy, if you just bother to think about it.

Many trainers use the buzzer technique these days, the only difference between our methods and theirs being that their animals are usually kept half-starved. There's something funny to a reader or listener in my saying that I reward the working cats and wolves with chicken necks, until you come across, as I did, an establishment where one fox's entire diet consisted of one chicken neck a day. I know a man who explains seriously that he can't allow anyone near his grizzly when he's working in a show, because the bear is always starved for a month beforehand. Even more than the casual, unquestioning cruelty, the most depressing element of the animal trainer's

Out for a stroll with Nehani's mate, Ophelia, and their daughters, Betty and Jean. Wolves are tremendously powerful and you can't teach them not to pull, so walking them was like constant whiplash. It was hard enough if they all went in one direction, but if they scattered, it was murder.

They tell me I've got the biggest grizzly bears that can be handled without restraints. Seymour here is seven, weighs half a ton and has claws five inches long. This picture shows the grizzly's true disposition when you don't harass them or deprive them of food to get your way.

world is the unrelenting *dumbness*. Morality completely aside, I would no sooner do a scene with a frantically hungry grizzly than I would trim my hair with a chainsaw. It isn't safe, and it usually doesn't film well at all.

Things limped along. The gift shop generally fed the animals, which was as much as I'd ever asked of it. Princess the jaguar came into heat, and we traded her to Bob Baudy for two bear cubs: Seymour, a grizzly, and a Kodiak female whom I named Phyllis, after my dog. Thumper the wallaroo died of pneumonia in the Montecito house, which was always too foggy and damp for a tropical animal. Michael Rennie went to Europe to work, and we never saw him again. He died there in 1971.

We hadn't been able to find either a place to live in Buellton or a buyer for the house in Montecito. The bank foreclosed on it, and we were told that we would have to move out within a week's time. We were resigning ourselves to putting down sleeping bags between the rack of dashikis and the case of Nigerian woodcarvings, when—in perfect accordance with our usual routine of being snatched from the sharks' jaws at the very last possible moment, so as to be saved for more sharks—someone brought Vince Evans, the owner of Pea Soup Andersen's, to meet us.

A few words about Vince. He used to be a screenwriter, and then he married a lovely, elegant oil heiress named Marge, moved to the Santa Ynez Valley, and became a gentleman cattle rancher. At that time, Pea Soup Andersen's was owned by the last surviving member of the original Andersen family, and it was failing badly. According to Vince, he was hanging out in the restaurant's bar, commiserating with the last Andersen, when the owner asked him for a loan to keep the place going. Vince made a counter-offer to buy the restaurant, and promptly turned Pea Soup Andersen's into the unquestioned gold mine that it is today. He's a tall man, a bit chubby now, with white hair and a strong, bricky Irish face. He yells a lot. I always liked him.

Vince liked us, and he seemed very much impressed by the cleanness of our cramped little zoo, and the health and gentleness of the animals. When he heard about our imminent homelessness, he offered us the use of a big old adobe house that he owned, about a mile south of Pea Soup Andersen's. He had been letting a local sheriff live there, presumably keeping it up in lieu of paying rent; but the man was being transferred to another district, and the house would be vacant in a day or so. We could move in whenever we chose.

I couldn't believe our good fortune. A house miraculously turning up at the last minute, all right—but *this* house! The adobe was visible from the highway, and I had never driven past it, going and coming from Montecito, without coveting it shamelessly and daydreaming about what it would be like to live there. It was a cool, spacious, rambling place: to enter it was always a little to walk into the shady, slow air of another time. A doctor built it in the early 1890s—the legend is that he used to tend wounded members of Joaquín Murietta's out-law gang, who would come down at night out of the hills just behind the adobe. The sheriff had left the house in great disre-pair, and for a while we just camped in one room, like timid exporers in a jungle clearing. We had almost no furniture now.

Shortly after we had moved into the adobe, Ivan Tors turned up at the gift shop. We had completely lost touch with Ivan in the past years, though I knew that he had gotten out of Animals, Inc. The final touch had been a fire—after those two floods—which destroyed the ranch almost totally. Ivan was now producing a children's television program called *Jambo*. It specialized in the most outlandish plots since late *Have Gun, Will Travel;* but it was essentially an animal show, and sud-denly there was a little work for us again.

Lenny Kaufman, Ivan's brother-in-law, wrote one *Jambo* show for me to do, and one featuring Ted. Ted played a wicked circus trainer who was cruel to Rijo, until the tiger finally turned on him. A young girl who loved the tiger and had made friends with him managed to call Rijo off, saving Ted's life. That was about average for *Jambo,* though my own show was somewhat more cluttered. I played a girl camping alone in the woods, studying birds. A cougar (Chauncey) gets into her tent and somehow hurts himself, whereupon she nurses him back to health. The cougar becomes her defender; and in the course of the show, Chauncey had to fight off bears (Murgatroyd and Sweet William) and a jaguar (Clyde, though I can't recall now how a jaguar got into the story). It must have been a great temptation for Lenny to throw Belvedere in there somewhere as the Hound of the Baskervilles.

We had to film Boris's big escape scene at a shopping center in Buellton. It was a very hot day, and Boris quickly lost interest in acting and abruptly plopped down right across the doorway of a large beauty salon. I'll always remember that window full of fluttering matrons with curlers in their hair and green cosmetic masks on their faces. It looked remarkably like an odd kind of pet shop.

As though to counterbalance the *Jambo* break, we began to have landlord trouble at the warehouse property, and it seemed likely that we might have to move our animals once again. When we mentioned the situation to Vince Evans, he told us that he had for some time—even before our arrival in Buellton —been playing with the idea of setting up some kind of animal park as a tourist attraction for his restaurant and the Valley in general. Cannily wary of risking his own money on the project, he took us to meet Jack Wrather, who owns *Lassie* (not the dogs, but the show), American Airlines, and heaven knows what else. Wrather was hesitant and noncommittal at first, which had the effect of making Vince even more enthusiastic, genuinely determined now to create a park around us and our animals. Eventually Wrather agreed to consider the possibility in detail, and Vince left it at that for the time.

At Vince's invitation—and with the aid of another, though far less frantic, caravan of friends—we moved the animals across the highway to the old adobe. We laid down a big strip of macadam on a rise of ground behind the house for the cages, and established the barn as a combination kitchen and hospital. It seemed very appropriate, since that was where the doctor was supposed to have treated Murietta's men by candlelight. The adobe itself was gradually healing and brightening, as we pushed our frontiers steadily back from room to room. I wanted very much to stay here.

Vince owned an abandoned building in Solvang that had once been a bowling alley, and he let us put our gift shop and training arena there. We would drive the animals into town on Saturday and put on continuous shows all through the weekend. The Johnsons would drive into Solvang ahead of us, and Jean would dust and clean the shop while Ora set up our battered and slightly menacing popcorn machine, and handled the sales. "Well, at least we're not a roadside zoo anymore," I remarked to Ted. "Now we're a traveling circus. I was always so sure we'd never be one of those, either, whatever happened."

One of the Johnsons' additional chores was to bring Spot to Solvang with them. Like most leopards, Spot hated being at close quarters with other animals, so we'd load him into an aluminum traveling cage and put the cage on the back of Ora's pickup. Ora would park behind the shop and wait for us to arrive and take Spot inside. One morning, a gust of wind whisked the light cage off the truck, skidding it along the ground like a tumbleweed. The door popped open, and Spot came out running. He bounded straight through the little shopping center—the shopping carts cleared out of his way like a flight of gazelles--and on into an open field beyond, where he halted to get his breath for a proper snarl. It was exactly like the scene we had filmed with Boris, except that this one was for real.

The Johnsons had been scared to death of Spot ever since his tumultuous arrival at Newhall in Johnny's truck. It was impossible to blame them: they knew that Spot's habit of charging all men when he was in his cage or out for exercise was an exhilarating game for him, but to understand all is not necessarily to relax. But the whole town was watching, surrounding the field, and for Spot's sake—let alone ours and the onlookers—there was nothing for Ora and his younger son

Jerry to do but go after him, while Jean ran to the telephone to call Ted and me. They had Spot's leash with them, and nothing else.

Jean and I were busy panicking on the telephone when her voice changed abruptly and she said, "Oh. I guess it's all right." Poor Spot was so bewildered at being suddenly loose in this strange place that Jerry, who was about fifteen then, was able to walk right up to him and put the leash around his neck. He almost dragged Jerry back to the cage, and he purred and washed and rubbed against the bars when he was inside.

I tell this story for a particular reason. The next time you read newspaper articles about deputy sheriffs armed with automatic weapons leading their posses on a hunt for some escaped lion or tiger, remember that the savage beast is invariably as terrified and lonely as a soul in Limbo. I have never known one that wasn't trying to find its way home, or that didn't know when someone was attempting to help it. We make them into creatures who fear the sky, who can't feel safe anywhere but within a few square feet of stone and steel and darkness. We are responsible for them, to them—it is absolutely the least we can be. But of course it's more fun to shoot.

Tanya's scratching at the old couple's door is one slightly odd example of the captive wild animal's conditioned need to be closed in again. Another is the story of Bela the buzzard. Pete Batten gave Bela to us; he had been brought to the San Jose Zoo with a badly broken wing, which Pete had set so well that Bela could fly again. He was a sweet, affectionate bird, who semed to love not having to hang around five miles up on a thermal current, waiting for something to die, and who didn't at all mind having his gargoyle head scratched. Buzzards are wonderful. I used to call Bela "The Buzzard of Happiness."

Bela's big wrought-iron cage stood near the fence, next to that of a macaque named Fred, who was one of the great safecrackers of our time. Fred specialized, not merely in breaking out of his own cage, but in springing any other animals he could reach. I came out for the evening feeding one day in time to see Fred crouched atop Bela's empty cage, seemingly waving goodbye to the buzzard wheeling higher and higher into the sunset. I wasn't as upset as I might have been. Ted and I had for some time been debating the question of setting Bela free, since he was whole and healthy and perfectly capable of readapting to the wild. Fred seemed to have made the decision for us. I waved to Bela myself, and turned away.

Two weeks later, we were standing outside with several friends when we sighted a big dark bird coming in low, with all the purposefulness of an airplane making its final approach to the runway. It was Bela, and he looked like a cartoon caricature of a disheveled, beat-up buzzard. His head and neck were bleeding, big swatches of feathers were missing from his baggy body—all that was needed would have been a few crossed Band-Aids here and there. His fellow buzzards had apparently reacted poorly to a cousin with the smell of human hands on him and incomprehensible stories to tell. He landed on the roof of the adobe and flapped ponderously up and down a few times; then he flew to the fence and back to the house again. He was making strange, thick noises, none the less urgent for sounding like a car with a dead battery.

"Oh, Ted," I said, "he's hungry!" Ted went into the house, returning with a chunk of meat which he threw onto the roof. Bela lurched into the air immediately, and I was certain that we'd lost him; but he flew to the fence once more and perched there, still making that grinding, clunky sound at us. It seemed suddenly to me that he was saying, *No, you idiots, I don't want food—I want to get back in my cage!* Since his escape it had been turned so that the door was against the fence. We turned it around again.

Bela didn't fly to his cage. I have six witnesses to the fact that he walked slowly down a double row of tigers, wolves, and lions, all slavering to get at him, taking absolutely no notice of their eager fury; and that he hopped into the cage

Einstein, the little barn owl whose love for me stemmed from the sad and persistent delusion that I was a barn owl too. I've always felt bad about those eggs she kept laying for me, because I never could do anything for them.

and stood in the doorway for a moment, making a different sort of noise now. His body couldn't have expressed greater relief if he'd wiped a wing across his bald brow and sighed, "Thank God, I'm home! Man, it's a *jungle* out there!"

Pete Batten also gave us Einstein, a beautiful little barn owl with a clubfoot and a white face like an acorn. I don't suppose that any animal has ever loved me in the same way that Einstein did. When she grew old enough to think about such things, she took me for her mate, crooning to me, cuddling against me, and performing heartbreakingly earnest and confident courting dances for my benefit. Barn owls mate for life. Einstein laid eggs for me every spring, and again in the summer, one a day until there were six or seven each time. It didn't seem to make her unhappy that they never hatched, but I couldn't keep it from troubling me. She was so patient, so secure in her choice of a mate, so certain that we were a pair of proper barn owls together. I always felt somewhere that I had failed Einstein. That isn't really a joke.

A middle-aged couple drove up to the adobe one day and announced, "We heard you had an animal place, so we brought you a lion."

"I don't want a lion," I said, but they were already lifting a crate out of the back of the car and prying it open. I knew it was renal rickets again before I ever saw the dwarfed body or the bowed, deformed hindquarters that seemed to ooze bonelessly out of the crate. The eyes tell you. Cats who suffer from renal rickets have a terribly lovely, immediately recognizable expression of dreamy, faraway peacefulness. The eyes are wide and limpid; they never seem quite focused, at least not on anything that you can see. Even the animals in the most pain have that look. In zoos they call them *stargazers.* It's most notable in young lions, perhaps because of the brown eyes and the long eyelashes. My little Scoo had looked like that.

"Oh, he's really good," the couple said. "We used to have a pet shop back in the Midwest, and we'd keep him chained out in front all the time. Pulled people in like crazy. You could do that here." As they drove off, they called back to me that his name was Lucky.

Lucky had a perfectly rotten disposition, as he was perfectly entitled to have; but a diet loaded with calcium and B-vitamins brought him around remarkably, and in time we became friends. I used to spend most of my weekday afternoons taking the animals for walks in the hills, after I had finished cleaning cages.

Phyllis the Kodiak bear loved to walk sedately beside me on a chain, while Seymour the grizzly ran loose, charging over the hills all the way to a little reservoir, where he would drink and then come rioting back to me. Lucky liked to run after me, making dives at my ankles and hanging onto my legs to be dragged along, as kittens will do. We made it part of the shows in Solvang: I'd call him out of his cage-wagon, and

Lucky the lion, who suffered from renal rickets and had that "stargazer" look in his eyes which this affliction produces.

he'd pounce on me and knock me down, and probably fall over himself, because he still couldn't stand up that well. Of all the lions, children always loved Lucky best.

We acquired a great many animals that year, most often in ways ranging from sad to completely tragic. An old friend named Julie MacDonald (she is a wonderful sculptress, and the only person I know who has successfully raised a baboon in her home) married a man with young children, and felt it best to give us most of her menagerie, which included a jaguarundi, a pair of bushbabies, and a Victorian lady of a kinkajou (a little raccoon-like creature) named Lucy Brown. And we were given a year-old leopard by two young San Francisco men who had raised him from cubhood with the run of their apartment and then, in the usual tradition, grown afraid of him. He had never been outside, never been really handled—the apartment was his jungle, and he ruled it in the very best leopard style, while his terrorized owners slunk along the walls to get to the kitchen or the bathroom. This is another one that sounds funny.

They brought him to us tranquilized—God knows how that pair ever managed it. You never, never know the right thing to do in such a situation, but we decided to let the leopard wake up in an outside cage and begin adjusting all at once to his new home, instead of doing it by degrees. He came out of the anesthesia, saw trees and grass for the first time in his life, and went berserk, literally breaking himself to bits against the bars. He wouldn't eat, and he wouldn't go into the den box that we had prepared for him. It was Banté over again, but a leopard is different from a cougar. He would have killed us if we had tried to sit with him.

We got more tranquilizers into him and brought him inside the house, but the same thing happened when he reawakened. All that poor leopard wanted was his apartment again: natural surroundings or not, it was the only thing in the world he had to cling to, and nothing else held any reality for him. After two weeks of trying everything we knew to make it up to him, we had to put him to sleep.

It was the leopard who finally made me acknowledge to myself the essential evil of the traffic in wild animals. At that time, having little money, we were buying very few animals directly from dealers, but generally accepting the gifts and the orphans as they came, and trading around like children with bubble-gum cards. Our rationale was that we were rescuing mistreated animals like Sweet William and adopting the sick, abandoned ones like the lions Joe and Lucky, and that we never took creatures out of the wild, nor forced any animal to work for us—the great majority, at all times, never worked a day. We were the good ones in the trade, the trainers who lectured to conservation groups; but it was a bit like the rum and molasses merchants of the eighteenth century, many of whom liked to claim that they had never bought or sold a slave in their lives, though their worlds depended utterly on the existence of slavery. We were in it too.

Ironically enough, it was just then that the Humane Society of the United States asked me to write a pamphlet condemning the exotic-animal traffic, to be distributed at the coming auction of Jungleland's assets. Hundreds of animals were to be sold to anyone who could pay for them, and the auction was being so heavily advertised that every idiot and madman in the country would be there to buy. I did write the pamphlet, but the auctioneer wouldn't permit the HSUS to hand it out. Having been to the auction, I doubt that it would have made a nickel's worth of difference.

I didn't want to go, but we had very little choice. Jack Wrather, the American Airlines millionaire, had agreed to go in with Vince Evans and us on building an animal park near Pea Soup Andersen's, and Vince felt that the auction offered a perfect opportunity to acquire a wider variety of animals than we had. In addition, I was terribly anxious about a couple of llamas: a female named Gladys, and her blind baby George.

George had been born in a field while we were at Jungleland, and was very nearly kicked to death by several horses before anyone found him. I used to worry myself sick about George, knowing that if he ever became separated from his mother, the other llamas would kill him, that being the way llamas are. If we bought no one else, we had to save Gladys and George.

The auction was infinitely worse than I had expected. I couldn't possibly have imagined anything that hideous and mad, and I still don't have anything to compare it to. I supposed an image of a *Walpurgisnacht,* a witches' Sabbath, comes the closest; and yet the truly dreadful thing was that there were no demons or familiars here—nothing but people off the street screaming to outbid each other for a tiger. A used-car dealer bought a hippopotamus as some kind of selling gimmick for his business; a wild-eyed old man bought a badger, and a nice-looking young couple with four small children cheerfully put down their money for two lion cubs. There was a man who kept buying animals and giving them to me—two phalangers, a slow loris I'd always coveted at Jungleland, bighorn goats, and an entire herd of black sheep—and a wealthy man from Hollywood who sat there with his taxidermist, consulting with him before he made any bid. *Animals make people crazy.*

Pat Frawley, who owns Schick and Technicolor, Inc., called to me and came over, saying, "I can't hang around here, you gotta shop for me." Pat is a formidable man, a rightwinger beside whom Ronald Reagan is a Trotskyist, but in a strange way he rather liked me. He peeled seven or eight hundred-dollar bills off a roll of them, saying, "Get me a beaver, a wallaby, a couple of otters if they have them. Keep the change." Vince was very impressed.

Gladys was offered for sale without her George, since the firm's policy was to auction the male and female animals separately. Ted and I made a hugely vulgar scene about it: me threatening the auctioneer with Humane Society lawsuits, horrendous publicity and physical assault, while Ted appealed to the crowd with all the stops out. "What kind of a place is this, selling a mother away from her blind son? What is this, a slave market? That little llama'll die without his mother—he's *blind,* he can't take a step without her, she's all he's got in the world." Then, wheeling on the auctioneer, "Bring him out here, why don't you? Let the people see what you're doing— let them get a look at that blind little baby llama with his mother. If you've got the *guts!*"

Even in the midst of all that brutal craziness, enough people backed us up that we won the point, and we bought Gladys and George together. The arrangement was that you paid for the animals on the spot, but you had to come back four or five days later to pick them up, meanwhile paying ten dollars a day for their keep. We returned with a truck, a trailer and a bunch of transfer cages on the same day that we were scheduled to do a quick scene with Chauncey for *Lassie.*

The pickup day was even worse than the auction itself, because it was totally chaotic. The auction firm provided no help at all: psychotics, sentimentalists, and innocents alike had to grab their wild animals and get them out of there any way they could. The noise and the sheer wallowing jam of people made any intelligent action impossible, and disaster almost inevitable. Someone who had bought a black leopard was backing a truck up to his cage when the desperate cat broke loose in the crowd. But the craziness all around him— the smell of it, I think—frightened him so much that he ran straight back into the cage and sat there shaking and moaning. I'm not sure that more than a few people ever noticed that he had been out.

There was a grizzly bear I loved, a female. She had been kept in a tiny shoebox of a cage most of her life, but it was her home and she was used to it. Somehow no wretchedness ever touched her courteous nature; she used to wave kindly at people through the bars, and they would throw popcorn to her.

The Hollywood man who had come with his taxidermist shot her right there, in the cage. Some of the children cried.

The horrible thing is that she and the other animals who went to that man almost certainly suffered the least of all. Animals either adjust to whatever pain and loss they have to accept, or else they give up and they die. The animals at Jungleland were survivors: like the grizzly, they had managed to retain their dignity and to make a kind of life for themselves in those stifling, miserable little cages. It was all they had known, the only world they understood, and now they were being ripped away from it at the whim of people who, for their own silly or sick reasons, just thought that it might be fun to have a bear. I'll always wonder how many of those animals starved to death in the first week, because their new owners had no idea of what to feed them. Or because they were too heartsick to eat.

Even the wisest of us think we're special. We may not believe in souls and afterlives much anymore, but we do still believe that we are the only creatures who can hurt inside. I tell you that it is not true.

One man came by while we were there to pick up a huge male chimpanzee that he had bought at the auction. A chimpanzee is a good bit more aggressive than a gorilla, and even stronger in proportion to his size; and grown males who have worked in shows—and usually been beaten to make them perform—are, quite simply, killers. The man was told that he would have to take the chimpanzee away himself, and he blinked mildly and said, "Oh. Okay." He unlocked the cage, walked in, took the chimpanzee by the hand, and led him off to his car. When last seen, they were driving north on Highway 101, with the chimpanzee sitting by the man in the front seat. The relationship may not have lasted as far as Ventura, but you never know.

Ted and I collected the smaller animals first, putting off

tangling with the llamas as long as possible. Pat Frawley's beaver came slowly out of his stone-floored cage, blinking in the light in a way to make your throat close. I don't know how long he'd been in there. When we turned him loose in the pond on Pat's Beverly Hills estate, he went out of his mind with joy, diving and surfacing, swimming around and around whacking his tail on the water, climbing out just so that he could plop in again. It was the only goodness that I remember from that day.

Llamas, camels, and the rest of that family are ornery, prickly beasts even in a good humor. They can bite your arm off, and they can also spew the contents of their capacious stomachs at you with the accuracy of Robin Hood. We backed the trailer as close to Gladys and George as we could get it, which wasn't very close in that madhouse. Ted said, "You grab the baby and run for the trailer with him. Gladys will follow you, and I'll try to grab her. Don't look back."

Gladys was as protective of her blind George as Thing was of that one runty kitten. I would far rather have tried to sneak a meatloaf past any given lion, but I scooped George into my arms and sprinted for the trailer with him yelling and kicking, and Gladys right behind me, spitting green bile at the back of my head all the way. Every so often, she'd turn around and nail Ted with a fusillade too, so that by the time we got the two of them closed in the trailer, we were both completely covered with a clinging, stinking, burning slime. We headed directly for the *Lassie* studios, cleaning ourselves off as best we could on the way.

The *Lassie* script required Chauncey to be driven off some raid or other by Lassie and a German shepherd friend. It was a very brief scene—they really just wanted a good shot of Chauncey closing with the two dogs—but Rudd Weatherwax unexpectedly demanded that Chauncey be muzzled. We explained that muzzling a cougar impairs his breathing, and that we'd never muzzled Chauncey and weren't about to start now. Things got very loud very quickly, but Bill Beaudine finally talked us into accommodating Rudd for the few moments that the shooting would take. Chauncey proved quite tractable about the muzzle, but I was ashamed, and afraid for him. This Lassie was the fighting one, and I'd seen him hurt other dogs in scenes like this.

But I had underestimated my dear Chauncey. When the dogs charged him, he tried neither to bite nor to escape, having sized up the situation perfectly and accepted it. Instead, he suddenly stood up on his always-wobbly hind legs and came down like thunder with a paw pinning each dog. For a moment I was sure that he had broken their backs. So was Rudd.

Somehow they eventually stitched together a fight scene out of the resulting bedlam (though they missed a beauty between Rudd and me). Finally they cut, and I had the muzzle off Chauncey and was loving him and telling him what a brave, clever fellow he was, when the director said, "Right, now we'd like to have the cat run out of the shot. You know, full-tilt, heading for the hills."

Chauncey never runs; and we would never have asked any cougar to run anywhere after the kind of exertions that Chauncey had just been through. I said angrily, "You didn't tell us you were going to want him for that. We'd have brought a double cat if we'd known. Forget it—Chauncey's through for the day."

Bill Beaudine intervened once more, saying in his soothing manner, "Well, let's just try it once or twice, anyway. If it doesn't work, it doesn't work, okay?" I did like Bill, and I felt that we owed him the extra effort. We agreed grudgingly to let Chauncey go through the scene.

Chauncey was as amiable as ever, but he had his own ideas of what we owed anyone. He was quite willing to walk out of the shot—he did it three times, serenely and stylishly, as befitted someone who had just beaten the hell out of Lassie. He would not run. The director finally said in a fury, "Look, for God's sake, just hit him in the head with a rock or something, that'll make him run."

"Get Chauncey," Ted said to me. "That's it, get Chauncey." And we walked out of the studio without saying another word to anyone. Bill Beaudine followed us to the parking lot, apologizing for the director, but we wouldn't speak to him. That was a bad day, except for the beaver.

14

But things began to look up for us immediately after the horror at Jungleland. Three or four *Lassie* shows were specifically written for our animals, as though by way of a peace offering; in addition, we were asked to come back and do the Cougar commercials again, as we have done ever since. Kenyon & Eckhardt's writers had finally gotten away from the beaches and hot rocks, and were developing the more sophisticated theme of the Girl and the Cougar. We went on location in San Francisco for the first new commercial, and the model drove through the streets with Chauncey sitting calmly beside her, and me lying out of sight on the floor of the car, to keep him company. He always liked driving, as long as someone he knew was with him.

Ground had already been broken for Andersen's Animal Park, and Vince Evans was determined that it would be open by summer. That time was much like the facelifting at Peaceable Kingdom, with construction workers all over the place, and altogether too many assistant designers huddling in every corner with their subassistants. Ted and I alternated between utter euphoria at the idea of someone else paying the feed bills, and nagging concern that our ideas of what an animal park should be were getting lost in all this grand confusion. For the most part, we let it go, being too overwhelmed by our bustling prospects, and too earnestly anxious not to make trouble. A sniff of security will do that to you.

Jack Wrather and his wife Bonita Granville—a former child movie star of the Shirley Temple era—used to come up once or twice a month, arriving in their converted Trailways bus accompanied by a cast of thousands. On occasion they brought their chief designer, Jim Buckley, with them. Jim was a delightful man, and we got along well from the first, which boded ill for the park. I might have been much more candid with him, and have fought harder to make myself heard, if we had been immediate enemies.

Putting it baldly, I would love to have Jim design a house for me, but not a cage. He never understood that animals are not stuffed toys, that they don't spend all day posed in one place, and that two of their main activities are eating and defecating. His park was a little jewel, as a purely aesthetic conception; but his cages made no allowance for the animals' needs, and his artistic sense wouldn't let him bend enough to leave much room for us to do shows, or to move the animals around comfortably. The fate of Andersen's Animal Park was implicit on the drawing board.

I did like going antique-hunting with Jim, looking at what surely must have been every old barn, stagecoach, and haywagon in two counties, his idea being to make some relic of this sort a central, functioning attraction of the park. Eventually he settled on a one-room schoolhouse—well over a hundred years old, it turned out to have a family of barn owls living in the belfry—which was established as a combined snack bar and gift shop. He also attended the MGM auction of classic movie props and costumes, and bought the tugboat that Marie Dressler piloted in her *Tugboat Annie* movies. By the time the boat had been torn down, transported to the park, and reassembled on a tiny artificial pond, it had cost the Wrather Corporation nearly $30,000. I somehow doubt that it ever paid its way.

Two of the dearest friends I have today arrived close together, shortly before the opening of the park. Simon the chimpanzee came first. He was three years old, and had belonged all his life to a couple in Vermont who adored baby chimps. There are too many people like that to do chimpanzees any good. They were kind to Simon, however, and they were wise enough to realize that chimps who have been raised totally with one family cannot make the transfer of affection to a new owner after a certain age. Ted flew to Vermont and spent two days getting to know Simon on his home ground before he brought him back.

Simon came to us towing a suitcase full of clothes, and accustomed to have his dinner with the family—he ate with a spoon, and dealt with spaghetti like a blasé *maître d'hotel*. Like all chimpanzees, he was a great tester of limits: the first thing he did on meeting me was to bite my arm. So was the second. For several days I avoided disciplining him, wanting him to accept the fact that he lived with us now before I began imposing a new set of rules on him. Besides, my experience with Judy "on the bell" had left me a little afraid of chimpanzees, as I never was of gorillas or bears.

The fatal moment came when Ted, Jean Johnson, and I took Simon to the drugstore in Solvang to buy diapers for him. (He always wore baby pants with diapers under his clothes.) Ted went in to make the purchase, leaving the three of us sitting in the car with the windows closed. Simon, who knew all about car windows, gave me a long, speculative look and started to roll down the one on his side.

"No, Simon, leave it," I said. He was at me before the words were out of my mouth, screaming maniacally and showing his big teeth. I braced my back against the door and put my boot straight up in his path. I didn't kick him, but he charged

Jerry Johnson and his friend Simon the chimpanzee. Jerry helps take care of all the animals, but he's closest to Simon; I call this a "father-and-son" portrait. Simon, by the way, not only uses a toilet but also flushes and then washes his hands.

straight into it and bounced back into the corner. Then I grabbed him by the arm, shook him hard, and threw him to the floor of the car. I'm neither proud of this nor apologetic; it had to be done, and it had to be all at once and over with if it wasn't to be done every other day. By the time Ted, who had heard the racket in the drugstore, came running back to the car, Simon was very well in hand.

I have never had to hit Simon again. We yell at each other now and then, but it's bluff on both sides, in proper chimpanzee tradition. He grows gentler and more affectionate every day. Full-grown at ten years old, he weighs a hundred and twenty pounds, and it would be both pointless and foolish for me to hit him. He could pick me apart like a boiled chicken if he wanted to, but he doesn't want to. It comes down to that, in the end.

Incidentally, his mother would have handled the situation in very much the same way. Chimpanzees, like bears, occasionally cuff their babies when it becomes necessary to remind them whose house it is. Elephant mothers, as in the *Just-So Stories,* really do spank rambuctious little ones with their trunks; and even the wolf—that most doting and indulgent of parents —will snap at a troublesome cub, after many patient warning snarls. A cougar disciplines her young by biting them firmly on the back of the neck—I've done it myself with cougar kittens. But none of these parents ever injure their children in the slightest, nor do they ever punish by withholding love. You just have to use some sense, as any wolf will tell you.

It's a surprisingly solid axiom that the biggest animals are generally the sweetest-natured, and the easiest to work with. Lions and gorillas, after all, have no natural enemies, and nothing to prove, while foxes, monkeys and the little jungle cats like caracals and jaguarundis, for instance, are nightmares of tangled nervous systems and territorial instincts. The average kitchen tabby is far more aggressive than the average lion.

Which is all by way of being a rambling introduction to my daughter Neena.

Shortly before the park was ready to open, Charley Franks, my old elephant mentor, called me. Charley had known Taj at Animals, Inc., and he knew that I had never stopped wanting another elephant, even when I insisted most loudly that I could never expose myself to that particular sorrow again. He told me now that a friend of his named Johnny Strong had just brought his family's little traveling circus to Santa Barbara for a couple of days. Charley had heard that the Strongs were going to have to sell their elephant, because she had grown too big to fit through the doors of the high-school auditoriums where the circus played so many of its dates. Vince Evans was dubious about the cost involved—after a tugboat and a school-house, you have to cut corners somewhere—but he came with Ted and me that same evening to see the Strongs perform at San Marcos High School. I'll always remember the name of the place, because Neena was there.

She was lovely. She did an act with Johnny Strong's twelve-year-old daughter, carrying the girl in her trunk as gently and thoughtfully as Chaplin holding a flower; and she danced, walked a plank, and did a headstand with the same grave, graceful slyness—Chaplin always knows exactly how appealing he is. Vince fell for her as instantly as I did, and I easily fina-gled the purchase price out of him for the noble creature. But Johnny Strong insisted that Ted and I first spend a few days getting acquainted with her at his headquarters in Thousand Oaks. He was candid about the fact that one of his reasons for selling Neena was her increasing penchant for sapping the circus hands—that is, slugging them with her trunk. "She's spoiled," he said, "she grew up with the kids, and they spoiled her. You've got to know just how to handle her."

At Thousand Oaks, however, he simply handed Ted a bull-hook and said, "Okay, take her for a walk." I sat on a bench watching them go off together, with Ted walking close on her left side, just behind the foreleg, which is the correct position for working an elephant. They strolled along in placid companionship, until Ted halted and gave Neena the command to turn. A split-second later, he was skidding along the ground almost twenty feet away, with all the breath slammed out of him, while the bullhook tumbled lazily through the air. Neena had rolled up her trunk and sapped him so fast that I never saw it happen, as I never saw the other three times that she got him that day. Yet she never seemed angry or malicious about it, nor did she even seem to be particularly trying to hurt Ted. My Taj had been an infant, but Neena was eight years old, and eight is the time for making up games.

We still wanted her—a bit nervously—after two exhausting days in her company, so Johnny sent her down to us in a furniture van, along with a man who had trained her for several years. He stayed with us for a week, showing us how to put her through her circus act and drilling us expressionlessly in a grimly impressive repertoire of things to do to her if she made any trouble. I had seen several of them before. He did know a lot about elephants—which is different from understanding them—but after a little while we were both desperately anxious for him to go away, so that we could get down to the serious business of playing with her.

The fascinating thing was that Neena obviously felt the same way herself. While her old trainer was with us, we were like schoolchildren together, silently allied against the teacher. I would catch her glancing drolly sideways at me during one of his lectures on the creative use of the bullhook, and have all I could do not to burst out laughing, as she seemed to want me to do. She did sap us both a couple of times that week (it feels like being clobbered with a tight roll of carpeting); but once the trainer had returned to Thousand Oaks, it was immediately as though Neena had come home. Whatever the game had actually meant to her, from that day on she never hit us again. I never used the bullhook on her, either.

The best way to make sure that she got enough exercise was to invite her to chase me up and down hills and crash through thickets of greasewood and manzanita to find where I was hiding. Charley Franks was appalled to the marrow of his elephant-wise bones, but the Great Chase quickly became the dearest part of our daily routine. We would stop to rest after a while—me sprawled on the ground, watching Neena rubbing against trees and happily throwing dirt all over herself, rocking on her legs with her eyes half-closed and her mouth hanging open, which is what she does when she is most ridiculously happy—until I said, "Come on, Neena, we'd better go back." She would be up instantly, rolling off toward the adobe and the old trailer where she lived. I always rubbed her feet with oil before I left her, because they have a tendency to crack. Elephants have surprisingly delicate skins.

Taking my head in her mouth was her idea. I'm sure it hadn't been part of her circus routine: it had to do with the need to embrace, to be closer than our ill-matched, unyielding bodies would let us come. It's a wonderfully surrounding feeling of utter warmth and restfulness; and there is a rumble that you can't really hear, but only sense down inside yourself. Elephants make that sound to one another when they are content together.

People have asked me so often for so long how I feel about the possibility of being killed by a wild animal that I have evolved a fairly standard answer: "Between one blow from Rijo's paw and a couple of years spent dying from stomach cancer, which would you choose?" Sometimes I add, "At least, if Rijo ever gets me, or one of the bears, it'll be my fault, it'll be because I made a mistake. I like that better than dying for no reason at all."

There's more to it than that. The fact is that if I couldn't feel safe held high in Neena's trunk, or with my head under her foot or in her mouth, I think I wouldn't mind if she killed me anyway. I never try to explain that part.

The grand opening of Andersen's Animal Park was treated

as a great event by the Valley people. Not only the local press, but newspapers from San Francisco to San Diego had run feature stories on the park, and we really had an embarrassment of dignitaries at that opening. In addition to official representatives from Solvang, Buellton, Santa Maria and Santa Barbara, there was a local Congressman present, and a generous scattering of movie and television faces, many of them in Jack Wrather's entourage. Lassie himself cut the ribbon at the entrance, and then Ted and I led a couple of thousand people into the park to see our first show. The crowd was too large to fit comfortably into the grounds—it was a genuine packed house, turnaway business. We thought that was a good sign.

During the last few months of preparation, I'd learned that I had at least some executive ability: that I could run things involving people and take responsibility for more than animals' diets and vitamins. Ted and I had hired and trained a number of girls to patrol the grounds and clean the cages. We'd start work at 7:00 A.M., five days a week, and have the cages smelling good by nine, when the gates opened. Each girl was in charge of five cages. They were instructed to be polite to the visitors, but never to tolerate the least harassment of the animals, whether it was rock-throwing, cigarettes tossed into cages—that's a popular favorite—or simply children screaming and making faces. A couple of Toulouse geese wandered around near the pond, acting as enforcers, and as protectors of the more vulnerable water birds. They used to account for at least two or three rowdies a day.

We did shows intermittently during the course of the day. I always began by standing in the doorway of my office, which was just across from Neena's big enclosure, and shrilling, "*Neena!*" at the top of my voice. Up would go her trunk, the great ears would shake out, and Neena would blare a greeting that once scared a small boy into literally jumping straight out of his shoes and bolting out of the park, leaving the shoes behind him. Then I'd go running into her arena, and we'd play

A favorite thing to do: I yell, "I love you, Neena" up her trunk, and then she embraces me with her forelegs.

together, with Neena picking me up and setting me on her head; doing her circus act if she felt like it, and not if she didn't. I'd put my head in her mouth, or yell up her trunk, "I love you, Neena! Can you hear me?" and Neena would bend her forelegs around me, and hold me.

It was a fairly set routine: I usually went in with Nehani the wolf and his mate Ophelia, and Ted with Joe. I'd wrestle Seymour the grizzly, and Ted would romp with Clyde, who loved him dearly; we'd do Chauncey's Lincoln-Mercury snarl —with Ted holding a microphone to Chauncey's throat so that the audience could hear him purring all the time—and take women in one by one to visit Spot, while their husbands snapped pictures of them timidly stroking a leopard's fur. Mike Pocceicha, a young falconer friend of ours, occasionally gave exhibitions, flying his redtails and lugger falcons to lures down in a long, grassy trench where we often exercised the cats. The show was as relaxed and unhurried as we could conveniently make it, and we went out of our way to talk to the audience, and to answer their questions.

Mr. and Mrs. Cute. We called each other "Mother" and "Father," and we made an awful lot of terribly corny jokes, especially when we were lining up all the children whose parents would let them file through Sweet William's cage holding fig newtons between their lips. (We generally saved him for last, and it never failed to twitch my heart a little to see him going solemnly to sit in his bathtub as the crowd approached his cage.) I'd chirp, "If the parents would like to come around to this side, you'll be able to get some really good last pictures of your little ones"; while Ted rarely missed a chance to inform them afterward that their children had just been nuzzling the only one of our animals who had ever attacked a human being. They always gasped properly.

But we did try to educate, as well as to entertain. We played to the children, giving their questions priority over those of the adults, and continually emphasizing that wild animals love their

This is Neena's "sit-up," a trick she learned in the circus, before I got her. She has a whole circus repertoire, which she runs through just for fun, without my even asking her. She can do all the tricks, but the point is, she doesn't have to do them.

families, that they are neither toys nor savage beasts to be afraid of, and that the best you can do for them if you love them is to leave them alone, and try to see that other people do too. I do like to think that we planted the seeds of fifth-column sabotage in the homes of a few hunters, anyway. There were thousands of children, and many listened very hard.

That was a good time for us, at least as far as security went. What an unbelievable luxury it was to wake in the morning without having to lie there wondering in cold, bland terror how we were going to feed everyone for one more day. We ourselves drew a regular salary from the Wrather Corporation, and were allowed to take time off to continue doing the Cougar commercials and *Lassie*. Utter, utter, absurd luxury! We worked as hard as ever for it, feeling responsible for every aspect of the park, but it was a pure oasis, and I was always grateful for it.

Ted's "Please don't bite me, kitty" stunt, which he did with Clyde at Andersen's Animal Park.

We bought an old Greyhound bus, and Ted reconditioned it into a sort of mobile home, complete with built-in cages, beds and cooking facilities, so that we could travel comfortably with several animals to location assignments. Ted loved that bus. We were coming home late one afternoon from working on a Cougar commercial when, just before we reached Buellton, Ted spotted a car-wash place and insisted on stopping there to hose down the bus. Mike Pocceicha, the falconer, helped him, while I grumped in a window seat, tired and grimy, dreaming of baths and listening absently to the purring of the cougar in the big rear cage.

It wasn't Chauncey this particular time, but Spike, his occasional understudy. Spike had a pink nose and an overwhelmingly bouncy disposition, like Tigger in *Winnie-the-Pooh*. There was no malice in him, but his idea of a good time was jumping on people. As far as he ever knew, they liked it as much as he did. His purr was always uniquely rich and theatrical, and in my drowsy state it took me a while to realize that it was growing a bit loud even for Spike. I turned and saw him strolling cheerfully down the aisle toward me, with the cage door swinging open behind him. He was looking for someone to play with.

I hurled myself at the front door, slammed it shut and turned to ward off Spike as he bounced at me, purring rapturously. We hit the floor together, and after that it got to be like one of those cartoon fights where you see a whizzing welter of arms and legs and heads going around like clothes in a washing machine. He wasn't biting or clawing me, but his happy strength was battering me dizzy against every solid object in the bus. I had nothing to hold him with—not a chain, not a rope, not even a dog-leash. Bobbing to the surface for an instant, I saw Mike Pocciecha staring through a window, his face absolutely bloodless. Mike, who could hold eagles and great horned owls on his hands, was terrified of Spike. I shouted to him, "*Tell Ted—get a rope!*" and was gone again as Spike swarmed jubilantly over me, his body as unyielding as stone under the sweet fur. You forget how hard they are, even when you touch them every day.

When I came up for a second time, Mike was just running back to the window. I shook free of Spike long enough to brace myself against the frame and hear him call, "Ted says he hasn't used up his quarter yet!" Then Spike had me again, waltzing me away through the bus.

Somehow—more or less dragging him by his tail—I got him back into the cage and locked the door properly. I was still collapsed on a bunk, counting my bruises and reassembling myself, when Ted came in, as bright and bouncy as Spike, full of pleasure over the way the bus had cleaned up. To my wheezing, furious charges of desertion under fire, he replied blithely, "Well, I knew you could take care of yourself, you're good with Spike. Anyway, it was my last quarter. Come on outside, she just looks fantastic now."

One of the *Lassie* shows was fun, because I got to act for the first time in a while. I played the wife of a forest ranger, bedridden with a broken leg and menaced—naturally—by an escaped tiger. I had to lie in bed and scream wildly for help as Rijo stalked toward me, puffing his usual hiccuppy greeting and saying, "Hello, Mommy, I'm glad to see you." Lassie rescued me.

Another *Lassie* had to do with a girl who ran a little animal park of her own, and was something of a veterinarian to boot. We had to stage the birth of a llama for that show, which necessitated tranquilizing good old Gladys, the Sweetheart of Jungleland. I was holding her back legs while our own vet gave her a shot; and as she started to go under, she gave one tremendous kick which knocked me five or ten feet through the air, landing on my celebrated tailbone again. The next morning, I couldn't stand up, and had to be taken to the hospital, where I turned out to have suffered a crushed spinal disc. Occupational hazard.

I was wrestling with Seymour the grizzly during one performance, when a boy in the crowd popped a balloon. Seymour and I both swung around to see what was happening, and Seymour's paw accidentally caught me across the nose, breaking it rather badly. It was certainly no one's fault; my nose was set and healed quickly enough, though the pain did last longer

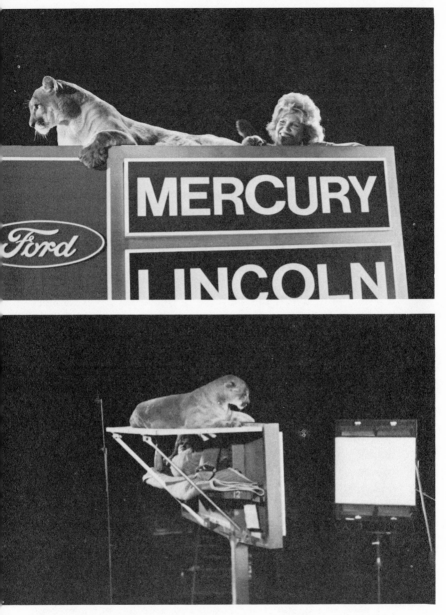

Just before they filmed Chauncey on top of the sign, I'd get him settled and calm. Then I'd duck down to my hidden platform just below him, where I could talk to him and soothe him. When he snarled, I'd tickle his tail through a hole in the platform, to make him twitch it. I used to call myself "the world's best-paid tail twitcher."

than the doctor had told me it would. But that passed in time, and I forgot about the incident almost entirely.

It was at this time, after we had gotten the Lincoln-Mercury job back, that Chauncey's identity as the Cougar on the Sign began to become established. Until then, we had used a dozen different cats, and nothing in the commercials had ever called attention to one or another of them as an individual. But Chauncey was always Chauncey: there was no mistaking him for any other cougar, and no missing the singular person in his eyes. People were already writing letters to the Ford Company about him.

Concerning that famous sign: it is eighteen feet high, and the cougar climbs up a huge staircase on runners to a five-foot-wide ledge at the top. I follow him to a smaller ledge just below his, after which the staircase is wheeled away. Chauncey disliked the whole business in the beginning, and wouldn't have anything to do with it, until my little ledge was installed and he became confident that I would always be there. Ted would give him his snarl-cue from the ground, while I reached through a hole in the upper ledge to tickle his tail. That was all there ever was to it, once he was sure of me.

It was also during this period of relative affluence that our marriage went under. I don't see much point in going into the causes—when you marry someone for the wrong reasons, knowingly, as we both had, you generally deserve what you get—but we had for some time found ourselves in the bad place of being Mr. and Mrs. Cute in public, leading a beautiful life with our beautiful animals, beautifully, and going our separate ways after the show. We were a lot of people's pet marriage, a kind of community fantasy, and that will turn you into stone in time.

I want to say something about Ted. Life has not ever been easy for him—how could it be for a lion in our times, our crazy streets? He doesn't belong here; there is no guile in him, no quick and supple adaptiveness. Like any lion, he reacts physically to whatever he wants, or doesn't like, or can't understand, and I have seen him staring at this world with a lion's angry eyes, needing to roar and smash something. I have often been afraid of him, but never as much as I have feared and sorrowed for him. Lions are doomed, all lions. I pity anyone who has never known a lion.

Our most serious conflict had, on the surface, little to do with the marriage itself. Ted and I had scuffled and mourned and gone hungry together for a long time, and we still got on well as business partners, respecting each other. But we were disagreeing more and more now about training methods, and that was the one matter that I couldn't compromise and remain myself. With other families it's drinking, or raising the children.

The dispute centered around the "hot-shot"—the electrified cattle prod that Ted has always tended to use on the big cats. He was coming to rely on it increasingly as the years passed, not simply as a means of discipline or reprimand—which was bad enough—but in anticipation of any trouble they might be thinking about making for him. We had endless, exhausting, repetitious fights about it, with me raging, "It's *stupid,* it's just so bloody stupid! There isn't one animal you need to use that thing on, not one. Rijo's going to break you in two if you do that to him anymore."

"Rijo's getting to play too rough," Ted would answer. "That's a seven-hundred-pound tiger—all he has to do is pat me on the cheek, and I'm gone. That doesn't hurt him, a little jolt like that. I'm just telling him to watch it with me. Just reminding him."

"It hurts him. It hurts him that you could do something like that to him. And Clyde. What were you reminding Clyde about? Ted, he loves you, he's like a baby with you, and you're turning him mean and scary. He doesn't know what's happening to him. He doesn't know why you're being like that."

Then Ted would wheel to face me and shout, "God damn

it, they're wild! They aren't babies anymore—they're too old, too big for us to keep playing Mommy and Daddy with them. We're the head lions, the top jaguars, and they need to know that all the time. They aren't what you keep trying to make them, they don't think the way you'd like them to think. They're wild."

"I know what they are. That's what makes it so crazy to put your faith in something like a hot-shot. All it does is anger the docile animals, and it won't back off anything that really wants to get you. Try it on Spot sometime, that toy of yours." He never did, but we never resolved the issue between us. It made our public united front an increasing burden to keep up.

It seems to me more and more that women are generally better with wild animals than men are. I'm not talking especially about myself, but about a sex who have had it forced almost into their chromosomes to smother their competitive instincts in the cradle. Most male trainers manage well enough up to the point where the animal's will crosses theirs. After that, it's war, and the male ego is often compelled to see the animal killed rather than admit defeat. Women don't have that particular problem. It has been so inculcated in them to let the man win, because it will break his pride not to, that it is much easier for them to understand why a wild animal always has to win. My entire philosophy as a trainer is based on that one idea. The animal has to win.

A digression here. People continually ask me, "Is that really all you use when you get in trouble, that flappy little dance step?" The answer is still yes, as a rule, but it depends on the situation. Christopher is currently in the feisty, pouncy stage that all adolescent cougars go through—it's less a danger than a playful nuisance, but they can hurt you when they get like that. I sometimes carry a spray bottle of Listerine in my hip pocket when I work Chrissie. The mist itself doesn't bother him, but the hissing sound of the plunger, seemingly coming from out of nowhere, confuses him and *changes his mind*. If I expect real trouble from an animal, I may have someone stand by the cage with another squirter, this one filled with plain sudsy ammonia. You aim at the nostril area—even if it gets in the animal's eyes, it doesn't hurt him. It's the strong smell that sidetracks him, filling his attention with something that isn't me at all. A whip or a hot-shot, on the other hand, tends to concentrate his mind wonderfully, to quote Dr. Johnson.

Incidentally, there's biting and biting. If you don't push an animal who's growing nervous or angry, if you're careful not to back him into a corner, you may well get bitten just the same, but it's rarely, if ever, a serious attack. Most people tend to think that when a wild animal bites you he's become a raging, unstoppable terror, mad with the scent of blood, who won't let you go until he's killed you. That isn't true. They usually bite once and then back off, saying very clearly, *leave me alone and I'll leave you alone*. It's a warning—and quite often it's playfulness, because that is how the carnivores play with each other—and it's unavoidable. The other sort of biting, almost always, is entirely a matter of human insensitivity.

As close to the ocean as we had been living all this time, we might as well have settled in Nebraska, for all the contact we had with it. (My one trip to the beach in several years had resulted in a feverish sunburn, and a conviction that other people's normal enjoyments were definitely forbidden to me.) This changed within the first months of the park's operation, beginning with a telephone call from a woman living in a local housing tract. Without any preamble, she announced, "There's a pelican in my backyard, and I want you to come and get it."

I didn't believe her. Gulls, yes; but pelicans hardly ever come even this far inland. But she was certain and insistent: "Yes, it's a pelican, all right, and it's out in the wading pool playing with my kids!" So I went over to her house; and, by Godfrey, it really was a genuine brown pelican, apparently uninjured, but unable to fly. I named him Peter, and kept him in a little pool which I had been using as a play area for the baby animals, bringing him fish from Santa Barbara. Eventually I gave him to Pete Batten, who had a female brown pelican up at the San Jose Zoo, and was hoping to induce them to mate in captivity. The California count was down to about sixty that year, as I recall.

Then some small children brought us a baby harbor seal, wrapped in a paper sack. She couldn't have been more than three or four days old—she still had traces of the lanugo, the soft, fluffy white birth coat, and there was no layer of blubber under her skin. She had crumpled little hind flippers like a mass of kelp, and her eyes were the size and color of plums in her pointed face. The children had found her on the beach at Santa Barbara, with no other seal anywhere around.

I knew she couldn't live. Mother harbor seals abandon their pups early enough, at three weeks of age, but they don't beach them this young unless there's something fatally wrong with the infant. They always know. I never had any choice but to love her, but I didn't have to give her a name—that was voluntary. I named her LuSeal, "my Easter Seal."

I didn't have the faintest idea of what to feed her, or of how I could possibly get anything down her at all. Over the phone from San Jose, Pete Batten told me how to use a stomach tube, and what LuSeal's formula should consist of (a blend of prepared commercial food, various vitamins, cream, and Ringer's Solution). I had never fed an animal through a stomach tube before, and I was terribly shaky the first time, fearing that the tube might hit a lung or let air into her stomach. But LuSeal caught onto the trick almost immediately, and within a week she was coming up to me asking for the tube, which she swallowed without a hitch. She always had an excellent appetite, but she grew only a little in the time she lived with me.

I kept her in the bathroom, since seals have to be protected from the heat of the sun. On the beaches and islands where they

Nibbles the white-tail fawn and LuSeal the seal grew up in a house together—ours—which has to be a little bit unusual. If I held one, the other was miserable, so the only answer was to hold them both at once.

normally sun themselves, there's always a cool sea breeze blowing; but living inland they can get sunstroke easily, because of all the subcutaneous fat that they store. I put salt in the bathwater for her. She was a demanding little tyrant: since harbor seals can't raise themselves up on their front flippers—as sea lions can—or bend their hind flippers under them, she would wriggle all over the house on her stomach after me, going *gaa, gaa,* like a crying human baby. When I finally picked her up, she would throw her flippers back over my arm and gaze up at me in rapture out of those dark eyes that seemed to get a little bigger every day.

Belvedere was crazy about her. He had been lonely at the adobe, because all the animals were at the park now, except for a mule deer fawn named Nibbles, whom I was raising in the house. I used to come home at night, make dinner, and then put on an old bathrobe and watch television, with LuSeal asleep across my lap, the fawn snuggled against my sides, and Belvedere stretched out in front of me, guarding us all, including the people on the television screen. When I left him to baby-sit for LuSeal in the bathroom, I usually returned to find her sleeping with her head on Belvedere's stomach, and him afraid to move because he might disturb her. They were always together in the house, the three of them, Belvedere and Nibbles and LuSeal.

We had to do a Cougar commercial in Las Vegas, where it was too hot to take LuSeal. For a week before our departure, I schooled Ora and Jean Johnson in the knack of feeding her with the stomach tube. They got good enough so that I took off feeling confident and unworried, which is rare for me. When it comes down to one individual animal, I've always been bad about delegating authority.

I had hardly reached the hotel in Las Vegas when Jean was on the phone, all but incoherent with alarm. From the moment I'd left the house, LuSeal had become a changed personality: not only did she absolutely refuse to take the stomach tube, she barred the door to the bathroom, growling like Nehani, and literally chased the Johnsons out of the house, wriggling at them with her little jaws stretched wide. Even Belvedere couldn't do anything with her.

It was perfectly typical baby-animal behavior, accepting no substitute parents. I thought of her imagining herself abandoned for a second time, and I was ready to turn around and fly straight home, leaving Ted to cope with the commercial by himself. But I called Pete Batten first, rousting him out of bed to hear him grumble, "Look, she's nice and fat, she won't starve in two days—just do your show and go home." A very hungry LuSeal greeted me at the door on my return, and I spent that whole day feeding her continuously and taking her with me wherever I went in the house. I told her over and over that she was the silliest seal in the world, and that I would never leave her again.

She died at the age of five months, of whatever her seal mother knew was wrong with her when she was born.

Like symptoms of a disease that you don't notice at first, and then don't want to notice, peril began to creep up on us again. The animal park's doom was built into it, as I've said—it was simply too small to accommodate the kind of audiences that would have enabled it to meet expenses. I learned a good deal about economics in the year and a half that the park survived (Vince Evans had had me doing the cost sheets for the construction company during the building of the park), and I came to understand very thoroughly that even the best-designed such place has no chance in the world of succeeding financially. The overhead is incredible, if you mean to treat the animals properly as well as maintain appearances. Attendance revenues can't keep up with it, unless you raise your ticket prices to the point where people would stop coming anyway. The few good animal parks, like the good zoos, always function at a deficit and go a little more into debt each year. People liked us, but that simply isn't enough anymore.

The death rattle of Andersen's Animal Park was signaled by the arrival of Jerry Luther, an efficiency expert hired by the Wrather Corporation to find some way of making the park pay off. Like most of the people who have caused me pain in my life, Jerry was a nice, likable man who didn't mean any harm. He was trying, naturally enough, to prove to a large corporation that he was worth all the money they were paying him, which brought him up against our pride and our hurt egos every five minutes or so. We had unquestionably made mistakes, but they had nothing to do with the inherent failure of the park, any more than dragging Simon around to the openings of supermarkets and gas stations—which was Jerry's idea of a gala promotion—was going to do anything to save it. I felt that we and the animals were being stupidly degraded, and our relationship with the Wrathers, and with Vince, became steadily more strained and sullen. It was a matter of time now.

One day during this period we were visited by several people from the San Diego Zoo. They had scheduled a chimpanzee act as the main attraction for their annual picnic, but the act had canceled at almost the last minute, and they wondered if we might agree to come down and do a show for them. The event fell on our day off from the park, and we had been feeling so downhearted lately that it seemed a rare delight to be wanted somewhere. So we took Rijo, Boris, Chauncey, Clyde, Seymour, Spot, and a shy young wolf named Sylvester, and we went to the picnic.

It may have been the funniest, silliest, most disastrous show we ever gave anywhere. It was staged at a performing-seal arena; and as it happened, we followed a seal act, so the stage was soaking wet for our cats and bears. We took all the animals backstage in their trailers, and Ted went out front to announce that he would begin with Seymour, one of the few working grizzlies in show business. I put a chain on Seymour and started to walk him into the arena. But we had to pass the seals—they were actually sea lions, as is usual—and they all started barking and lunging around as soon as they saw Seymour. Whereupon he panicked, turned around and bit clean through my hand. That's how grizzlies panic.

Once I got him out on stage, he was fine. I rode him and wrestled with him, all the while talking to the audience about affection-training and keeping my bleeding hand wrapped out of sight in my dress. Ted couldn't understand why I was working with just one hand, and kept whispering, "What's the matter with you? Use both hands, you'll lose him!" We were separated from five thousand people only by a moat, and Seymour was eminently at home in the water.

Everything went wrong. We turned Chauncey and Clyde loose to do their famous simulated fight, confident that they wouldn't go anywhere near the water encircling the stage. Neither of us had considered the possibility that the cats might not know there was any water in the moat. Chauncey promptly fell in, and actually swam a bit, hoping to join spectators before we could fish him out. The whole show went like that, but the audience loved it. We entertained them—one way and another—and we scored point after point for our ideas of working with wild animals; and our grand finale with Rijo and Boris finished to the biggest standing ovation that we had ever known. It scared Rijo so much that he bolted down the ramp leading offstage, dragging Ted after him with his feet hardly touching the ground. That got even more applause, and I waved prettily and began to follow him with Boris. *All part of the show, folks, part of the show.*

I don't know why it is, but Siberian tigers sometimes have odd problems with their visions; objects and movements that don't frighten other cats can spook them like horses. Something hanging overhead on the ramp—I think it was part of the sound system—brought Boris to a dead stop halfway down. Not only would he not go any farther, but he began backing up, step by step, and there wasn't a thing I could do but go with him. He backed us straight out onto the stage again, and five thousand people stopped putting on their coats and wiping their children's hands and faces, and sat down again to see what would happen next. So did Boris, and so did I, in the center of the stage. Ted would have to come back sooner or later.

According to Ted, he was too occupied to notice anything unusual until he had Rijo calmed and put away in his trailer. Then he looked around at last, saw no Boris and no me, and came tearing back up the ramp to the stage. The audience applauded his arrival, and I flipped a hand at him and offered him Boris's lead chain. Ted took a firm hold of it, said, "Okay, come on, Boris, no more messing around," and started to pull.

A balky horse or donkey generally just plants his feet and won't budge; but the more you haul on an obstinate tiger, the more he backs up. That might be worth knowing sometime. Ted kept tugging on the chain, and Boris kept retreating, until —with thousands of people chorusing, "Look out, *no!*"—he backed majestically off the stage and into the moat. He gave a doleful little yip of dismay as he went under.

Ted still had hold of the chain, which was something anyway, even though there was no chance of our pulling a five-hundred-pound tiger out of the water by main force, as we had done with Chauncey. The arena had turned into Bedlam, with everyone shouting suggestions at us (I remember references to helicopter rescues and pontoon bridges), and Boris barking desperately as he paddled to stay afloat. Siberian tigers can swim quite well, but Boris had never been in the water before, and the increasing uproar frightened him even more. His great head looked grotesquely enormous, bobbing about as though there were no struggling body attached to it at all.

"You've got to go in and get him!" I yelled in Ted's ear, certain that Boris was drowning as we stood there. Ted, entirely understandably, kept mumbling, "Well, I don't know, maybe he'll come out by himself." But Boris couldn't get a grip on the wet stage, or enough leverage in the water to do more than scrabble wildly and fall back again. He never took his eyes off us, even in his greatest terror.

Ted went in. He dived deeply and came up under Boris, making a kind of raft to support him and give him a moment's rest—then he pushed up as hard as he could, and I threw all my weight on the lead chain, and Boris, with a good purchase on Ted's back, popped out of the water and sprawled at my feet, panting and coughing. The audience started to applaud, but it trailed off as though everyone had had the same second thought at same time. What price affection-training now, with an extremely upset Siberian tiger about to eat up a foolish lady trainer, as soon as he got his breath back? Suddenly the only sound anywhere was those bloody seals carrying on under the stage.

But I had completely forgotten that we were doing a show. Boris stood there before me, trembling, with his head hanging, looking like a drowned puppy, and all I could think about was how sorry I felt for him. I cried out, "Oh, my poor *baby*!" and fell to wringing the water out of his tail. I used both hands for that, because you have to.

They did applaud then, far longer and louder than before; and if they were laughing with relief too, so were we, heaven knows. But we had made our point, more dramatically and effectively than we probably could have any other way. What could have kept those cats, that grizzly, that wolf, putting up with those unbelievably incompetent, bungling trainers, if it wasn't love?

15

So many doors, opening and closing. We had worked animals for movies and television, been both a roadside zoo and a sort of traveling show; we had enjoyed the undeniable luxury of having an animal park more or less of our own; and now it looked as though we were in for another winter of scavenging around the meatpacker's in Saticoy. Jack Wrather had grown increasingly sour on the park when it failed to make money for him—he claimed now that he had been deceived, and that he had never imagined that the operating expenses would be so great. I thought that he might better have addressed himself to Jim Buckley's taste in tugboats, but it hardly mattered at this point. Ted and I dug in and waited. We had been here before.

But you never do go back through the same door. At the time that we gave the show at the San Diego Zoo, the Lincoln-Mercury people had contacted us to ask if we would bring Chauncey to Las Vegas for a weekend, to be the guest at their semiannual banquet for their dealers. These are always elaborately presented occasions, at which the dealers are introduced to the new line of cars and presumably fired up to go home and sell them. Jerry Luther allowed us the two days off, and we drove to Las Vegas in the first new car we had ever owned. It was a Chrysler station wagon.

Chauncey was a great hit at the banquet, and from that week-end on, our relationship with Lincoln-Mercury began to become significantly warmer and more personal. Up to that time, our only communication regarding the Cougar commercials had been with the Kenyon & Eckhardt production group, who made the films and signed our paychecks. None of the people from Detroit had ever seen Chauncey, except on their television screens. Car dealers and Ford vice-presidents alike were coming up just to look at him, and to touch him as shyly as children. Chauncey affected people like that.

But the big thing—though we didn't know it then—happened in the parking lot before we even got into the hotel. I don't think we were quite out of the station wagon when a husky, blond man came storming up to us, demanding, "What is our cat doing in a competitive product?" I blazed up immediately and roared back, "He isn't your cat, he's Chauncey!" and that was how we met Owen Bombard.

Dear, fierce, amazing Owen. A French-Canadian from up-state New York who worked as a gandy dancer—a railroad laborer—among a great many other jobs, to put himself through school, he was head of public relations for Lincoln-Mercury. (Today he is head of public relations for the Ford division of the Ford Motor Company.) Owen knows everything, because it makes him happy to teach himself things. It's hard to explain his kindness to us over the years, so we don't try. He issued a ukase that first day, and from then on Chauncey had his own Colony Park station wagon every year to drive in wherever we went. Owen always insisted that it was Chauncey's car.

Not long after that weekend in Las Vegas, we were summoned to meet with Jack Wrather, who told us flatly, "I don't know whose fault it is, but this whole animal park business just isn't working out the way I expected. I have to tell you,

I'm disenchanted." Then he announced that we had something like thirty days in which to get our animals out of the park. He had a new lock put on the gate, and we were allowed to go in only to feed and clean under the strictest supervision.

We were back in the position of having nowhere to keep the animals, except in the extremely inadequate quarters at the adobe—and heaven only knew how much longer we might be able to stay there. Braced as we were for it, the blow had fallen more shockingly than we could have anticipated. Eliza was definitely running out of ice floes.

Enter Mrs. Harriet Nugent. That isn't her name, because she is a nice woman in many ways, and I truly wouldn't want to hurt her feelings. For the same reason, I won't give the name of the service organization she headed—obviously it has something to do with animals, or Ted and I wouldn't have been speaking at the dinner where we met her. We didn't say anything about our current troubles to her then; but she came to see one of the last shows that we gave at Andersen's Animal Park, and afterward Ted told her everything. Mrs. Nugent was very sympathetic, and very angry on our behalf. "You must come and talk to my husband," she urged us. "I'm sure he'll be able to work something out for you."

Her husband turned out to be a retired admiral, even wealthier in his own right than she was in hers, and the sort of man who worked out business propositions for many of the reasons that other people solve chess problems. "What I suggest," he told us, in the way that admirals suggest things, "is that you establish a nonprofit organization, to be called something like —oh, say, Orphans of the Wild. It would function as a temporary or permanent refuge for sick, maimed, and displaced wild animals. Perhaps, when funds permit, it might also serve as a sort of specialized graduate school for veterinarians, and even as a breeding center for endangered species." He took a measured, commanding turn around the living room, increasingly pleased with his new toy, and with us for bringing it to him.

"Harriet will, of course, take charge of the fund-raising," he continued, "that being her area of competency, so to speak. You two would naturally be on the board of directors, while I—" he eyed us almost shyly over the rim of his liqueur glass. "—I would propose myself as chairman of the board, if you have no serious objection. To begin with, I would immediately purchase Mr. Edwards's old adobe, as well as the surrounding acreage, out of my own pocket, to serve as organizational headquarters." He beamed briskly at us, as though the matter were already entirely accomplished.

And so it was, as far as we could see. The admiral and his lady really did make a down payment on the adobe, and foot the bills for all the expenses of moving the animals back there, of building proper cages and facilities for them, and of setting up Orphans of the Wild. We got an astonishing amount of volunteer help in all this from local people, who had come to take more pride in us—and to have more concern for the animals—than I had ever looked up to realize. It was a shock to me. Since my childhood I had had no real experience of feeling part of any human community.

Because our slapstick performance at the picnic had been such a success, we were approached by representatives of the San Diego Zoo with a firm offer to give shows there every weekend. In spite of being one of the best and most celebrated zoos in the country, they were in a bad way at the time, with attendance down to seven or eight thousand on Saturdays, and a bit more than that on Sundays. We jumped at the offer, and the first show was scheduled for the weekend of January 8, 1972. The Zoo had a one-minute commercial made from film clips of our television work, and saturated the airwaves with it for weeks in advance. I felt like a detergent.

Those shows at the Zoo made us stars, or as near to it as I

ever expect to come. The first one was unbelievably well-attended: there were over twenty-one thousand people on Saturday alone, and they mobbed the stage afterward like fans at a rock concert. It overwhelmed me, after so long a time of knowing exactly what miserable meanness and stupidity animals call out of human beings, to find that there were still so many who wanted only to be close to a bear, or to sit and watch someone loving a tiger. It had to be that, because our shows themselves were never anything much as shows (except now and then, given a moat and a few seals). We were simply there on the stage, being with the animals, as we were with them every day with no one watching at all. As long as he got his chin scratched properly, it was all the same to Chauncey.

Amazingly—almost suspiciously—nothing bad happened to us at the San Diego Zoo. We didn't go hungry, we didn't lose a single animal, we got along quite well with the Zoo employees and officials alike; and the one mishap in all that time occurred in our huge, ancient Greyhound bus when Sydney, our young black leopard, bounced over Ted's head and accidentally raked Ted's scalp with a tooth, necessitating five stitches. But that was

While Ted did this stunt with Fred the lion at the San Diego Zoo, I would say to the crowd: "Most trainers put their head in the lion's mouth. Ted likes to be different."

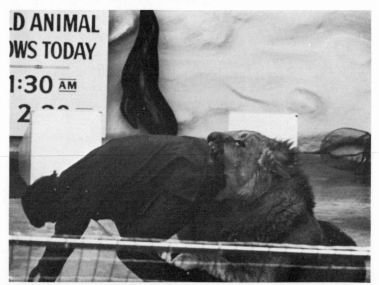

it for misfortune—we lived well and rewardingly for fourteen months. It took getting used to.

We moved our larger, older animals down to the Zoo, and hired Billy Redlin to live there and look after them. On Friday afternoons, we would load the others into the bus, drive to San Diego, and reach the Zoo at about ten in the evening. We'd sleep in the bus, and then spend Saturday morning helping Billy clean cages and preparing for the three half-hour performances that we would give that day. I remember that I spent my first night in the Zoo lying awake and listening to a fascinating cacophony of screams, whistles, growls, grunts, roars, giggles, and squeals, all unquestionably coming from the same nearby cage. I thought *hyena*; and then, *no, gibbon,* because gibbons seem to have the widest vocal range of all the apes. In the morning I found out that the sole begetter of the entire racket was a two-thousand-pound Pacific walrus named Fred.

Fred loved everything. I came to think of that carrying-on every night, all night, as Fred's canticle of thanks to the Great Walrus who had made this excellent world and him in it. His affectionate nature made him something of a menace: the keeper who had raised him warned me that if you went into Fred's cage to work, he was likely to sit on your foot and effectively keep you from going away from him again. He could truly squash you with love, but it was impossible for me not to go in most days and sit watching as Fred played with the little harbor seal who lived with him. They used to race madly up and down their pool, and the harbor seal would leap high out of the water over Fred's back, while Fred peered around in muzzy straight-man surprise each time, looking remarkably like a one-ton rubber boot with whiskers. When he got tired of that, he'd come over to be told what a beautiful Fred he was; and he always nodded at me as I spoke, occasionally squealing *meeeee*. He knew, of course, but he liked to be told again.

I spent a great deal of my free time in the baby-animal nursery. Almost all zoos have one—there's not much choice, considering the large number of animals who breed readily in captivity—and under Joanne Thomas, the one at the San Diego Zoo was a joy. I remember especially a pair of baby orangutans who were literally never seen apart; they clung together every waking moment, like two halves of a puzzle. Orangutans are like that, the great clutchers and cuddlers among the primates. Joanne once made a birthday party for the little female—I think her name was Karen—and I brought Sylvester the wolf, who was still young enough to like parties. Everything was very mannerly, until Sylvester started to eat the birthday cake, and Karen hit him. Joanne was pleased, in a way, because Karen had always been such a timid creature, but I gave Sylvester some of my own cake. Fair's fair.

I would be happy to be the baby-animal nurse at a really good zoo, like the one in Cincinnati, or the San Diego Zoo while we were there, before Dr. Charles Schroeder retired. The occupational hazards are twofold: the first obviously, being the parting with the babies when they're grown enough to be given to keepers. But there is another, and it comes when the animals reach a certain age of plain finkiness—it's five or six months in the case of a grizzly bear, for instance. They aren't adults, or even really adolescents, but they have become aware of themselves as grizzlies or leopards—no matter how deeply they may have imprinted with their human foster parents—and suddenly nothing matters but finding out, now, this minute, what it is that grizzlies and leopards are. Mostly, it amounts to a sort of aggressive teasing and little more; but this is the time when people begin to grow frightened of their adorable exotic pets. Even sensitive, experienced nurses don't quite know what to do with them at this age, and their relationship with the babies is rarely as close and confident again. It's hard on the animals, who still need their mothers.

I'd love to give a course for zoo-nursery workers, not just teaching them to deal with recurring situations like this, but perhaps to give the sort of non-shows that Ted and I do. I think it could create a tremendous amount of public interest in the zoos, who will one day have to face the fact that they are in commercial competition with outfits like Lion Country Safari and Marine World. The good zoos could do wonderfully well simply exhibiting the rapport between individual animals and their keepers, which does exist, though the public almost never sees it. That was all Ted and I ever did, and I'll never forget the great hunger with which we were received.

Anyway, for those fourteen months we were stars. It was fun, and it was restful to be catered to, to be special again for a while; but I was always aware that the audiences were coming, not to see us, but to be in the presence of Rijo, Spot, Chauncey, Seymour, and the others. The animals knew it too, and during that time they all became delighted hams like Nehani, padding their parts shamelessly. Sydney, the black leopard, made her routine of bouncing about on a diving board more of a Hollywood production with each performance; and Sylvester worked out a show-stopping number in which he ran between a double line of children, deliriously licking every face he could reach. His timing was incredibly professional: he would pause at exactly the right peak of audience interest, deliberately choose the smallest child there and roll on him as though he were wet morning grass or a patch of sunlight. Rijo, in contrast, often did nothing theatrical at all; but when I petted him the whole arena sighed, and I could feel them in my hands, touching him through me.

Harriet Nugent was having trouble funding Orphans of the Wild. I think there were just too many other demands on her time—she belonged to an incredible roster of worthy organizations, and had recently been honored for her work in raising money for them all. Most of the considerable money that it took to keep the orphanage running came directly from the admiral, and the drain on his resources was becoming too great. The Nugents had felt from the beginning that our working at the Zoo made for a conflict, but we couldn't afford to give up the

San Diego weekends. And even if we could have, they were such fun. We thought everything was going beautifully.

But suddenly it was all over at the Zoo. Dr. Schroeder, that wonderful kewpie-doll martinet who demanded instant obedience from everyone, and had it coming, retired, and was replaced by another sort of man altogether, an efficiency specialist. Soon after Schroeder left, the little harbor seal was moved out of Fred's pool. I forget what the actual pretext was, but I remember that Fred died. Our contract with the San Diego Zoo was not renewed. The new director told us, "I'm sorry, but it doesn't seem to me that attendance has picked up enough over the summer to warrant continuing the association. In candor, I expect our audiences have been growing a bit tired of your act." We were on the loose once again, and rather out of shape for it this time.

Very shortly afterward, Harriet Nugent called a special meeting of the board of directors of Orphans of the Wild. It was held, not at the adobe, but at the Nugents' home, where, with much rustling of papers and parliamentary fidgeting—she was not at all an unkind woman—she finally made her proposition to us. "I'm afraid that the only way for me to raise the amounts we need is for the people I approach to understand that I am in complete control of the orphanage's affairs. So I'm afraid I have to ask—request—if you two will resign from the board and leave Orphans of the Wild entirely in my hands, I will guarantee to do everything in my power to keep it going. Even if that means funding it myself. Otherwise—" She rattled the sheets of parchment bond again. "—I'm afraid that my husband and I will have to disassociate ourselves from the project. Immediately." She folded her hands and looked at us in genuine appeal.

I think that Ted and I were more relieved than anything else. We never suspected bad motives, and we still don't. We were still so ignorant of the way in which money and organizations

work that we hadn't even really known what to be afraid of
when the Nugents summoned us to the meeting. We said, "Oh.
All right, fine—whatever you think." Neither of us had ever
been cut out to be a board member or a director of anything.
Just as well to be rid of that pointless responsibility, anyway.

Some two weeks later, we were awakened by a telephone
call from our lawyer, Joe Agapay. "Hey, I hate to start your
day off like this, but you're not going to have too much time to
waste sleeping for a while. The Nugents just put your outfit into
bankruptcy."

"Oh," I said. "I'm sorry, Joe, I'm still asleep. The Nugents
what?"

"Bankruptcy, kid. Liquidation, closing up shop, creditors
taking over. Didn't they tell you anything?"

"No. No, they didn't tell us—we thought everything was
going to be all right. After we resigned from the board—"

"Right," Joe said. "Sure."

"Well, I guess if they had to do it, they had to. I guess their
lawyers or somebody told them it was the best thing."

There was a silence. Joe said slowly, "You're taking it pretty
calmly, considering the animals and everything."

"What about the animals?" I sat up in bed, suddenly dry-
mouthed and shivering. Ted was saying, "What is it? Let me
talk to him a minute, Pat."

"Oh, Jesus," Joe said. "You didn't know."

"What about the animals?"

"They're classed as assets of Orphans of the Wild. They'll
be sold at public auction, like everything else. Pat, I'm sorry.
I'm sorry."

All I could think of was Jungleland. In the following days,
while Ted and I blundered around in almost speechless shock,
trying to understand that we were somehow $50,000 in debt,
what inhabited me entirely was not fury at the Nugents—they
had probably done their best—not even tears, but the image of
the man from Hollywood aiming his rifle at the grizzly bear

through the bars of her cage, while she sat there rocking herself and waving to people. Our conversation became reduced to vague, hopeless mumbles of "What if we called . . . ?" and "Who was that woman at the party—the one who said if we ever . . . ?" I remember that I was thirsty all the time.

Ted couldn't sleep. I could, but I didn't want to. My dreams were always of the grizzly, and of that black leopard, escaped and small among grabbing, yowling maniacs. Lying awake all night long, I devised and discarded one lonely scheme after another, from bank holdups to blackmail, extortion to chain letters, to all of us hiding out in the Los Padres National Forest. But our helplessness and terror functioned as a sort of anesthetic, keeping us from thinking clearly about anything except the one reality in the world, which was that we couldn't protect the animals. The thing we had always been most afraid of had happened at last.

Only Joe Agapay never gave up. He came to the house a few days after his telephone call to tell us, "All is not yet lost. I've been going round and round with the judge and the creditors all day, and I finally made a breakthrough. You get up something like a quarter of the outstanding debt, and they'll give you a ten-day extension on the court order. Not a bad day's work, for an aging Hawaiian."

We stared at him for a moment, and then Ted exploded. "Damn it, Joe, what the hell's the good of that? We can't raise $10,000 any easier than we could raise the whole amount. And even if we could, what's the use of ten lousy days? What kind of a stupid, pointless deal *is* that?"

"Ted," Joe said, utterly unperturbed by his outburst. "Friend. Look. The creditors don't want your animals. They want their money. Auctioning the animals is a big drag for them, and it won't bring them in anything like what you owe them. They'd much rather have the full amount, even if it takes a bit more time to get it. *If* they think there's any real chance of getting it. You get me that first $10,000 to show them, and I can stall them off a whole lot longer than ten days, believe me. I know what I'm doing."

"How much time do we have?" Ted asked.

Joe's assurance faltered for the first time. "You got a week. I couldn't do any better than a week."

"We can't make it." I don't know which of us said it. We sat in silence for a long time after that. Belvedere came in and lay down by me, whining nervously at the darkening air. Then I turned on a desk light, groped around for a pencil and a piece of paper, and sat down again. The others looked at me.

"I'm writing an advertisement," I said. "A newspaper ad, asking people for money." Joe cleared his throat. I said, "All those people who came to the park, all those people at the Zoo. People who know Chauncey and Rijo, people whose children's faces Sylvester licked. People who never touched a wild animal in their lives, except for Spot. I'm asking them to help us."

Joe said, "*Rrrmmp.* Um. Hate to sound cynical." Ted said, "Pat it's a waste, you can't raise that kind of money through the mail like that, not in a week. We can dig up enough to buy back maybe a couple of animals—why spend any of it on newspaper ads?"

"Which couple?" I asked. "Rijo and Boris? Clyde and Neena? Chauncey and Sweet William? Just name two." Nobody said anything for another long time. "Look, they are not going to the auction. None of them, none of them are going to be sold at any goddamn auction. I don't know what I'll do if this doesn't work. I'll do something. But they are not going to that auction."

I took the biggest space that we could afford in the *Santa Barbara News-Press.* The advertisement ran as follows:

DEAR ANIMAL LOVERS:

To all of you who believe in our work and who have helped us before, we are directing an appeal which we felt we would never have to make. Unless we can raise

$50,000 within the next 60 days, our animals will be sold or destroyed and the wildlife refuge discontinued. Since there is little time left to salvage the animals and our work, we are appealing to all of you.

We need your help DESPERATELY, as we are at present unable to cope with the entire financial burden which has been thrust upon us through the bankruptcy proceedings which have been initiated by the Board of Directors of Orphans of the Wild, much against our wishes.

All your donations will be used to prevent the sale or destruction of the animals. . . . Please understand that such donations or contributions cannot be tax-deductible; therefore our plea is, of necessity, on a personal level. If you believe in us and our work, PLEASE HELP.

And after that, we just sat and waited. I know that we must have taken our meals, worked with the animals, and done our cleaning and feeding chores as usual, but what I remember of the next couple of days is sitting in a kitchen chair, hour after hour, not moving, not thinking, staring straight ahead like Banté or Sweet William. I think I was something like a sick animal during that time: so frightened as to be past fear, past thought or anticipation, just waiting to live or die.

I remember how cold and drowsy I felt going with Ted to the post office, and I remember the first letter, the first one we took out of our box. It was hand-written, folded neatly around a check for $100, and it said, "This is not much help to you, I know, but perhaps it can pay for euthanasia for the animals, if you cannot save them. They should not be sold, as I am sure they would never be happy, except with you. I wish I could send more, but this is all I can afford."

The second envelope contained $300, and no note. The third had $25 in it, with a letter that said, "I would like this money to be used for the big black bear, the one that ate the cookies from the children." Our box was choked with mail, and there was twice as much waiting for us at the counter. Most of the donations were for small amounts, but the total came to slightly less than $2000.

Ted had tears in his eyes. I didn't cry, for a wonder; but when we got home, I went out to Neena and stood with her for a long time, pushing in close between her forelegs and letting her hold me hard with her trunk, claustrophobia or no. For the last several days I had only gone near her to feed her and check her feet, which had been bothering her, and almost run away again. I was ashamed to let her look at me.

By the next day, the *Los Angeles Times* had picked up the story, and we began getting contributions from all over southern California. They came in all sizes, large and small alike often accompanied by letters saying that this gift was to help save the wolf, or the blind llama, or the elephant. After four days we had raised nearly $6000, and at the end of our week's grace the donations combined with our own savings exceeded the necessary $10,000. Joe Agapay, as he had promised, won us a further extension after the ten days were up, and kept on tap-dancing and sweet-talking our creditors, continually managing to buy us more time. Our personal funds had vanished into the ransom, and we couldn't move the animals until we had paid off the remaining $40,000 or so, but at least they were out of danger for a while. As for poor old Mr. and Mrs. Cute, they went back to being broke and scared.

How strange our normal emotions—ordinary confusions, accustomed fears, familiar daily elations and exhaustions— seemed to us after that time of calm despair. The animals had grown skittish, smelling the emptiness in us, and it took days for us to be easy with them again. When your one feeling is of having betrayed and doomed what you love most, it's oddly difficult to accept your life back, to believe in mercy.

On the day after the *Times* ran its story about my advertisement, we got a telephone call from two total strangers named Liz and Larry Hovey. The Hoveys live in Los Angeles, where Larry is a training manager for a large bank, and Liz is some-

Ted and Cheryl Baca with Chauncey. The Bacas came to us in our hour of need—and they're still there, always helping. The nicest thing about having animals is the fantastic people you meet.

thing important in the telephone company. They said, "We love animals, and we'd like to be some help. Can we come and see you?" I think I almost said *no*. I was so tired, and it was still hard for me to talk to anyone.

The Hoveys brought their friends Ted and Cheryl Baca with them when they came up to Buellton. None of them were experienced animal people (Ted Baca is a civil-rights specialist for the Treasury Department, and Cheryl was then working in public relations for Carnation Milk), but they knew a great deal more about money than we did, and they were resourceful and energetic where we were feeling emotionally brittle just then. They suggested that we incorporate ourselves as a nonprofit animal refuge again, this one to be called Love Is an Animal. It gave us a better legal position from which to protect our animals; and besides, we could use all of the old Orphans of the Wild publicity brochures that way.

The fact that so many of the mail donations had been sent specifically to one or another of our animals gave Cheryl Baca an idea for helping to feed them. "Why don't you set up something like a foster parents' plan—some way that people could pledge themselves to contribute a regular amount to support a particular animal? I think the reason people responded so strongly to that ad of yours is that so many of them felt they knew your animals as individuals. I think they'd love a chance to be personally involved with them that way—to feel special about one wild creature. Remember, Ted and I get dibs on Sylvester. I want to be Sylvester's mother."

The plan succeeded far beyond our imaginings: within a very short time, each animal had at least one "parent" sending five or ten or fifteen dollars a month to help defray expenses, which had risen to about $5000 a month by then. Many were older women, living alone, and none were wealthy. I mention this because it occurs to me now that the Nugents and our other acquaintances of that type never really could see the animals as individual personalities. They were in the habit of supporting good works in the mass, of contributing to faceless worthiness, but they never become involved with Murgatroyd as Murgatroyd: one particular bear who was neither Seymour nor Candy nor Sweet William. But the old woman who sent Lucky five dollars out of her Social Security check every month would never have mistaken him for Joe, or for any other lion in the world.

Whenever we could manage it, we gave picnics for the foster parents at the adobe. They would ride buses up from Santa Barbara and Los Angeles, bringing gifts of fruit and Karo syrup for their bears, and chicken necks in paper bags for their cats. I wish I could tell those good people what curiously comforting times those were for me. It wasn't just the money, but their faces when Simon or Sylvester kissed them, and the look of slow, tired, disappointed hands touching a tiger at last. People shouldn't have to wait all their lives for a tiger.

During one of those picnics, I heard a scream, and a plump, matronly lady came shooting out of our bathroom in considerable disarray. I had completely forgotten to warn her about Marcus Wallaby, who lived in the bathroom, slept behind the tub, and loved to jump onto laps when the opportunity presented itself. I always held him and played with him myself—he made much better company than *Playboy* or *National Geographic*—but I suppose you did have to be prepared for his arrival. The poor lady never would use our bathroom again.

Which inevitably reminds me of my other toilet story, from our time at the San Diego Zoo. Ted and I had been shopping in Lompoc one afternoon, buying produce for the animals, and on the way out of town we stopped at a gas station so that I could use the restroom. I was sitting on the toilet when a woman pulled the unlatched door open, looked in, said, "Oh, excuse me," and withdrew. The door had just swung shut behind her when I heard her gasp, "Oh, my God!" A moment later she opened the door again and stood there pointing at me. "You're Pat Derby!" I sort of wiggled my fingers at her.

She reached back and yanked three children into the doorway with her, absolutely gabbling with excitement. "Do you *know* who that is? That's the lady at the zoo, remember? You went up on the stage and petted the wolf and everything, and I got my picture taken with a leopard—" The children sucked their candy and stared, and I covered myself as best I could, smilingly prepared to sign autographs, while that woman prattled along. "Oh, you just don't know how we enjoyed your show, you can't imagine what it means to us to have had the chance to meet you!"

Stardust, the Big Time, the Broadway Melody! If only Uncle Nigel could see me now!

Between the foster parents' plan, a new Cougar commercial, another performance at the Earl Warren Showgrounds, the tireless help of our friends, and Ted playing drums and singing with a trio in Solvang, we fed everyone through the summer and fall of 1973. We couldn't make any headway paying off the bankruptcy, however: it chilled every corner of our lives and made every day something to be scurried through on tiptoe, panic-stricken at unexpected phone calls or strange cars in the driveway. Having been so pampered and secure, even for a little while, made it infinitely worse than the simple old days of sneaking around cattle ranches in the hope of finding a dead cow. (Does it count as rustling if the *corpus delicti* is all over green gunk? I always wondered.) Ted developed a stomach ulcer that summer.

Ted's seventeen-year-old daughter by a previous marriage came to live with us during this time. Fairly shortly afterward, I moved out. It was bound to happen sooner or later—comparatively few business partners share a bedroom. I didn't get on well with the daughter, and I was nervous about her friends, some of whom I knew to be drug users. I was afraid to leave them alone around the animals.

About narcotics. I don't have anything moral against their use, but all the experience of my life recoils from them. Everything that has ever mattered deeply to me—acting, dancing, working with animals—depends so totally on earning and maintaining control that I don't dare to play games with the anarchy that is quite probably my natural condition. A wild animal knows when you're out of control, whether the agent is wine, cocaine, sorrow or a sinus condition, and it may frighten him or excite him, depending on his nature and your relationship. Either way, you can get killed; and Neena needs me.

It was a rather odd separation. I rented a house at Flag Is Up, a large thoroughbred ranch only a couple of miles from Buellton, but I spent every day at the adobe, as always, working with Ted. The Hoveys and the Bacas were there on weekends, and Ora and Jean Johnson had long since moved into the area and come to work for us on a full-time basis. So little had changed from the old days, and yet the old days were over.

When I arrived at the adobe on one late-summer afternoon to check on the animals, I saw Boris lying down in his run. I called to him, but he didn't answer, which was unlike him—Boris always responded to his friends' voices with a one-tiger riot of puffing and calling and barking. Going closer, I saw that his jaws were slack and drooling, and that he was breathing with enormous effort, as though his body had to keep reminding itself of how this was done. I screamed for someone to get Ted, and I ran in to Boris, trying to gather all of his limp five hundred pounds onto my lap.

Ted called our vet, Dr. Craig Larsen, who asked for a blood sample, since he had no more idea than we of what could be wrong with Boris. Ten minutes after Ted had left for Los Angeles with the sample, Boris died in my arms. He was in a coma by then, and never moved at all, but I felt him go away, like water sliding through clenched fingers back into the sea.

The lab analysis showed an overdose of barbiturates. We never knew how they got into his food, but they could have been given to him only by someone familiar with his eating habits, who knew him well enough to call him over to the dish —Boris was shy of strangers. There were a number of possible suspects hanging around the adobe all the time now; and it's so much a pillhead's sort of joke: "Hey, *yeah,* let's get the tiger high, see how he trips." I'm sure whoever did it had no special intention of killing him. I'm sure they never thought about it, one way or another.

He was such a silly tiger. Would it have made any difference at all if even one of them had known how silly he was?

16

In September of 1973, Owen Bombard asked if we would bring Chauncey to a news conference at the Del Coronado Hotel in San Diego, to introduce the new Lincoln-Mercury line for 1974. We took Christopher with us as well this time—he was then about two months old, and was already appearing in commercials for the new Comet sedan. Chrissie was the joyous limb of Satan that Chauncey had never really had the time to savor being: the struggle to live, and to learn to walk again, had imposed dignity and wisdom on him at an age when he should have been climbing the curtains. But Christopher climbed things and got into things and bit people, and even his raspy little snarl sounded like an urchin burlesque of Chauncey. He seemed sometimes to be having a childhood for both of them.

That San Diego appearance went even more successfully than the one in Las Vegas, and Owen began to sound us out about the possibility of our going on a cross-country tour with the two cats. Driving next year's Cougar XR-7, we would visit dealerships, be guests on talk shows, hold press conferences, and eventually wind up at the Detroit Auto Show on November

23. A white Cougar—definitely a white one. We could call it "Chauncey's Cougar Caravan."

Owen had become such a good friend in the last months that we had no hesitation in explaining our financial muddle to him, especially the treadmill impossibility of our ever raising enough money to pay off the bankruptcy claim. Owen brooded over the matter for a while, and then came up with a further suggestion: Lincoln-Mercury would pay us $300 a day while we were on the road, and the car would later be auctioned off in Detroit, the proceeds to be given to Fund for Animals. We could increase the car's collector value—this part is purest Owen—by having movie stars, politicians, athletes, and other celebrities autograph it along the way; and we could make the tour itself a forum for endangered wildlife. "Sure, it's good publicity for everybody, but it'll be fun for Chauncey too. He likes traveling, he loves getting the royal treatment—look, he's been a hard-working professional cat for six years, I think we ought to do something nice for him now." Owen was already working out a rough schedule on the tablecloth.

We knew from the beginning that it wouldn't be any vacation for us: the chaotic month of preparation was exhausting in itself, let alone the fact that we would be hitting some twenty-two cities in thirty-five days, while covering close to seven thousand miles. But apart from our need for money, we were both looking for an excuse to get away for a time from ourselves at the adobe and the continuing question of our partnership. My coming over to work every day wasn't proving to be a satisfactory arrangement, and what was at odds between us where animal handling was concerned had been growing worse since Boris's death. Ted said to leave it for now—"let's talk about all that stuff after the tour's over." I was glad to agree with him.

The tour was to begin on October 12 with three days of personal appearances in Los Angeles. Cleveland Amory, head of Fund for Animals, came out on the eleventh to have photographs taken with us, and to be the first to autograph the white Cougar. Cleveland is a charming, clever, genuinely dedicated man, but he and I favor different ways of promoting conservation of wild animals. Like most of us, he tends to preach to the converted and scream damnation at the rest. I don't think it works—you can't get the average hunter to stop killing animals by calling him a sick, vicious barbarian. I think you have to get him somehow to like or identify with a single deer or bear, or whatever it is that he kills. That may sound crazy and hopeless; but otherwise it's just words, just numbers, like six million Jews and all the starving children in India who'd love to eat your cauliflower. Numbers don't make us care, and neither does hellfire. Individuals sometimes do.

Almost on the eve of our departure, Christopher came down with coccidiosis, which is a disease caused by intestinal parasites. He wouldn't eat, and he kept crying in bewilderment, because he had never felt bad before. I sat up with him all the night before we left for Los Angeles. I thought he was going to die.

The tour officially began at the Ford plant in Anaheim, where Chauncey gave out awards to schoolchildren, and some actors from the show *Emergency* signed the white XR-7. It seemed rather anticlimactic, but it picked up when we went on to the USC–University of Washington football game, and to a hockey game with Owen that evening. I have a great and absurd weakness for games, even when I don't understand them; and I've always really wanted to be a feather-headed, inanely grinning part of the halftime show, as I was with Chauncey. It had never occurred to me that I also dreamed of sitting on the hood of a car with a cougar and Gordie Howe and being pushed out onto an ice rink, but I loved it. I'm very corny.

We spent our last day in Los Angeles running around Universal Studios, getting autographs from Rock Hudson, Elizabeth Montgomery, Lucille Ball, Richard Boone, Robert Young, Julie London, and absolutely anything else on the lot that looked like an actor. They all used colored felt-tip markers to sign with; the autographs were then solemnly sprayed with a fixative that smelled like bananas. In the evening Cleveland Amory was the host at a Universal reception for Chauncey, who stalked among the famous smiles with the benign air of one who knows that he has top billing, script approval, and a stranglehold on the gross receipts. Owen had a toy jungle built for him, complete with waterfall, and Chauncey lay there calmly during the reception, his paws crossed, watching everything. All the cougars I ever knew were fascinated by human behavior; the *conquistadores* called them *"los amigos del Cristiano"* for their harmless curiosity, and shot them. Pacing in and out of countless auto showrooms, blazing television studios, and smoggy city rooms, Chauncey never tired of watching people perform for him.

We set out the next day, with Ted and Chauncey in the station wagon, and Owen, Christopher, and me in the white Cougar. Chrissie was still sick, but his medication seemed to be taking effect, and he was beginning to eat again. The first day was eminently typical of the entire tour: we made appearances at the Lincoln-Mercury dealerships in Oxnard, Ventura, and Santa Barbara, were interviewed on a television program in Santa Maria, arrived in San Francisco around midnight, and were up at five the next morning to do a breakfast show. I learned then that Owen Bombard functions on three hours' sleep, and when you're with him, so do you.

During the whole month of the tour, we averaged two television talk shows before noon every day, and might or might not manage lunch before the newspaper and radio interviews began. At the Lincoln-Mercury dealerships we visited, we continued to blink into cameras and talk about why people need cougars, and why the presence or absence of whales and lion-tailed macaques matters in all our lives. We never used Chauncey to sell cars.

I like to remember a small town called Rock Springs, Wyoming, where we stopped for dinner on our way to Cheyenne. The diner was full of Saturday-night cowboys, and every pickup parked outside had a gun rack mounted across the rear window. Chauncey had a twenty-four-hour guard in every city of the tour; but Rock Springs was an unscheduled stop, and Ted and I took turns running out to the station wagon every few minutes to make sure that everything was all right. Naturally, we attracted more attention this way than we could have gotten with a public-address system and topless dancers. The cowboys began to come out in curiously shy, shuffling groups to look at Chauncey, and to touch him. A few made the obvious jokes, but most just stood staring, asking what we fed him, and if that was really purring he was doing now, like a cat. As many as they must have chased with dogs and shot down from trees, they knew less about cougars than many children who came to our shows. Maybe it helped that some of them learned that evening what a cougar feels like under the hand, alive, looking at you. I choose to think so, this once.

Salt Lake City, Cheyenne, Denver, Wichita. The Ramada Inn in Wichita had a flashing marquee that read WELCOME, CHAUNCEY! and the dealership reception was so mobbed that twice as many security guards had to be sent for. I waded through the crowd in real panic, holding a snarling, hissing Christopher over my head. (He had perked up considerably, enough to begin tearing up our motel room every night.) Chauncey took the confusion completely in his stride, accepting it all as his due. About ten miles before we reached whatever city we were heading for that day, he would leisurely start to groom himself: the matinee idol making up in his dressing room. Owen swore that he could see Chauncey counting the house at each reception.

And so it went—Topeka, St. Louis, Memphis, Nashville (where Chauncey was formally presented with the key to the city). Chattanooga. Atlanta (where Georgia's Governor Jimmy Carter signed the car).

Washington, D.C., was a highlight because of Sue Pressman. Sue is my best friend in the world. She used to be a veterinarian, but as long as I've known her she's been working for the Humane Society of the United States. She is as tough and cynical and determined as a cross between Lucy B. Stone and an African buffalo; and if you are mistreating an animal anywhere on this continent or in Puerto Rico, Sue Pressman will parachute down your chimney on Christmas morning and beat you up. I love her.

By Philadelphia, cigarette smoke, flashbulbs, microphones, handshakes, and winter were catching up with all of us except Chauncey. It was freezing cold as we stood outside our hotel amid a swarm of photographers, waiting for Muhammed Ali and Joe Frazier, who were in town for their second fight. They arrived almost at the same time in black Cadillacs, each accompanied by shoals of beautiful women, all of whom made our presence there rather ironic by wearing enough furs for a small Eskimo village. Of the two, I preferred Frazier, who had a knack for cryptic, caustic one-liners which went right by Ali. Besides, he actually looked at the cougars.

I posed between the two fighters, holding Christopher in my arms. As soon as the cameras began to flash, Ali started throwing punches past my nose at Frazier, which frightened me and had Chrissie furiously poised to take a chunk out of somebody. All the way up in the elevator to the reception, they sparred from corner to corner, with Ali howling, "I'm gonna whup yo' ass, man, *whup* yo' ass, gonna whup yo' ass!" Chauncey ignored them magnificently; but if Chrissie could have gotten loose, George Foreman might still be the heavyweight champion today.

On our first day in New York, we taped two shows in succession at the National Broadcasting Company studio: first *Today,* with Gene Shalit, and then *What's My Line?* The studio employees were so frightened of Chauncey that we had to build a cage around him in the elevator before they would take him

Joe Frazier signed the hood of our Cougar XR-7 during our cross-country tour in 1973 as Muhammed Ali needled him. Right after that they pretended to trade punches over my head, and Christopher, then three months old, got excited and tried to join in.

up. He did have his own dressing room, though, and at the sight of its central feature—an enormous naugahyde-covered couch, his ears went up and his tail began to twitch without any prompting from me. Chauncey's weakness was always leather.

He stalked that couch every time we took our eyes off him even for a moment. We would slam our hands down on the cushions just before he attacked, saying loudly, *"No,* Chauncey!" and he would retreat in a dignified manner and lie down again. But Ted and I were in and out of the dressing room all morning, taping the two shows in rather disjointed segments; and at the end of *What's My Line?* we had to leave both cougars with Nick Busch, a Lincoln-Mercury employee, and go back onstage to shake hands with everybody. I instructed Nick that Chauncey was not to eat the couch, or my leather purse, or my favorite leather coat. Nick nodded confidently. He had become greatly fond of Chauncey on the tour, and was proud that they were friends.

When we returned with Owen after the show, we met a white, trembling Nick in the hall, leaning against the dressing-room door, his eyes closed and his hands behind him gripping the knob. We cried in unison, "Nick, my God, what *happened?*" and he stepped silently aside and let us open the door. It was like a scene out of another Dracula movie, with Chauncey just about to sink his fangs into the quivering, pulsating, helpless couch, and us bursting in just in time. He looked so disappointed that I found myself wishing that we had arrived a few minutes later—maybe just in time to save my coat. Chauncey deserved a weakness, like everyone else.

"You know, it's funny," Nick said to us afterward. "I've traveled with Chauncey, I've stayed in the car with him, I've run crazy errands for him in the middle of the night, and for a P.R. flack I really do know this one particular cougar pretty well. Those big eyes of his, and the way he talks all the time. I just know who he is, you know? He made a couple of passes at the couch after you left, and I did that thing—*slam,* cool it, Chauncey. Chauncey's cool, I'm cool. Old Nick, the lion tamer. I was all set to retire you guys and take the show over myself. Right—suddenly here comes Chauncey one more time, and this time I swear there's a whole different look in his eyes. He's smiling at me, and he's saying, *You know something, Nick? You're not Ted, and you're not Pat, and the more I look at you, the more you just look like poor old Nick Busch, who used to play football.* So I slam the couch, I yell at him—back, back, you devil! Chauncey just keeps coming along, smiling at me. My whole life passes before my eyes. I say in a loud, firm voice, 'Okay, Chauncey, I tell you what—you can have the couch, and you can have Pat's coat and her purse, and I'll even throw in your leash, how about that?' And then I went outside very fast, to get some air, and I don't want to be a lion tamer anymore. Not even for Chauncey."

We had Saturday off, so Ted drove up to Auburn, New York, to visit his parents. I stayed in the motel, having decided to

Jimmy Stewart's wife, Gloria, got the big treatment from Christopher at a wildlife conference in Washington.

spend my free time writing postcards and reading. That afternoon, Owen arrived unexpectedly, while I was in the shower. "Pat, dear," he said, when I finally opened the door, "I hate to spoil your holiday, but I just had a million-dollar idea. Let's take the boys and have our own little parade down Broadway. Everybody's doing matinees today—Debbie Reynolds, Carol Channing, Zero Mostel, Christopher Plummer. We'll catch them all at intermission and get so many signatures the car'll count like a petition. And I'll take you to the Tavern-on-the-Green afterward."

So we drove into New York, where Owen's million-dollar idea worked perfectly: almost every actor on Broadway came out to autograph the white Cougar, and we stopped traffic, and I caught cold. I was sniffling and wheezing all through the appearances in Pittsburgh, Cleveland, Chicago, and the last one in Detroit. It was definitely time to stop talking and go home.

And yet, as draining and noisy and occasionally silly as the journey had been, I liked it all. It was theater; it was as close as I had come in more than ten years to the old days of touring with a nightclub act. We had made some dent at least in the bankruptcy debt, and we had talked about the rights of the wild unhuman before larger audiences than we could ever have reached in any other way. And I was with Chauncey every day for all that month, and saw how a king carries himself in a world that will never quite measure up to his standards of behavior. I will always be grateful that we had that time together.

In Detroit there were great welcomes for Chauncey at both the Ford Motor Company and Lincoln-Mercury headquarters. Bill Benton, the general manager of Lincoln-Mercury, presented him with a scroll at the latter reception. Bill is a tall, attractive man with an air of authority which Chauncey seemed to recognize as something special. Bill was a friend of Chauncey's from some years before, when he had insisted on being allowed to lead him into a press conference by himself. Chauncey had balked at the lights and the applause before he was quite onstage, leaving Bill standing alone in front of the reporters, holding onto a leash that seemingly ran off by itself into the wings. Bill seemingly gave the leash a strong tug and roared, "Ah, come on, Chaunce, don't be dumb!" The *lèse-majesté* of it all so astounded Chauncey that he followed Bill on without another moment's hesitation. Bill had faked him out, as Chauncey was later to fake Nick out over that naugahyde couch at the NBC studios. That's how it's done.

This time, Bill came hurrying up as Chauncey reclined on a table at the reception. He shoved the scroll under his arm and grabbed both of Chauncey's front paws in his own, greeting him exuberantly, "Chaunce, old boy, great to see you! How've you been, you old scoundrel?"

Nobody touched Chauncey's paws, not ever. It was the one liberty that ever angered him, and even at his most affectionate, neither Ted nor I dared to trespass on that special frontier of his dignity. And here was Bill Benton squeezing and shaking his paws and saying, "Looking good, you old rascal, looking good!"

Oh, marvelous—seven thousand miles to have him bite the head off the general manager of Lincoln-Mercury. Talk about a wow finish.

But Chauncey only blinked at Bill, studied him calmly for a moment, and then began to purr. *Oh, it's you,* he said. Whatever he recognized in Bill, he never acknowledged it in any other of the numberless, scurrying human beings who bent down to yell and grope at him and breathe smoke in his face. *As long as it's you,* he said.

Dear Chauncey, I still wish I had let you eat that stupid couch.

17

In looking back, I'm struck once again by the almost metronomic alternation of good times and hard in our years with the animals. It feels to me now as though some kind of divine justice said to us long ago, whether we listened or not, "If you are going to keep wild creatures, then you must live exactly as they live." And so we have, really, for their natural lives are also bounded by greenness, when the rains come, and the cubs, and there is game for the predators, grass for the browsers, berries on bushes for the bears; and the silent brown days when things die. Aesop's grasshopper aside, wild animals know when winter's coming, and spring too, but both times always take them by surprise anyway. We lived to that rhythm too, always —green and brown, savor and survive.

The white Cougar was sold at the Detroit Auto Show to a collector named Floyd Moore. I think he bid about $6000, however much that works out to per autograph. The success of the tour had made Lincoln-Mercury extremely aware of the cougars' drawing power; from that point on, personal appearances became our primary source of income, as they still are. Almost as soon as we got home, late in November, we began going out again, mainly to dealerships in the Midwestern states, places like Cedar Rapids, Iowa. Chauncey drew ten thousand people into the Lincoln-Mercury showroom in Cedar Rapids. Customers who couldn't find anyplace to park their cars walked miles through the snow to see him. The dealership shows took us up to Christmas, feeding the animals well and keeping me too busy to think much beyond dinner and the alarm clock. But with the holidays came word that my mother was ill with cancer, and failing rapidly. I called her at the old house in Sussex. I said, "I'll be there in three days. We'll have Christmas Day together, and New Year's Eve."

The voice was the same, running water in sunlight. Only her breath had changed. "No," my mother said. "Don't come. I don't want you to come. I don't want you to remember me the way I am now. You used to think I was so pretty. Don't come home, Patricia, please."

"But I can take care of you," I said. "I'm a good nurse now, I know how to take care of tigers, gorillas, mothers, anything. Why can't I just come and be with you?"

My mother was silent for a long time. "I'm tired," she said at last. "It's been twenty years without your father, and I think that's fair enough. It's all right, Patricia. People bother me now, but I love you. Don't worry about me at all."

Flag Is Up had been sold while Ted and I were on tour, and I moved into another ranch house near Buellton. I had two lion cubs, Hannibal and Percival, with me; and I also had Christopher Two, who was three weeks old—our original Chrissie having grown too big to continue posing as "the little Cougar in every Comet." Just after Christmas, Murgatroyd got his big show-business break in the pilot film of a program called *Sierra,* which was about park rangers in Yosemite. We were booked for more auto shows at the time, so we hired Mike Pachica, our falconer friend from the animal park, and Billy Torgeson, who had worked for us at the San Diego Zoo, to go on location with Murgatroyd. He played the part of a quirky, cranky, destructive giant named Old Cruncher. Murgie was always an amiable bear himself, but the rest of it was type-casting.

One scene required him to rip up a Volkswagen sedan. Billy and Mike set the stage by loading the car with chicken necks; they shoved them into the glove compartment, under the seat cushions, the floorboards, and everywhere else but the brake linings. Murgatroyd toppled the car over and plucked doors and fenders off it as though he were defoliating an artichoke. He had truly found his calling.

Shortly afterward, Owen Bombard called with an offer for me to take Christopher Two to St. Petersburg, Florida, to make a promotional appearance for the Lincoln-Mercury dealer there. I arrived in St. Petersburg when the fuel crisis of early 1974 was at its peak, far worse than I had ever seen it in California. The lines at gas stations were three and four hours long, and there was an air of panic and murder that almost condensed on your skin. The dealer had provided me with a new Comet to get back and forth from my hotel on Treasure Island, but he apologetically left me on my own as far as gasoline was concerned. On my second morning in town, I joined the shortest gas line I could find, which was just beginning its second loop around the block. We had been inching along for an hour or so when I halted momentarily to let a van cross through the line to the street. Then I shot straight ahead before anyone could cut in front of me. I was wearing platform wedgies, and one of them slipped off and caught under the accelerator, jamming it down. Briefly, I hit a Corvette, which plowed on into a Porsche and disintegrated; beyond that, the falling dominoes become a little vague.

No one was hurt, but I had to wait with my victims until a policeman arrived, as Florida law requires. He checked first on the passengers in the other cars, and then came over to ask if there had been anyone with me. I was standing by the ruins of the Corvette, staring at it in hazy fascination.

"Oh, no," I assured him, "there was just me and the—oh, my gosh, the cougar!" I had completely forgotten about Christopher Two in the back seat.

"Cougar, right," the policeman said, making a note of it. "What *cougar?*"

Christopher's transfer cage had tipped over, and he was on the floor, unhurt but furious, baring his milk teeth and making noises like a Disposall. The policeman gaped, started to open the car door, changed his mind, turned and bellowed to half St. Petersburg, "Good Gawd, they really *is* a little cougar in that Comet!" Everyone looked around for the cameras, and the man in the Porsche asked me, "What do you do, ma'am— travel around for Lincoln-Mercury and wreck cars so you can run a commercial?" He was quite serious about it, and rather respectful.

After two days, I went on to the Chicago Auto Show. Ted

I raised Christopher, at left, with two lion cubs, Percival and Hannibal. For the first year of his life, poor Chrissie thought he was a lion.

met me there with Chauncey; but for once it was Christopher Two who stole the show, running back and forth on the car tops and playing with Chauncey's tail. Chauncey would snarl at him indignantly, and Christopher would back off for an instant and then pounce at the lashing tail again. He was obviously having a marvelous time, and yet I had begun to worry that something was seriously wrong with him. He often cried out when I picked him up, or even when I played gently with him, stroking his back and stomach. Two Chicago veterinarians assured me that he was in great shape.

I flew back to Los Angeles for a few days on business, while Ted made a couple of dealership appearances with the two cougars. During the loading process at O'Hare Airport, both of their crates were dropped; and I returned to find Chauncey with a cut on his face and Christopher Two outwardly unmarked, but now in constant, terrible pain. He screamed hideously every waking moment, whether handled or left alone, and could sleep only under heavy sedation. The local vets could still find nothing the matter, so I took him back to California with me to see Dr. Larson. The only available flight would arrive after 1:00 A.M., but Christopher couldn't wait until morning.

All I could think of in my own sleeplessness was renal rickets and an intestinal stoppage, especially since Christopher hadn't moved his bowels for three days. Before boarding the plane, I telephoned Cheryl Baca and left a message with her answering service, asking the Bacas to get together all the equipment needed for an enema and meet me at the airport. The answering service transcended itself on that one, garbling the message so that it came out: "Take an enema and wait until I call." Ted and Cheryl are loyal friends, but they fulfilled only half of that request.

At two-thirty in the morning we were in an all-night drugstore, where the clerks speculated almost audibly on what possible perversion could involve one man, two women and all *that*

In the "Sierra" TV series, Murgatroyd played a bear who tore up everything. It was type-casting.

stuff. They might have been even more bewildered to see us an hour later, dancing wildly around the Bacas' bathtub, where Christopher Two had at last produced a two-foot-long stool. Cheryl said, "I never knew the true romance of the wild until now."

The bowel movement did relieve some of Christopher's immediate pain, but it had no effect on the basic cause. Dr. Larson's examination revealed the same inbred weakness that had kept Chauncey half-paralyzed for the first year of his life. Sue Pressman calls it "Saran-Wrap bones." I will never know how long Christopher had been breaking his bones and half-healing without my becoming aware of it; but the accident in Chicago had fractured both his back and his pelvis. Dr. Larson inserted fourteen steel pins in Christopher's hind legs and said, "I don't know. Take him home and keep him quiet. I don't know, Pat."

That effectively ended my traveling for the next few months. Ted did the dealer shows with Chauncey, and I sat home watching late movies on television most of the night, with Christopher Two asleep in my lap, sucking on my thumb. Today, at a hundred and fifty pounds, he has Chauncey's walk and Chauncey's look, and it seems appropriate that he should have succeeded Chauncey on the Lincoln-Mercury sign. But he still sucks my thumb, with a fierce concentration that closes out the universe and says, *I'm just a baby, and you still love me.*

Sierra became a regular series, giving Murgatroyd a steady job in Yosemite and Ted and me our first weekly source of income in a good while. Once it became obvious that Christopher was going to live, that was one of the nice green times.

In May the World's Fair opened in Spokane, Washington, and Lincoln-Mercury decided to send us to the opening to draw attention to their exhibit. Ted drove up with Chauncey, but I took Christopher Two on the plane. I didn't want him tossed into any baggage compartment ever again, so I asked if I could purchase an extra seat for his carrying cage, as I used to do for my bass fiddle long ago. Several shocked clerks informed me that this was against all Federal regulations, as well as being unconstitutional, and we finally compromised on my putting Christopher in a much smaller carrier, which would fit under my seat. Christopher didn't like that at all, and neither did I, but it was the best we could do.

The real trouble began over my own seating, rather than Christopher's. We were flying first-class, and I had asked to be placed in the No Smoking section, with a seat on the aisle, because of my claustrophobia. When I got on the plane with Christopher Two, the stewardess showed me to a window in the Smoking section. I called her back, saying, "I think there must be some mistake. This isn't the seat I purchased."

"I know," she said in candid embarrassment. "I'm afraid you've been bumped out of your seat so we could get the computer on the plane." I began to make Christopher noises. "Well, there's a man taking this big computer to the World's Fair, and your seat was the only one where they could strap it in adequately, I guess. I'm really sorry about it."

I went into orbit. It was a classic, certified old-time, doubtless inexcusable Pat Derby explosion, the gist of which was that giving up my place to a human being was one thing, but no computer was about to grab an inch of my space in the world. The whole first-class section was staring at me as I trumpeted, "The day computers take over from people is the day I leave! I'll go to Mars, I'll get in a cage with my animals, I'll just *leave!"*

The stewardess, as it happens, was totally on my side. She called in a public-relations man from the airline, and he and I went at it, him conciliatory and me in full cry. Eventually the pilot came back to see why the takeoff was being delayed. Along with the public-relations man, he reminded me that the other passenger had, after all, purchased a seat for the computer. It was the one point that could possibly have made me angrier than I already was. 'You sold space to this man for a contraption which is just as dangerous if it falls off the seat as my carrier would have been. Then you turn around and force me to cram this animal with a broken back into a cramped little shoebox, even though I was willing to buy a place for him. This cougar is a living creature, with feelings—that computer is a machine, and *I hate computers!"* I lost a few potential allies with that last outburst. Blasphemy is still possible, even in this secular age.

"This plane flies by computers!" the pilot shouted back at me. "For your information, in ten years, fifteen years, the whole world is going to be run by a computer, what do you think about that?" I told him what I thought about it, and we went at each other with the cabin increasingly in an uproar, divided between the pilot's supporters, mine, and those passengers who, like the public-relations man, just wanted to get the plane off the ground. But the pilot was like me: a fanatic heart, a person of principle. We understood each other very well.

"I suppose you feel that computers will someday replace people," I challenged him, and he replied, "They're already

doing it! And I'll tell you something else, let me ask you something else—what *good* are cougars, anyway? What good are
animals?"

That did stop me for a moment, although the question had
really been being asked of me all my life, in one way and another, beginning with Uncle Nigel. I said, "What good are trees
and grass?"

"They're *no* good! The only things on this earth that make
any sense are mechanized objects that serve humanity." We
went on and on like that, delaying the flight for at least an hour,
until at last a businessman who had the seat directly behind
the computer stood up and said, "Madam, I will take your
seat, and you and your tiger can have mine. Let's just get on
our way and get to Washington." He was so courteous about
it that I was glad to agree. The pilot stamped back to the cockpit, and the plane grumbled into the air.

When we stopped briefly in Seattle, I got the stewardess to
heat a bottle of milk for Christopher Two. She had asked if
she could see him during the flight, and had immediately fallen
in love with him. I had him on my lap, drowsily pawing at the
bottle, when the pilot came out of the cockpit again. He took
one look at Christopher and said, "Okay. Right. You get
that cat right back in his cage."

I was trying not to make any more trouble for anyone. I said,
"Why? As long as we're on the ground—"

"Listen," he said grimly, "it was only out of the goodness
of my heart that you were allowed to keep this animal on the
plane. You get him back in his cage, or I swear I'll throw him
off myself." But he had overdone it: the stewardess was in open
mutiny now, and six or seven passengers rose angrily to Christopher's defense. He glowered and stalked off, while I continued
to feed Christopher until he fell asleep, snoring milkily.

But he couldn't let bad enough alone. Halfway to Spokane,
I looked up to see him standing in the aisle, demanding, "What

do you think about those grizzly bears that just killed those two people up in Yellowstone?"

"It's the first time since 1901 that grizzlies have hurt anybody," I answered. "The records of people being killed by wild animals—and especially grizzlies—are so minute that we hardly bother to keep statistics. But machines are killing people all over the world, every day, hundreds of them every second. Nobody ever says they ought to hunt down the machines and wipe them out."

"That's different. You can't argue—that's entirely different!"

"No, it isn't!" I was on my feet, restraint and maturity vanished over the windmill. "They're going to go in there now and start shooting every bear they see, because of what happened. But that country belongs to the bears, and people can't go blundering in there, feeding them and taking pictures and just racketing around, and not expect to be hurt." I was almost crying, but the words were coming too fast. "People have no right to trample all over the earth, leaving no place at all for grizzly bears to live alone. Man has no right to believe that everything is here for *him!*" Christopher Two woke up under the seat and yelled for my thumb.

"Well, I hope they kill all the grizzly bears," the pilot said. He waited for my reaction, but suddenly it was impossible for me to talk anymore, or even to be angry with him. I sat down and looked away from him. "They will," I said.

When I returned from Spokane, an offer was waiting from the Cincinnati Zoo to do shows through the Fourth of July weekend. I jumped at the chance, because the Cincinnati Zoo is one of the good, restoring places for me. It's smaller than the San Diego Zoo, and somehow a bit warmer and more intimate. The director, Ed Maruska, has the highest rate of breeding gorillas of any zoo in the world, and the first white tiger cubs ever born in captivity. And very pink cheeks.

I had been corresponding for years with Anne Southcomb, the baby-animal nurse at the Cincinnati Zoo. When I was there, she was raising a tiny gorilla who had been rejected by his mother. I never saw him detached from Annie's shoulder: he was like a furry, silent, wide-eyed growth, unquestionably benign, but not removable except by major surgery. He must weigh at least two hundred pounds by now, and I'm certain that Annie is still wearing him. Another of her charges was a week-old pygmy hippopotamus named Libby, who weighed three pounds and looked exactly like a pink china piggy-bank. Libby loved to sit on laps—as far as she knew, that was the natural habitat of the pygmy hippopotamus. I wonder about her, too.

The animal nursery was backed onto the amphitheatre where we gave our shows, and I used to walk through it to get to the dressing room. A big silver-backed male gorilla became fascinated by my red hair, and it was part of our daily routine for him to play with it, turning the strands between his fingers with the same immense carefulness with which Shamba had always touched me. And there was an ancient orangutan named Sam, who asked very little of life except to have his hand held. When orangs are content, they make a deep, dreamy humming sound, something like a spinning wheel. I used to sit for a long time holding Sam's hand, feeling his pure happiness moving through me, and not thinking at all.

When I returned to California, Ted and I continued to work together, beginning a new series of shows at the San Diego Zoo, and a new Cougar commercial with Chauncey. The new model in the Cougar commercials was a lovely woman named Farrah Fawcett. She is the wife of the actor Lee Majors; and by a curious coincidence, we were hired at that time to work on an episode of his *Six-Million-Dollar Man* show. It was shot on location in Kanab, Utah, and had something to do with the last cougar in the area. We took Chauncey and three other cougars, but most of the action scenes were done by Christophe One, now half-grown, big for his age, and extremely active. The show needed a lot of shots of the cougar running, and we used to get Chrissie started by letting him chase Ted. One afternoon he caught him. This excited him so much that he began jumping all over Ted, not meaning to hurt him, but hurting him. A fang caught Ted's upflung arm and laid it open. Ted's nephew Ricky, who occasionally worked with us, had Chrissie on a pickup rope but still couldn't get him off Ted. I ran over to help Ricky, and as I pushed Chrissie away his head came up and smashed me in the nose, breaking it for a second time. It didn't hurt as much as the other time had. I made fighter jokes with the crew, and forgot about it.

But shortly afterward, when Ted and I came back from Utah, I passed out at the wheel of my car and wrecked it totally. The blackout spells and headaches that followed finally brought me to a doctor, where I learned that the scar tissue from the first injury had developed into a fibroid tumor in my brain. There would have to be surgery.

I'm afraid of hospitals, and of being ill. I put the whole matter as far away from me as I could, and immersed myself in a new job: a movie for television called *The Runaways*. It was about a boy who runs off from an orphanage and a series of foster homes, and befriends a leopard who has escaped from a wild-animal park in a thunderstorm. Ted was doing some extra work on the *Six-Million-Dollar Man* when shooting began, so it fell to me to report by myself to the location, which was a farm near Solvang. We had no other grown leopards besides Spot—Lucifer and Lucrezia were cubs then—so I brought Clyde along as well, to serve as a double.

On an impulse, knowing that I was certainly going to need help, I rounded up ten or twelve young girls, all students from a school that Ted and I had recently instituted for people who wanted to learn our techniques of working with animals. They were very sweet, and completely green, and we must have looked like the Trojan Women when we arrived with the two cats. There were at least a hundred raucous, hard-nosed film people waiting for us, and the most prominent among them was Faye, the trainer from Animals, Inc., who used to club the bears to make them work. Seeing her there, leaning up against her big car with its battery of airhorns, guffawing with the electricians and the grips, immediately threw me back to my beginnings in hopeless ignorance and terror, and the fallow deer fawns dying as I held them. Everything I had so painfully learned and become in ten years suddenly seemed a watery sentimental daydream. The reality was still Faye, wearing her necklace of bear claws.

Before we began shooting I called the company together and told them all I could about what leopards are. I warned them in particular to let me know before they made any noise shifting equipment or moving vehicles; and I added, "I'm sure you're laughing because we're a group of ladies here—but I would advise you, if you have any fears while the cats are loose, to get behind the nearest lady you can find. One other thing about leopards is that they seem to like women a lot better than they like men." Everyone laughed some more.

For the first shot, the director wanted the leopard to come down a hill and stalk in among a field of horses. (There just aren't that many original scenes in animal films, let alone scripts.) We used Clyde for that one, because Clyde always came when you called him. The society of horses bored him, however, and it showed; so for the close shots in the field we went to Spot, who enjoyed horses very much indeed. We worked like that all morning, alternating between Clyde's dramatic deliberateness and Spot's furious activity, and when we broke for lunch the attitude of the whole crew had changed completely. Now I was Sheena, Queen of the Jungle, because a jaguar would come to my call; and they were also very respectful of the girls. Considering how many of them had taken my advice about stepping behind a lady whenever one of the cats even glanced at them, I don't see what else they could have been.

The director took me aside before we left to consult with me about the next day's central shot: the leopard escaping from a house by crashing out through a window. "We're using the regular candy-glass, of course, but I'd just like to know how you're planning to spook him through. So nobody gets hurt, I mean."

"I don't spook my animals," I said. "Look, Spot is like this. If he's in his cage and there's a sudden noise, he'll go straight up in the air and bounce around the cage four or five times. Then he'll sit down and look straight at you, as though he's saying proudly, *My God, was I ever frightened—did you see how upset I got?* Leopards enjoy doing that, it's a kind of a game. We'll have to build a solid box, like a cage, framing the entire window—about five feet by six feet, with a couple of little holes in the bottom. When I put Spot in the box, you get your cameras ready, because I'm only going to do this for you one time. I'll stick the compressed-air thing from a CO_2 gun into one of the holes under Spot, so that he'll hear a funny soft hiss like air escaping from a tire. He'll zip around that cage and fly right through the window. One time."

The director couldn't keep from asking, "What if something happens and we blow it? Why can you only do it once?"

"Because the first time it's a surprise and a game," I said. "The second time, he'll know it's me doing it, and he'll think he's being punished for something. I won't do that to him."

Ted arrived the next morning, took one look at my window-box and roared, "Man, what are you doing? That gimmick's never going to work—I never saw anything that crazy!" The director looked from one to the other of us, saying dubiously, "Well, I don't know, Pat *said* it'd work . . ." Ted stormed over to me, and we had it out in front of anyone who cared to catch the show. I was nervous and equivocal, already more than

Spot jumping through the candy-glass window. It showed that an "impossible" shot can be achieved without abusing an animal if you think it out and have the full cooperation of the studio. (Photo by Santa Ynez Valley News)

half-wishing that I had asked his advice and shared the responsibility for setting up a shot this risky. But I held my ground, because I heard Faye laughing.

It went beautifully. Spot came sailing through that peanut-brittle window like a dolphin breaking water, landed soundlessly, ran off a little way, and then turned to say to me, *Wow, talk about* scary! *Did you see me?* And I ran up to him then and loved and comforted him for a long time, crooning baby-talk reassurances that were meant for both of us, and nobody laughed, not Faye, not anybody.

It's strange. Millions of people who never knew him will remember him as the cougar who lay on top of a billboard and snarled into the camera. In fact, he hated heights, and his snarl was a game he had played all his life, with no more ferocity to it than a baby's gurgle. He never could make it sound menacing, and they had to dub in Diablo's old fury every time.

Chauncey died on Tuesday, August 19, 1975. He was nine years old, which is the prime of life for a cougar; but in his last months the paralysis of his cubhood returned, coupled with an inner-ear infection which in time destroyed his sense of balance. Almost to the end, I still clung to some tatter of hope, because he himself never gave up even for a moment. Every morning, while he could stand at all, he'd come tottering and careening out of his cage in the garage, as excited and eager as a kitten to get to the little turfed yard and his beloved tree, his sunlight, his nesting birds in the flowerpots, his wind over the valley. He seemed to understand how important it was for him to exercise: I came outside constantly to check up on him, and often found him plodding around and around that patch of grass, his head swaying like an old horse's head; endlessly falling over, but never complaining, and always, always getting up as quickly as he could. *Keep moving, keep moving. It can't catch you if you just keep getting up and going along in the grass.* He knew.

Every day came to revolve around him for me. It was almost funny, in a sense: rather like living with an aged parent, or grandparent, who must be forever babied into taking his nap, taking his pills, going outside with a little radio to sit in the sun. In another way it was horrible, as that other is, because it's the end of dignity and independence, the end of being a man or a woman, or a cougar. I couldn't bear to watch Chauncey flopping around the yard, to see that soul patiently dragging a dead body after it like a grinning trap. I didn't want him to see me looking when he fell down and got up and toppled over again, or to know that I heard him grumbling quietly to himself sometimes because he couldn't make his legs work right. But I did watch, and he would look up into my eyes—his eyes were always the first pale, hesitant green of fuzzy spring—and come reeling toward me, purring and purring, to have me scratch the old best place, under his chin, and say his name.

Finally he could hardly move, and I fed him by hand and spent the better part of an hour each time manhandling his two hundred pounds of helpless weight out to the yard and back again. I think there was some brain damage from the infection. But nothing that was truly Chauncey was ever damaged or defaced: to the last, the same green spirit looked out of him at me, proud and wise and untouched by human silliness, except where he chose to let it touch him. I saw him looking at death in the same way, as at one more tailless, furless inferior being, to be treated with kindness and courtesy, like all the poor others who did their best and couldn't help not being cougars.

How can there not be Chauncey? I can make myself understand everything else, except that part.

18

Brown and green and brown again. In October I was operated on to remove the brain tumor. I was in a coma for four days, and at one point my heart stopped. I wonder if it was then that I found myself out of myself, watching from somewhere beyond *up* or *down* as figures bustled and clucked around something on a table. I knew that they thought it was me.

It took me a long time to come back. Weeks later, everything still seemed to be happening at the other end of a long, echoing tunnel, and I couldn't make anything matter. A friend who had been through the same experience warned me with great earnestness, "It's very dangerous to be where you are now. Some people just get stuck out there. Think about something important, something you love, make yourself be thinking about it all the time. I mean it, Pat. Otherwise it's—I don't know—it's such a *temptation*. Think about something really important."

It had to be Neena. I had gone under the anesthetic talking about her, mumbling worriedly about a cracked toenail on her left hind foot. I kept concentrating on her smell, on her pink mouth and the wet black tip of her trunk, and the place between her forelegs where I fit. My friend was right—whatever

Rocky the bobcat, symbol of still another car. The day this picture was taken, I had just come out of the hospital after surgery to remove a brain tumor. Rocky spooked Chauncey and I had to go chase him.

that other place truly was, it was the deepest temptation I have ever known. But Neena is still my home. When I returned from the hospital, she came to me and held me in her trunk more gently than she ever had, as though she feared that I might break and vanish. Tears began to roll out of her eyes.

Sierra had been canceled before I went into the hospital, but we still seemed to be doing well enough financially, in spite of the deepening national recession. I had been home for one day when Lincoln-Mercury called, saying that they wanted to take some still photographs of Chauncey and Christopher Two with Rocky, the bobcat who was the symbol of their newest car. I weighed less than ninety pounds and tottered even when I was lying down, but I went out to the ranch and worked Rocky with the cougars. He and Christopher played together like kittens; but Chauncey's sheer size was too much for him, and Rocky attacked him, which is what the smaller cats do when panicked. Poor Chauncey turned and fled, and I went reeling after him, while Jean Johnson ran after me, certain that I was going to collapse and die before her eyes. We all rescued each other, and somehow we did get the stills of Chauncey and Rocky together. Then Jean took me home and put me to bed.

That job, such as it was, was virtually the last one that came in for the next several months. Lincoln-Mercury's sales were down, like everyone else's, and they were cutting back sharply on their publicity expenditures. All the zoos were suddenly in deep trouble, and the television programs that had employed us regularly in the past were all off the air. Our savings from the period when we seemed to be working every day vanished almost to the last dime when we paid off the bankruptcy claim. With that settled, Vince Evans promptly hit us with a foreclosure and a demand for us to vacate the adobe property by the end of December. I never blamed him for doing it—he'd been unable to use the land for two years—but the action left us back in our classic situation: no money, no hope of money, and nowhere to keep the animals. Winter comes that fast sometimes.

Ted and I had been talking for some months—especially since my operation—about separating professionally as well as personally. We still worked well together on routine matters like the Cougar commercials; but the old sore points, like declawing and hot-shots and CO_2 guns, were still sore, and our attitudes toward the whole question of working the animals had become entirely opposed. Ted enjoyed studio work as an end in itself, while I was finding it harder and harder to justify renting the animals out at all, and to go on with the old juggle of catering to directors' whims while trying to protect the animals at the same time. Wherever I had been for those four days, I had returned with some new understanding about time and hard choices. We decided that we would each find a piece of land to build on, and divide the animals between us.

I suppose we managed it as well as possible, and better than most divorced couples with children, but it was horrible, and the beginning of a worse horror. I'll try to talk about it as though we were just splitting up the books and records. There was no question about my taking Neena, any more than there was of Ted keeping Joe, who loved him, and Sebastian, the young Siberian tiger, who was much better than Rijo now for studio work. Rijo has grown progressively centered around me through the years, and had even become occasionally agressive towards Ted. I kept him, and I took Spot, who has always been my cat; Ted got Clyde, which was fair, but rough on me, and Sydney—she was originally my Christmas present, but Ted was hers. In the same manner, I eventually got to keep Chauncey, though Ted took him first. We did try to follow the animals' preferences.

I took the two grizzlies, both Christophers, Sweet William, and Sylvester. Ted got Tawnee and Clover, our breeding pair of cougars, Murgatroyd and his sister Daisy, Bud, Humphrey the Malayan bear, a young wolf named Rhoda. *Lucifer and Lucrezia to me, Hannibal and Percival to Ted, I want Clancy and Mildred* . . . Reciting it like this doesn't tell you what it was like. I don't want to.

That wasn't all of them, of course. There were so many—wolves, lions, bears, foxes, coyotes, deer, llamas, owls, hawks, a wild boar—and each one had a name. Our orphans of the wild. We had been blind and insanely self-indulgent ever to acquire so many; even working full-time on every front, it had gradually become all but impossible to care for them properly, and we were not working anywhere now. It wasn't that I had ceased to believe in the miracles—the green times—that had rescued and sustained us for so long. It was rather that even miracles weren't enough anymore.

We began trying to find homes for as many of the animals as we could. I called zoos and reputable parks all over the world, and most of them had the same answer for us: *We'd love to take them, but we can't—there's no money*. We did place a few animals that way, but we were luckier with individual volunteers. The Johnsons took Simon the chimp. Sam, our aging, near-blind bobcat, went to a lovely couple in Santa Barbara, who built him a one-acre run where he's living out his last days in utter contentment. We gave Horace, a little fox with brain damage, to one of the students from our school, who has spoiled him as rotten as Horace always deserved to be spoiled. There were times that winter when I clung desperately to the knowledge of Horace's happiness and safety.

Of course, it was the smaller animals for whom we were most successful in finding homes. Who would be wealthy enough, crazy enough, to take a lion, a cougar, a grizzly? Oh, there are people. I gave several of the big cats to various Hollywood couples whom I knew at the time only wanted them for the kicks and status that their possession conveyed. I don't have any excuse for this. I was growing frantic with the fear of having to put the surplus animals to sleep, and at that point I would probably have rationalized giving them to Lester, the trainer who had hurt Taj's ears. Yet I knew then, as I had known since Banté, that it's only people who choose life at any price. Animals aren't like that. It is harder for me to live with the memory of that time than with what finally happened to the ones I couldn't give away.

Pete Batten came out to administer the lethal injections. It rained all day.

There's no choice, we have no choice. I can't feed Neena if I don't put the lions down. I hid in the adobe or wandered miserably back and forth in the rain, telling myself that Candy was getting old, that Lucky was definitely beginning to suffer from his chronic renal rickets condition. *It's a kindness to Phyllis, you know that. She sits all day tossing her head that way she does now, wanting out, out of here. What the hell did you ever expect, keeping a Kodiak bear in a cage?* If I was going to be supporting a tiger, I couldn't have more than the two grizzlies—*that means Sophia has to go. It's better than auctioning them, it's better than screaming maniacs dragging them away. I know that. I'm responsible.*

But the wolves. Oh, God, the wolves. They lay out there, shrunken, rumpled heaps under the rain, and even though I knew it didn't matter to them now, I couldn't bear to see them without shelter. Pete Batten walked past me, going back for another syringe, and he was crying. I didn't cry—Pete had the right, and I had none—but I wished with all my heart that I had never come back from wherever I went, those four days in the hospital.

Then Jean Johnson came running down the hill, calling to me. "Pat—Pat, you better come quick, Sheba's having her babies!"

It would be Sheba. The dumbest wolf in the whole world. She always managed to have her cubs in the rainy season, and she always drowned them. Not intentionally—it was just that she was too dense ever to give birth in a den box, or anywhere else but in a shallow hole scratched in the mud of her run with her front paws. It would fill up with rain as she lay there, and we'd find her in the morning, curled confidently around her dead babies. Oh, it had to be Sheba. Who else could it possibly have been, on this day?

It took three men, fending her off with a table, to hold Sheba away while I picked up the eight soaked cubs, backed out of the enclosure, and ran down to the adobe. I dried them, put them on heating pads to get warm, fixed beds for them; and all that time I kept thinking, *Saticoy, it's Saticoy and the meat-packing house all over again. Spend the whole day killing animals because you can't feed them, and here you are with your arms full of wolves one more time. Their mother would have saved you and them so much pain if you'd just arrived a few minutes later.* I was crying now, breaking in pieces, but I was already finding names for them.

With Neena—the best place in the world for me.

I kept two of the wolf cubs, and Cheryl Baca ran herself to exhaustion finding good homes for the other six. My two are named Jennifer and Jeremiah. Jeremiah has a slight harelip, which somehow makes his face occasionally look achingly human, as a bat's face can look. Jennifer is black, and her face seems almost concave, like the face of an Abrabian horse. She is shy, and she always waits for Jeremiah to tell her that it's all right before coming out of the den box to sniff at new hands.

Ted kept his animals in a barn near Buellton for a time, and currently lives in Tehachapi. We're friends; we still do the Cougar commercials and the auto shows together. When I could find nowhere to move by the end of December, the Johnsons—to whom so much of this book belongs—offered me the use of their five-acre ranch. The animals are still there at this writing. It isn't what I want for them permanently, but there are hills to go walking in, and it will do until I can buy some land of my own.

I don't intend to acquire any more animals. The ones I have now need me, not just as a source of food, but as mother, mate, companion, pack, or possession. Rijo would die without me. That's not said proudly, but in sorrow and some shame. I wish I could give them something more than myself.

If I've tried to do one thing in this book, it's been to combat the romantic nonsense that so often leads people to try raising wild animals in their backyards, garages, and one-bedroom apartments. Because of that, inevitably, this has been a book full of death and loss, pain and sickness, cold and rain and animal poop. But I hope that it also holds something of the kindness and courage of gorillas, the deep humor of elephants, the old-fashioned family responsibility of wolves, the sweetness of cougars (one cougar in particular), the joyous silliness of Siberian tigers. And the acceptance and understanding of who they are and what is right for them that belongs to all animals, no matter what we do to them, as it should belong to us all.

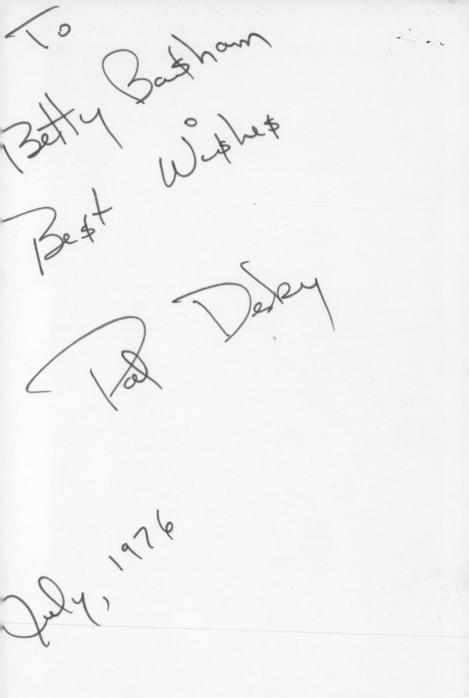

To
Betty Basham

Best Wishes

Pat Derby

July, 1976